Early praise for *Create Your Successful Agile Project*

Johanna packed this book full of wise insights for agile practitioners at all levels. She explains why agile practices work, and how to successfully adapt agile to fit your individual situation. If you're leading, managing, or working with agile projects, you should read this book.

➤ **Kathy Iberle**
    President and Principal Consultant, Iberle Consulting Group, Inc.

Create Your Successful Agile Project is a pragmatic and action-based book that bridges the gap between theory and practice. This is the book I wish I'd had when I started my first agile project!

➤ **Leland Newsom**
    Agile Coach, CapTech Ventures, Inc.

Johanna brings much-needed pragmatism to the agile community. *Create Your Successful Agile Project* is no exception. From cover to cover, she shares deep insights and valuable practice that will certainly help any agile team looking to inspect, adapt, and improve.

➤ **Ryan Ripley**
    Host of the *Agile for Humans* Podcast

There are not many books that provide a methodology-independent view of agile/lean principles and practices. This book does a great job of introducing the most important principles in steps that will help any leader build an agile team and then an agile workflow.

➤ **Mark Kilby**
  Agile Coach

Johanna's latest book is packed with suggestions, approaches, and ideas for how to successfully structure an agile project tailored to your organization's unique needs.

➤ **Joanna L. Vahlsing, PMP**

If you're a project manager and want a pragmatic guide to using agile ways of work, you will likely find this book quite useful. Johanna strikes a good balance between introducing fundamental concepts, developing appealing explanations, and offering expert suggestions.

➤ **Horia Sluşanschi**
  Strategist and Agile Coach

Create Your Successful Agile Project

Collaborate, Measure, Estimate, Deliver

Johanna Rothman

The Pragmatic Bookshelf

Raleigh, North Carolina

Many of the designations used by manufacturers and sellers to distinguish their products are claimed as trademarks. Where those designations appear in this book, and The Pragmatic Programmers, LLC was aware of a trademark claim, the designations have been printed in initial capital letters or in all capitals. The Pragmatic Starter Kit, The Pragmatic Programmer, Pragmatic Programming, Pragmatic Bookshelf, PragProg and the linking *g* device are trademarks of The Pragmatic Programmers, LLC.

Every precaution was taken in the preparation of this book. However, the publisher assumes no responsibility for errors or omissions, or for damages that may result from the use of information (including program listings) contained herein.

Our Pragmatic books, screencasts, and audio books can help you and your team create better software and have more fun. Visit us at *https://pragprog.com*.

The team that produced this book includes:

Publisher: Andy Hunt
VP of Operations: Janet Furlow
Development Editor: Katharine Dvorak
Indexing: Potomac Indexing, LLC
Copy Editor: Candace Cunningham
Layout: Gilson Graphics

For sales, volume licensing, and support, please contact *support@pragprog.com*.

For international rights, please contact *rights@pragprog.com*.

ISBN-13: 978-1-68050-260-2
Book version: P1.0—October 2017

To Mark, as always.

Contents

Acknowledgments   xiii

Introduction xv

1. **Why Agile and Lean Approaches Work** 1

    Software, We Have a Problem   1

    Agile Is a Cultural Change   4

    The 12 Principles of Agile Software Development   7

    The Two Pillars of Lean   8

    Iteration- and Flow-Based Agile   9

    Integrate the Agile and Lean Principles   11

    Now Try This   17

Part I — Create a Successful Agile Team

2. **Build the Cross-Functional, Collaborative Team** 21

    The Project Team Is a Product-Development Team   21

    Agile Changes Team Roles   23

    Team Size Matters   24

    Ask Teams to Organize Themselves   27

    Facilitate the Team's Social Contract   28

    Agile Teams Become Self-Organizing   30

    Keep Teams Together   32

    Recognize Team Traps   33

    Now Try This   39

3. **Build Teamwork with Interpersonal Practices** 41

    How Agile Team Members Are Similar   42

    Team Members Practice Continual Feedback   43

    Team Members Coach Each Other   46

    Recognize When the Team Needs an External Coach   47

Does the Team Need to Track Collaboration?   48
Help the Team Members Build Trust   49
Create a Team Environment of Safety   50
Recognize Interpersonal-Skills Traps   54
Now Try This   57

4. Agile Requires Different Project Leadership 59
How Leaders Serve the Team   60
Agile Project Managers Facilitate to Serve   61
What Product Owners Do   64
How Roles Change in Agile Projects   64
Consider Your Team's Need for Management   65
Recognize Leadership Traps   66
Now Try This   70

Part II — Design and Manage an Agile and Lean Project

5. Start Your Agile Project Right 73
Charter Your Project   74
Identify Your Product Type   78
Assess Your Project's Risks   79
Start Architecture Thinking   81
Recognize Project-Startup Traps   82
Now Try This   84

6. Teams Deliver Features 85
Plan at Several Levels   86
Release for Learning, Feedback, and Value   88
Deliver Value Through the Architecture   89
Create a Walking Skeleton   90
Deliver Value to Someone by Using Features   90
Define Stories So You Can See the Value   92
Experiment and Spike to Explore   94
Write Small Stories   95
Create Rolling-Wave Roadmaps   96
Use a Feature Parking Lot to See Possibilities   98
Consider Minimum Viable Products and Experiments   99
Recognize Value Traps   101
Now Try This   103

7. **Rank the Work** **105**
    Rank the Shortest Work First   106
    Use Cost of Delay to See Value   106
    Rank by Valuing the Learning   109
    Recognize Ranking Traps   110
    Now Try This   112

8. **Visualize Your Work with a Board** **113**
    Start with a Paper Board   113
    Iteration-Based Boards Show Team Commitments   115
    Kanban Boards Show Team Flow and Bottlenecks   117
    Make Your Own Board   120
    Visualize Problems with a Board   121
    Create Visible Boards for Geographically Distributed Teams   122
    Recognize Visualization Traps   123
    Now Try This   126

9. **Create Technical Excellence** **127**
    How Much "Quality" Does Your Product Need?   128
    Integrate as Often as Possible   130
    Consider Continuous Delivery   130
    Refactor Every Time You Touch Code or Tests   131
    Work as a Whole Team to Create the Product   131
    Test at All Levels So Change Is Easy   136
    Beware of Technical Debt and Cruft   138
    Work at a Sustainable Pace   140
    Use Technical Excellence to Speed Development   141
    Recognize Excellence Traps   142
    Now Try This   145

10. **Agile Estimation: The Good, The Bad, and The Ugly** . . .   **147**
    Understand Velocity   148
    Learn to Estimate with Relative Sizing   149
    Use Relative Estimation for Iteration-Based Estimates 152
    Count Stories Instead of Points   153
    Consider Cycle Time to Create More Accurate Estimates 154
    Know the Purpose of Your Estimation   155
    Create Approximate Estimates for Management   156
    Estimate Support Work   157
    Use Previous Data to Inform Your Next Estimate   158
    Consider the Value of #NoEstimates in Your Organization   159

Recognize Estimation Traps   159
Now Try This   163

11. Know What "Done" Means **165**
See the Different Levels of Done   166
Define Acceptance Criteria for Each Story   166
Define What "Done" Means as a Working Agreement   167
Consider When You Can Release to Customers   168
Understand When Customers Can Take Your Releases   168
Building a Product Toward "Real" Doneness   170
Recognize "Done" Traps   170
Now Try This   172

12. Agile Team Measurements **173**
Teams Learn from Their Measurements   173
Understand Burndowns and Burnups   174
Burnups Show You the Rate of Finishing   178
Iteration Contents Show What the Team Completed   180
Cumulative Flow Shows Where the Work Is   183
Cycle Time Shows How Long Work Takes   185
Velocity Is a Capacity Measurement   188
Agile Approaches Change the Meaning
of Defect Measurements   189
Recognize Team-Measurement Traps   193
Now Try This   194

13. Help Your Meetings Provide Value **195**
Retrospectives Provide Valuable Data   195
Walk the Board   199
Standups Create Recommitment and Collaboration   200
Solve Problems Outside of Standups   203
Demonstrations Show Progress and Value   206
Plan the Backlog   207
Create or Refine the Stories as Preparation for Future Work   208
Organize the Team's Meetings   208
Measure the Value from Meetings   210
Create Learning Opportunities   211
Recognize Meeting Traps   213
Now Try This   214

14. **Report Your Project State** 215
    Show Working Product 215
    Show Feature Progress 216
    Show Other Requests in to the Team 218
    Show What's Done but Not Yet Released 219
    Visualize Your Project's Delays 220
    Measure the Effects of Delays 222
    Recognize Project-Measurement Traps 223
    Now Try This 225

Part III — Help Work Groups and Managers Use Agile

15. **Create an Agile Work Group** 229
    Work Groups Meet Differently than Teams 229
    How Will the Group Visualize Its Work and Data? 230
    Visualize Work for a Management Team 233
    Product Development Is Cross-Functional 235
    Every Group Decides How and When to Reflect 235
    Now Try This 236

16. **How Managers Help Agile Teams** 237
    Managers Resolve Impediments the Team Escalates 238
    Managers Help Create the Workspace Your Team Needs 239
    Managers Move from Resource-Efficiency to Flow-Efficiency Thinking 240
    Managers Help with Team-Based Recognition 242
    Avoid Management Mayhem 243
    Recognize How Managers Can Help Agile Teams 244
    Now Try This 245

17. **Start Somewhere** 247
    Limit the Work in Progress 247
    Ask People to Work as a Cross-Functional Team 248
    Start with Yourself 248
    Last Thoughts 249

A1. **Glossary** 251

    Bibliography 253
    Index 259

Acknowledgments

No one writes a book alone.

I thank my workshop participants for their questions throughout the years. I learned from your questions. I also thank my clients, whose agile approaches reflect their uniqueness. We explored your approaches together. I also thank my Managing Product Development blog readers.[1] Your comments made my ideas better.

I thank my reviewers: Zvone Durcevic, Balaji Ganesh, Lorie Gordon, Matt Heusser, Carl Hume, Kathy Iberle, Mark Kilby, John Le Drew, Vikas Manchanda, Leland Newsome, Ryan Ripley, Amitai Schleier, Horia Sluşanschi, Rich Stone, Michael Tardiff, Joanna Vahlsing, Carl Weller, Terry Wiegmann, Serhiy Yevtushenko.

I thank my editor, Katharine Dvorak. In addition, I thank the rest of the Pragmatic Bookshelf staff who prepared and shepherded my book through to publication: Janet Furlow, Candace Cunningham, Potomac Indexing, and Gilson Graphics.

Any mistakes are mine.

Johanna Rothman
Arlington, Massachusetts, August 2017

---

1. http://www.jrothman.com/blog/mpd

Introduction

You know your current approach to managing projects isn't working. Your releases are too slow. The products have too many defects. People are multi-tasking all over the place. It's a mess. Is an agile software product-development solution the answer?

Maybe.

Agile solutions come in many flavors. You can even combine some of those flavors to create your own agile context for your project inside your organization. Don't fall prey to the notion that you can "just" adopt one agile product-development approach or framework wholesale, regardless of your context. That approach ignores your organizational, project, and team contexts.

I have yet to see a project team that could not adopt an agile approach. And I have seen many successful teams that have created their own agile approaches. These teams rejected the idea of "agile" by framework or book. They found the agile principles and practices that work for them.

You might be a project manager, a technical lead, a manager, and yes, even a Scrum master. Whatever your role, you are an organizational leader, trying to discover how you might use agile principles in your project. Your job, as an organizational leader, is to understand the agile and lean principles. You can then use those principles to improve your projects. Even if you don't fully embrace all that an agile approach delivers, you can still improve your projects with frequent delivery, feedback, and collaboration.

When you improve the projects, you can see more value from the products your organization delivers.

This book focuses on the team—the product-development team—and ways the team can learn to deliver value, over and over again. The book is divided into three parts:

- Part I addresses the creation of the agile team and how teams can learn to work together. If you are team lead of some sort (project manager,

Scrum master, coach, technical lead, first-level manager) do start here. If you are a mid- or senior-level manager and are wondering why agile teams are different, this part will help you learn why.

- Part II addresses the options your team has for designing its agile approach and delivering value throughout the entire project. This is where you can design your agile project. This part includes how to charter a project, plan the work, visualize the work, build in quality, use velocity to guide estimation, know what "done" means, add value to your project meetings, and report progress outside the team.

- Part III addresses agile approaches outside the project team. Work groups often design a different agile approach than project teams. In addition, managers are key to helping an agile team succeed. And if you or your team aren't sure where to start, I have some suggestions in the last chapter.

If you are a manager, you might want to start with Chapter 1 to better understand the agile and lean principles, continue to Part I, and finish with Part III.

If you are part of a geographically distributed team, read this book and determine what you can use and where your problems arise. Pay special attention to Chapter 8, *Visualize Your Work with a Board*, on page 113, to develop a cadence for retrospectives and learn as you experiment.

Scaling is the big idea now in agile approaches. My suggestion is to have *each* team learn how it can create a successful agile approach first, and then consider what needs to scale. I do not recommend every team use a "standard" agile approach. Each team is unique and can select from alternatives, as long as the team delivers value often.

If you want agile approaches to creating a program, where several teams collaborate to achieve one business objective, read *Agile and Lean Program Management [Rot16]*. If you want to understand how to manage the project portfolio in an agile way, read *Manage Your Project Portfolio [Rot16a]*.

If you need more ideas, please read my six-part series about what scaling agile means. (The summary post is "Defining 'Scaling' Agile, Part 6: Creating the Agile Organization."[1]) Remember that scaling is not creating or using a prescriptive framework, but instead is the ability to deliver value across the organization, every day.

To solve the problem of the individual team being able to use agile approaches to reliably and consistently deliver features, read this book. Let's start the fun.

---

1. https://www.jrothman.com/mpd/agile/2017/06/defining-scaling-agile-part-6-creating-the-agile-organization

CHAPTER 1

Why Agile and Lean Approaches Work

If you're thinking of implementing an agile approach, maybe you've had these
or similar problems:

- You get most of the way through your project and *bam*—key requirements
  change.

- The team started with an agreement about the architecture or high-level
  designs, but then realizes the agreements are insufficient for the problems
  it's encountering now.

- The team can't release anything at the desired release date, or even weeks
  later. Everything is partially done and nothing is fully done.

An agile approach can help you fix these problems and more. But what kind
of agile approach should you use? Some people swear by iterations, often in
the form of Scrum. Some people swear by kanban. Others say, "Agile doesn't
work. Never did. Never will."

Before we start to think about which approach to use, let's discuss why agile
and lean approaches exist.

Software, We Have a Problem

We can't develop and release a product without knowing what it will be, right?
Except we, as an industry, have a terrible time seeing the requirements before
we create some of the product and get feedback on what we developed.

Back in the '70s, when I started to work as a software developer, we created
"simple" products. The only input was the command line. We had no windowing
systems until the '80s. Cameras had only eight bits of grayscale, no color. The
mouse didn't exist until the mid '80s, and computers were much less capable

than they are now. We created our own unique networking systems. (TCP/IP didn't ship with computers as part of the operating system until the '90s.)

Even in these "simple" projects, I needed to provide myself—never mind others—with prototypes and/or delivery of small chunks of value to make sure I was on the right track.

In the late '80s and early '90s, with more computer power, our projects became more complex. Many teams had trouble finishing projects, and the bigger the project, the worse it was.

Carnegie Mellon developed the Capability Maturity Model (CMM) in the mid '80s to solve the problems of teams not delivering. That model has evolved into the Capability Maturity Model Integration (CMMI). At the same time, the Standish Group started to release its Chaos Reports, claiming that most projects had some form of failure. The projects were under scope, over budget, and over time.

No one was happy.

I became a consultant in 1994, after having worked in organizations for almost 20 years. I assessed projects and processes. I helped projects deliver with project training and consulting. I found similar problems across many clients:

> People—well-meaning people—thought they could hand a software team a big requirements document and the project would magically deliver exactly what the requirements stated. Architects thought they could work on the architecture and hand it off to a team to implement as designed, as if by magic. Developers thought they could hand off code to testers and it would all "just work" as if by magic.

You can see the problem: Working sequentially provided comfort, and it caused magical thinking. By magic, one person could hand off work to another person or team and it would all "just work."

Nothing could be further from the truth.

By the '80s and '90s, many of us working as developers, testers, or project managers realized that trying to predict everything and hand off from one person to another didn't work.

Here are some realities for software projects: There are no one-person projects. At the very least, software requires a developer and a user. More often, software requires a developer, a tester, and a user. That means there is a project team (developer and tester) and a user who need to collaborate to complete something useful.

Another reality is that we can try to predict everything about the project, but we often learn about the product as we proceed. We discover that the requirements depend on each other and interact to create a product that does—or does not—meet the desired performance.

Software isn't the only kind of product that requires interaction, collaboration, and feedback on value as the project proceeds. Hardware and mechanical projects require the same things. Even event planning often requires substantial interaction between the event planners and the people who want the event. Any time the people developing the product learn as they develop, a serial approach to delivering value doesn't work that well. That's because a serial approach only encourages one delivery, at the end. When teams deliver more often, they have an opportunity to learn more often.

I used staged delivery, an incremental feature-driven approach to projects, starting back in the '70s. I didn't have a name for it at the time. I only knew I couldn't conceive of the entire product at the beginning of the project and deliver what my customers wanted. I needed to deliver a little, get some feedback, and repeat. (I discuss this staged-delivery life cycle in detail in *Manage It! [Rot07]*.)

Many other people had similar experiences. For example, Hirotaka Takeuchi and Ikujiro Nonaka published *The New New Product Development Game [TN86]*, which included the first mention of the word "Scrum," in 1986. Christopher Meyer published *Fast Cycle Time: How to Align Purpose, Strategy, and Structure for Speed [Mey93]* in 1993.

Several books applied lean thinking and principles to product development in the '90s:

- James P. Womack and Daniel T. Jones published *Lean Thinking [WJ96]* in 1996.

- Don Reinertsen published *Managing the Design Factory [Rei97]* in 1997.

- Preston Smith and Don Reinertsen published *Developing Products in Half the Time: New Rules, New Tools [SR98]* in 1998.

Starting in the '90s, some notable people wrote books about how software teams might take advantage of nonserial approaches to work:

- Gerald M. Weinberg published his series of *Quality Software Management [Wei92]* books, discussing "steering" as a way to guide projects to success, starting in 1992.

- Steve McConnell published *Rapid Development [McC96]*, which discussed incremental approaches and small chunks of work, in 1996.

- Jim Highsmith published *Adaptive Software Development [Hig99]* in 1999, about how to create an adaptive project.

- Kent Beck published *Extreme Programming Explained: Embrace Change [Bec00]* in 2000, explaining XP.

- Andy Hunt and Dave Thomas published *The Pragmatic Programmer: From Journeyman to Master [HT00]* in 2000, explaining how normal developers could use pragmatic approaches to deliver value.

I published *How to Use Inch-Pebbles When You Think You Can't [Rot99]* in 1998 and wrote *Release Criteria: Is This Software Done? [Rot02]* in 2002. I wrote these and other articles based on many years of successful project experience using iterative and incremental approaches from rolling wave, deliverable-based planning to frequent releasing to teams swarming on work.

Agile and lean thinking applied to product development is not a new idea. Many of the ideas have been around for decades. However, these ideas ask the people on the project teams and in management to relinquish prediction and control, to embrace change and team organization.

That's a tough request for many people.

When the Manifesto for Agile Software Development was signed in 2001,[1] the authors articulated what many people had tried bits and pieces of in their organizations already. Agile and lean approaches for product development exist because these approaches help teams deliver working products for their customers. When teams use agile and lean approaches, they deliver products faster and better.

Here's the truth about an agile approach: Any number of agile approaches might work for you and your project. In fact, you might need several agile approaches to manage the risks for your project. What matters is your context.

There is no One Right Way to create an agile project. Let's first talk about what an agile approach looks like, then talk about what you might do to design your agile project or your agile approach.

Agile Is a Cultural Change

Agile is not just a different life cycle. Yes, agile uses an iterative and incremental approach, *and* agile approaches require a cultural change. Regardless of your previous culture, an agile approach creates a culture of working with

---

1. http://agilemanifesto.org

transparency, driven by value, collaborating across the organization. Those approaches enable a team to deliver value often.

This transparency, value, and collaboration might be quite different for your organization, and the focus on frequent delivery for feedback can be challenging to people, teams, and organizations.

First, let's see what an agile approach looks like. The general agile picture, shown in the following figure, illustrates what happens when a project adopts an agile approach. People in the organization have many ideas for the product. A responsible person (often called a product owner) collects those ideas and creates a smaller subset of those ideas into a ranked backlog for the cross-functional team.

General Agile Picture

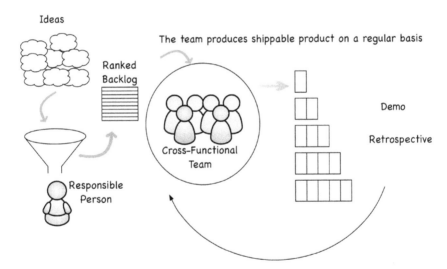

The team works on that ranked backlog, in rank order. The team creates and delivers releasable product on a regular basis. The team demonstrates its work on a regular basis. That's how the team receives feedback about what it completed. And the team retrospects on its work, also on a regular basis. At some point, the team ships the product.

These key ideas make agile approaches work: The team collaborates to deliver. The team limits its work in progress (WIP), either via iterations or with specified WIP limits. The team delivers releasable product often. The team reviews its work product and process on a regular basis.

All of these ideas create the agile culture, which allows the team to learn and gain feedback on its work. You can realize agile benefits for projects if you fulfill all of the following conditions:

- You have a cross-functional team with all the necessary capabilities and skills so that the team can release working product.

- You have one person (such as a product owner) who provides the team with a ranked backlog. That person might manage the input from several other people, but the team only has to listen to and work with one person.

- The team finishes valuable chunks of work often. I find that teams who can finish deliverables in a day or so make more progress faster than teams who take longer to deliver. The value of finishing something every day helps the team to assess its progress and to receive feedback on what the team completed.

- The team can release working product often. (I like every two weeks at a minimum.)

- The team reflects on its work process at least as often as the team releases working product.

If you cannot fulfill these conditions, you might be using an iterative (where the team iterates over refining features) or incremental (where the team delivers features regardless of feature size) approach that is not yet agile. That iterative and incremental approach might be better for your teamwork and delivery than anything you did previously. But don't fool yourself. Unless you can fulfill each of these conditions, you are not using agile approaches. Instead, you have *agile traps*. I describe common traps in each chapter as you might encounter them.

Work Groups Are Not Teams

Keep in mind that teams are not the same as work groups. Teams have interdependent work and goals. The entire team has one goal that the team delivers. In addition, team members make commitments to each other about the work.

On the other hand, you might work with other people, but as a work group. For example, support, sales, and HR are often work groups. Each person has his or her own goals. Group members might work together to finish work, but the group members do not need each other to finish the work on a regular basis. See Chapter 15, *Create an Agile Work Group*, on page 229, to help you see how to use agile approaches for a work group. Also see *The Wisdom of Teams [KS99]* and *Behind Closed Doors: Secrets of Great Management [RD05]* for more information about work groups and teams.

The 12 Principles of Agile Software Development

Agile principles help a team collaborate. If you live up to the principles, you will see increments of your product working every day or so. Those increments allow you to get feedback from your customer and provide feedback and learning within the team. The following list paraphrases the 12 principles of agile software development.[2]

1. Deliver early and often to satisfy the customer.

2. Welcome changing requirements.

3. Deliver working software frequently.

4. Business people and developers must work together.

5. Trust motivated people to do their jobs.

6. Face-to-face conversation is the most efficient and effective method of conveying information.

7. Working software is the primary measure of progress.

8. Maintain a sustainable pace.

9. Continuous attention to technical excellence and good design enhances agility.

10. Simplicity—the art of maximizing the amount of work not done—is essential.

11. The best architectures, requirements, and designs emerge from self-organizing teams.

12. Reflect and adjust at regular intervals.

Part of agile is the idea of sustainable pace and continuous attention to technical excellence. When you build small increments and ask for feedback often, you can welcome change. The change might be in the product or in the team's process. Agile teams fine-tune their work and the product when they reflect and adjust at regular intervals. The principles create the conditions for success, as mentioned in *Agile Is a Cultural Change*, on page 4.

---

2. http://www.agilemanifesto.org/principles.html

The Two Pillars of Lean

For many teams and organizations, the agile principles are not enough. These teams and organizations need lean thinking to help solidify how agile might work for them.

For many years, people assumed lean was about manufacturing. Because of the Toyota Production System (see, for example, *Toyota Production System: Beyond Large Scale Production [Ohn88]*), some people thought lean was a bunch of tools, specifically for manufacturing. Lean is much more than specific tools such as a kanban board, or a principle such as single-piece flow.

There are two pillars of lean: respect for people and a commitment to continuous improvement. (See the Lean Primer for the pillars as well as an excellent and brief explanation of lean.[3]) The two pillars of lean help us create an agile culture. Lean principles apply to knowledge work as well as manufacturing.

Many teams stumble if they try to use only the 12 principles of agile software development when they adopt an agile approach. When people add the pillars and lean thinking, they can make agile work better for their context.

Lean thinking—using the lean principles—helps agile teams use agile approaches to create better products and deliver more value. Lean thinking helps people and teams realize they need to visualize their flow of work and think about value as they apply the agile principles. If you're wondering about the source of lean thinking, I recommend reading *Lean Thinking [WJ96]*, *Lean Product and Process Development [War07]*, *The Toyota Way [Lik04]*, and especially *This Is Lean: Resolving the Efficiency Paradox [MÅ13]*.

These are the lean principles of software development from *Lean Software Development: An Agile Toolkit for Software Development Managers [PP03]*:

1. Eliminate waste.

2. Amplify learning.

3. Decide as late as possible.

4. Deliver as fast as possible.

5. Empower the team.

6. Build integrity in.

7. See the whole.

---

3. http://www.leanprimer.com/downloads/lean_primer.pdf

These principles specifically address the flow of work and the idea that cross-functional team works together. The agile principles say to work as a collaborative cross-functional team and to deliver often.

Iteration- and Flow-Based Agile

Teams use agile approaches in one of two primary ways: iterations or flow. Yes, you can combine them, too.

An iteration-based agile approach means a team works in timeboxes of the same size for every iteration (as shown in the following diagram). The team fixes the duration of the iteration. Teams often work in one- or two-week iterations (the timebox). Every two weeks, by definition, the team is *done* because the timebox is over. The team doesn't change the duration because the team can't estimate what it can complete in a timebox if it keeps changing the duration.

Iteration-Based Agile

Requirements Analysis Design Build Test Release Deploy	Requirements Analysis Design Build Test Release Deploy	Requirements Analysis Design Build Test Release Deploy	Requirements Analysis Design Build Test Release Deploy	Repeat as needed ...	Requirements Analysis Design Build Test Release Deploy	Requirements Analysis Design Build Test Release Deploy

Each timebox is the same size. Each timebox results in running tested features.

In iteration-based agile, the product owner and the team manage the work in progress by estimating the number of stories (and other work) the team can commit to in a timebox. When the team estimates, the product owner receives feedback on the estimated size of the work. The product owner then has choices to make more stories or ask the team to swarm or mob on the work.

Note that I have included all of the work in a timebox: requirements, analysis, design, build, test, release, and deploy. Teams perform all of those activities to deliver finished value. (Sometimes teams release internally but do not release to customers or deploy each iteration.)

You might think a team does these activities sequentially. Not necessarily. The team often performs these activities as a team, on one or two features at a time. I'll explain more in Chapter 6, *Teams Deliver Features*, on page 85. The team performs all these activities, but not necessarily in sequential order for a given feature. Here's a quick example: During a planning meeting, the team—as a team—discusses a couple of possible designs for a given feature, because the time needed might change depending on the design. A tester might sketch some possible tests. Even before the team "starts" work on that feature, the team estimates, designs, and tests—just a little bit. That's what I mean by a nonsequential approach to the work.

An iteration-based agile approach provides a cadence—a project rhythm—for teams to deliver and learn, retrospect, and plan.

In a flow-based agile approach, shown in the next diagram, the team maps the flow of value through the team. The team sets a WIP limit for each column on the board and tracks the team's cycle time—how long features take on average. The team and the product owner manage the work based on those limits. After finishing some work, the team delivers and learns, retrospects, and reviews what it wants to improve.

Flow-Based Agile

Feature: Clarify Req't, Analysis Design Build Test Release Deploy	Feature: Clarify Requirement, Analysis Design Build Test Release Deploy	Feature: Clarify Requirement, Analysis Design Build Test Release Deploy	Repeat as needed ...	Feature: Clarify Requirement, Analysis Design Build Test Release Deploy	Feature: Clarify Requirement, Analysis Design Build Test Release Deploy

In flow, the team limits the number of features active at any time with WIP limits for each team activity. There is no timeboxing built into flow.

Flow focuses on the continual pulling of work; iteration more often focuses on pulling a limited set of work into a defined timebox.

Neither the flow nor the iterations approach is *right*. Neither is *wrong*. It's all about what your team needs to see the work, release valuable product often, and get feedback.

I happen to like a flow-based approach inside of some cadence. I like seeing working product *at least* every two weeks, which is what I do for my collaborative projects. I deliver value more often for my personal projects—at least once a day. I want to see where the work starts, where it waits, how long it waits, if there are any cycles, and so on. Flow and kanban boards can show you that. Iterations—by themselves—don't show you details of where work is stuck.

Distinguish Between Cadence and Iteration

I said that iterations are timeboxes of a week or two, maybe longer if you don't need more frequent feedback. I also said that a cadence provides a rhythm for a project. Let me explain the difference.

Many teams appreciate a cadence for delivery, retrospectives, and more planning. Not every team needs the focus of a timebox to do that.

One team I know delivers several times during the week. It plans weekly, but not the same day each week. When the team has finished three features, it plans for the next three. It takes about 20–30 minutes to plan. It's not a big deal. This team retrospects every Friday morning. (I would select a different day, but the team didn't ask me. See *Organize the Team's Meetings*, on page 208, to see why I prefer midweek cadences.)

Notice that this team has two separate cadences: at least once a week for planning work, but not the same day each week; and once a week for retrospectives, on the same day each week. The team isn't working in iterations; it's working in flow. The team uses the idea of a cadence to provide a pulse, a rhythm for its project.

If the team used iterations, it would always plan on the same day, at the beginning of the iteration. The team would always have a retrospective on the same day at the end of the iteration. This team doesn't do that, and that's great. Teams don't have to follow prescribed ceremonies, especially if the team's context is different from other teams'.

A cadence is different from an iteration. Decide what fits for your team.

Integrate the Agile and Lean Principles

Think about what the agile and lean principles together buy you. These principles say to use a collaborative cross-functional team structure so that the entire team works on features. The principles emphasize seeing the work as it proceeds to get feedback on the work and the process. The principles caution you to not start more than the team can complete in a short period of time. And you deliver working product often and as fast as possible to see progress, increase customer collaboration, and receive feedback.

How can you think about the agile and lean principles for your project? How can you build respect for the people and continuous improvement into how your cross-functional, collaborative team can deliver small chunks of value often? That way, your team can not only deliver often, but also receive feedback often.

Consider How an Agile Approach Might Work for You

I often hear people describe their projects as being "agile/Scrum." Let me clarify: "agile" is an umbrella term that encompasses many agile approaches, one of which is Scrum. Some of those approaches are defined in the following table.

Named Approach	How the Approach Works
Extreme Programming	Primarily a collection of technical practices guided by these values: communication, simplicity, feedback, courage, and respect.
Scrum	Timebox-based project-management framework for delivering working product often.
DSDM (Dynamic Systems Development Method)	Timeboxed approach to delivering functionality. Facilitated workshops to determine the requirements and gain agreement on them.
Crystal	Focus on the people. Depending on the size of the project team and the product criticality, select the approach that fits for the team, the business people, and customers.
Feature-Driven Development	Deliver functionality incrementally after creating a (low-fidelity) framework for the architecture or object modeling. Focus on building value for the customer.
Kanban	Visualize the flow of work, work by value, and manage the work in progress. Deliver incremental value as the team completes the value.

Table 1—Some Agile Approaches

There are more agile approaches, but these are well-known approaches for teams.

Scrum is one project-management framework that helps a team adopt agile techniques.[4] Many teams start with Scrum because it is the most famous approach to agile. Scrum works for collocated teams who work on one project at a time, and where the team has all the cross-functional skills and capabilities it requires. And Scrum creates the need for cultural change. However, I have found teams that meet the following criteria are not good candidates for Scrum:

• Your team works on more than one project at a time. Or the team needs to provide significant interrupt-driven support or maintenance.

• Your team is distributed across more than four time zones.

---

4. http://www.scrumguides.org/index.html

- Your team is not cross-functional. That is, you have a team of developers trying to collaborate with a team of testers, often across time zones. Or you have a work group instead of a team.

- Your team does not have the skills or capabilities it needs. You have a scarcity of some necessary role, such as UX or DBA.

- Your "team" does not need collaboration. All the work is independent, not interdependent.

In these cases, I do not recommend Scrum as your agile approach. (Can you make Scrum work? Of course. It's more difficult than an agile approach has to be, but you can try.) I recommend you integrate flow into your agile design. You might also use iterations for a cadence of planning and delivery.

As described in *Iteration- and Flow-Based Agile*, on page 9, iteration-based agile uses timeboxes to manage the scope of work the team will complete. Scrum is similar, and also offers specific roles, such as the Scrum master and product owner. In addition, Scrum incorporates several events, including these:

- The daily standup

- The preiteration planning meeting (which Scrum calls the Sprint Planning meeting)

- The backlog-refinement meeting before the next iteration

- The demonstration to show and explain what the team completed in the last iteration (In Scrum, this is the sprint review and includes the team's assessment of whether it achieved the sprint goal.)

- The retrospective at the end of the iteration

You might decide these events are for you. However, you don't need to use Scrum to use an agile approach—even an iteration-based approach—that works for you. You might find that given your context, choosing an alternative or designing your agile approach works better.

I have seen people and teams use the agile and lean principles to progressively move to agile approaches as it fits for them. I recommend you do, too. The more your team is resilient and adaptive, the easier it is to create a great project that delivers a successful product.

You do not need to name your agile approach. I recommend you design an agile approach that incorporates the values and principles of agile and lean, rather than try to stick to a framework, regardless of its fame.

Keep Your Iteration Duration Short

If you decide to use iterations or cadence for planning, improvement, or retrospectives, how long should an iteration be? Iterations and cadences are about feedback. How much time would you want to elapse before you could know if everything the team did was wrong?

Pick an iteration length that would make it okay if you had to throw everything away. If you plan on a cadence, make sure that cadence is short enough that you're not replanning too late to accommodate change.

Maybe you've considered the ideas presented in the Potential for Release Frequency graphic on page 78, and you know your customers can't take product releases more often than once every six months. Should you wait to release once every six months?

I don't recommend that. In fact, regardless of when your customers can take releases or how much external releases cost, I recommend you release internally at least once every two weeks—ten business days.

Many teams decide that one or two weeks is the right iteration duration. That's five or ten workdays. Some teams choose three or four weeks, fifteen or twenty workdays.

 Joe asks:
Why Count the Business Days in an Iteration?

You've noticed I count five days in a week, not seven. That's because we work for five days out of seven. (I'm not counting people who work four 10-hour days. You folks can do your own arithmetic.)

If you count all the days, including the weekends, people are likely to work all the days. That's a problem. It's impossible for people to work all seven days in a week for any duration of time. It's possible for people to race to a deadline for maybe a couple of weeks. It's not possible to sustain that pace.

Count the days in the week you work. It doesn't matter if you work Sunday–Thursday or Monday–Friday or some other option. Count just those five days.

In my experience, it's easy for a duration of more than 10 days to lead to the *Trap: You Have Iterations of Waterfalls*, on page 125. Be careful of iterations more than 10 business days long.

If you decide to use iterations, select an iteration duration you can standardize on. That will allow you to gather data and become more predictable for your planning.

If you are using flow, consider a cadence for retrospectives and improvement activities. I assume if you use flow, you will release internally every time you complete a feature.

To start the iteration, you have a short planning meeting, where you either have enough user stories for a ranked backlog, or you develop them. The team agrees it can complete them in this iteration. At the end of the iteration, you meet with the product owner (responsible person) and conduct a demo, showing your completed features. The team conducts a retrospective so the team can inspect and adapt its process. Either at the demo or at the retrospective, the team and the product owner can agree to inspect and adapt the backlog for the future.

Loop until you meet the release criteria for the project. Note that since the product is releasable, you can release at any time.

Create Your Agile Mindset

A mindset is the values, beliefs, and principles you hold that guide your actions in a situation. (See Gil Broza's *Agile Mind-Set [Bro16]* for more information.)

An agile mindset means you value the collaboration and feedback in an agile team. You believe that small steps and frequent checking of progress will help. You believe that people collaborating can deliver a terrific product. You use the agile and lean principles of collaboration, delivery, and transparency to guide your work.

I had a challenge when I first used agile approaches for my work. I had perfection rules—I had to have the work perfect before I allowed anyone to see it.

That doesn't work. Instead, I needed to create the mindset that I could build something, release it to someone else to gain feedback, and then use that learning from the feedback to decide what to do next, as illustrated in the figure on page 16.

I have found that using Carol Dweck's growth mindset ideas, as described in *Mindset: The New Psychology of Success [Dwe07]* and outlined in the table on page 16, helps people see that exploration and learning are critical ideas for agile success.

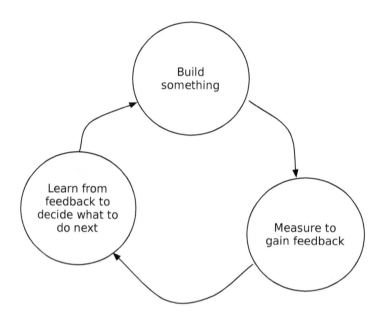

Fixed Mindset	Growth Mindset
We are born with fixed skills or talents.	Skills arise from hard work. We can improve.
Avoid challenges. In the face of challenge, give up.	See challenges as an opportunity. Persist until we get it right.
Coast by; don't bother with effort.	Effort is essential to mastery.
Get defensive with feedback.	Learn from feedback.
Blame others for setbacks. Get discouraged by setbacks.	Setbacks are something we use to try harder the next time.
Feel threatened by others' success.	Find inspiration in others' success.

Table 2—Fixed vs. Growth Mindset

Agile builds in adaptation to your projects and daily work. You can make this adaptation work if you adopt the growth mindset. When you work as a team, adopting the growth mindset and the agile and lean principles, values, and beliefs, you often discover you can experiment and learn from your experiments.

The agile mindset is one that says, "What small experiment can I learn from and make progress based on the outcome?"

Avoid Frameworks Until You Understand Your Context

You might be wondering, "Why can't I just use a framework?" If you can find a nonprescriptive framework that fits your team, go right ahead. Many of the current frameworks might work for your team. In my consulting, I have found that many frameworks are too prescriptive and do not create the agile mindset for a team. And management thinks the framework is all the team needs.

Instead of "installing" a framework, look at your team and see what your team needs to use an agile mindset and create its agile culture.

Now Try This

1. Think about iterations and flow and what you think might work best for you and your team. You might decide to create transparency in your work, even before you ask a team to transform its culture into an agile culture.

2. Consider your organization's culture. Keep in mind that an organization of finger-pointing and blame will make it much more difficult to adopt an agile approach. I'll discuss that more in *Avoid Management Mayhem*, on page 243.

3. Think about what you need to do for *your* agile mindset. How can you create a mindset that includes the agile and lean principles?

Now that you understand a little about agile and lean principles, let's talk about what the team looks like.

Part I

Create a Successful Agile Team

Build the Cross-Functional, Collaborative Team

Here's a familiar situation: You have a Very Important Customer waiting for a feature. The developers are done. The testers are not. Why? Because they're backed up with other work, testing other fixes, trying to keep up with projects, support requests, and who knows what else.

Maybe the lack of testers isn't your problem. It could be that you don't have enough UX people or DBAs working alongside the developers. You are missing the one element vital to a successful agile project: a fully skilled, cross-functional, collaborative team.

The cross-functional team is the heart of an agile approach. Cross-functional teams can deliver working product. When you don't have a cross-functional team, delivering anything seems impossible. Let's see how to create the cross-functional team your project needs.

The Project Team Is a Product-Development Team

You may think you have a project team or a feature team. A feature team can deliver features without depending on anyone else across the organization.

One way to make sure your team can deliver features is to think of your team as a *product development* team. When people think about *product* development instead of *projects*, they often realize that they need other skills and capabilities (possibly in the form of other people) on the team.

What kind of product do you have?

If you have a product with a database, you need people with database skills on your team. You might need database administration or data modeling skills. If your product includes user documentation, you might need the skills for creating that documentation.

What if your product is based on performance or reliability? You might need architecture or design leadership skills. (I prefer that the team learn how to assess performance or reliability or any other system quality by itself, without needing an external architect or designer.)

Because your product and organization are unique, I can't tell you exactly who should be on your team. For example, all projects need project-management skills, but your team might not need a specific project manager. I do recommend your agile team have a full-time product owner with sufficient time to dedicate to the team.

Product owner is a Scrum term. And because it's so pervasive in the industry, I'll use it here to describe the one person who interacts with the team to create and rank the backlog.

Think Capabilities, Not People

Many agile approaches say, "The team has all the roles it needs." That might mean the team has many people because no one has overlapping roles.

Instead of roles, think "capabilities" and "generalizing specialists." People can have more than one capability. (See *Trap: The Team Consists of Narrow Experts*, on page 34, for more information.) Both *The Nature of Software Development [Jef15]* and *More Agile Testing: Learning Journeys for the Whole Team [CG14]* discuss the idea of capabilities and skills rather than roles.

Developers might not be good system testers, but they might be able to contribute to creating test-automation frameworks and being able to develop and think about testing through the architecture. Maybe someone on the team has talents in the UI and can extend those skills to working through the application layer into the middleware. Maybe a platform person can also work in the database area.

Each of us has areas we prefer. In addition to those preferences, can we add more capabilities to our expertise?

Your team might also benefit from a coach, especially if the team is new to agile techniques. Agile approaches require people to change their mindsets and culture. Many people find a new culture a challenge: how to integrate the new thinking and the new practices?

Cross-functional teams have—at minimum—developers and testers. Think about the skills and capabilities your team needs to deliver the product often. If you don't have all the skills and capabilities on your team to release shippable product, that's an impediment. It might not be easy to remove that impediment. If you have cross-functional teams but not feature teams, consider measuring the time it takes for people to cycle through the features. Refer to *Visualize Your Project's Delays*, on page 220, to understand the effects of not having feature teams.

I call everyone on the team "developers" because that helps people realize their job is product development. Some people write code that ships. Those people are software developers. Some people write code that stays. Those people are testers. Some people write documentation. Some people help the team integrate. But everyone has a single purpose: to enable the entire team to release features on a frequent basis.

If you have a nonsoftware team, you have people who develop the product (or event) and people who check to make sure the product is working properly.

Agile teams fulfill these requirements:

- The team has all the people (with their skills and capabilities) it needs to complete the work.

- The team does not change people for a given feature.

- The team has a shared goal for its project.

- The team "owns" its work. Members commit to their work and they own their artifacts, including the code and tests.

- The team does not change people inside an iteration.

- The team is stable, so the people can learn to work together and can learn their product area(s).

- If the team uses iterations, no one changes what the team commits to for that iteration.

Your feature team needs enough product developers and product testers to maintain technical excellence as it delivers working product frequently. Who you need depends on the kind of product you are working on.

Agile Changes Team Roles

You might be accustomed to project managers who decide on dates. You might not have seen a product manager since the last millennium. That all changes in agile. In agile, the product owner or customer decides which features (including technical debt or defects) the team will work on and when.

Joe asks:
Do I Need to Have Stable Feature Teams?

If your organization is based on resource efficiency, you may have trouble convincing your management that you need to have stable, cross-functional teams to release features. However, the more you change team composition, the more the team will revert to forming or storming. (See *Keep Teams Together*, on page 32, for more information on forming and storming.) It takes time for people to learn to work together and trust each other. The more you change team composition, the more each feature costs.

If you have cross-functional, component teams, someone or some team still has to integrate work so that you can release features. You will incur a cost of waiting for the experts you need.

Stable, cross-functional feature teams that work through the architecture can develop and release features faster than any other team.

The team then is in charge of *how* the team does the work. The team makes all the architectural and design decisions. The team is free to attempt to change the product owner's mind about when to do something to make it easier to implement a feature.

No one outside the team designs for the team. That includes UX people, product managers, and architects outside the team. The team makes its own decisions. (See Chapter 9, *Create Technical Excellence*, on page 127, for ideas about how the team knows it creates useful and maintainable work.)

There is a role for architects and project managers in an agile project. They are part of the team and deliver code as part of the team. See more about this in Chapter 4, *Agile Requires Different Project Leadership*, on page 59.

Because the team delivers on its own, the team needs to be a reasonable size for the team to work together well.

Team Size Matters

I like small teams, between four and six people. Here's why.

I've observed over the years that teams of more than nine people didn't have what I call the "intimacy" of smaller teams. Teams of three people or smaller didn't always have the ideas needed, but teams larger than nine people lost something that was common to smaller teams—an ability to easily communicate with each other. There is a reason for that: the number of communication paths in the team.

Beware of Too-Small Teams

 Too-small teams—three or fewer people—might not have enough diversity to solve their problems. They don't have enough ideas. Too few people can be just as bad—although differently bad—than too many people.

Collaborative teams need pair-wise communication, where everyone talks to everyone else. There is no restriction on communication, and we want people to talk to each other. Following is a picture of the paths in a six-person team. I numbered the paths going around and then from the top to the bottom, starting on the left side of the image.

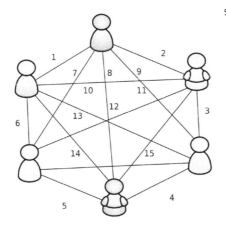

Six-Person Team Requires
15 Unique Paths
for Full Communication

The number of communication paths in the team does not increase linearly as the team size increases. Team communication paths square when the team increases linearly.

Here is the calculation where N is the number of people on the team: Communication Paths = N*(N-1)/2. That means you have these communication paths for these team sizes:

Team Members	Communication Paths
4 people	(4*3)/2=6
5 people	(5*4)/2=10
6 people	(6*5)/2=15
7 people	(7*6)/2=21
8 people	(8*7)/2=24
9 people	(9*8)/2=36
10 people	(10*9)/2=45

Five people require a total of 10 communication paths. Eight people require 24 communication paths. Once we get past 21 paths, many of us don't talk with the *entire* team—we choose who to work with and who to ignore. Once a team gets to 10 people, the number of paths is 45, which is unmanageable for most of us.

Can some people manage this number of communication paths? Sure. But not many of us, which is the problem. That's why "teams" of 10 people don't work.

If you have a group of 10 people, they will naturally divide into smaller subteams of people who can work together. They will not divide themselves evenly, as in five and five. Oh no, that would make life too easy. If you are lucky, they will divide by features. If you are not lucky, they will divide by architecture or by function, or even worse, by clique.

What do you do if you have a large team? Organizations create large teams for any number of reasons: they envision large features or the necessary expertise is distributed throughout the organization. Sometimes the organization has a program, a collection of projects that fulfill one business objective. (See *Agile and Lean Program Management [Rot16]* for ways to organize a program other than to create a very large team.) Often it's easier to organize the features so that smaller feature teams can deliver the results than it is to create a larger team.

Consider these alternatives to create smaller cross-functional teams:

- Make the stories smaller so the team can be smaller. See *Write Small Stories*, on page 95, for more information.

- Organize by feature or feature set. If you've been organizing by architecture, reorganize the *teams* to be feature teams. Aim for a feature team size of no more than six. For example, think about these feature sets: search, admin, billing. Each of those feature sets might need just one team. If your feature set is too large for one team, consider organizing as a program around smaller feature sets. For example, you might need a feature set for "simple search" and another feature set for "search within results." Both would be search feature sets and the team members might need to work or speak with each other.

- If you have already organized by feature and the team is still larger than nine, check for team skills and capabilities. The team members might not realize that it's great if they "cover" other areas of the code or tests.

- Should this team break into several other teams and organize as a program? Sometimes when teams become large, it's time for each team to take a feature set (or two) and focus on those features. (See *Agile and Lean Program Management: Scaling Collaboration Across the Organization [Rot16]* for ideas.)

If you still need a large team, consider measuring the team's throughput and see if the team waits for people outside the team or for people on the team. That will help you see if there is a problem with experts, as discussed in *Trap: The Team Consists of Narrow Experts*, on page 34.

Ask Teams to Organize Themselves

If your organization has always organized by function (development, testing) or by architecture (front-end, back-end, middleware), consider asking the teams to organize themselves to become feature teams.

Too often, managers want to assign people to cross-functional teams. Instead, ask the people to discover how to create feature teams that make sense for them.

 Joe asks:
Why Shouldn't Managers Assign People to Teams?

Too often, managers don't have enough information about the people. Managers might not know what a team member wants to learn. They only know what a person has done since that person started to work for that manager. People have many more capabilities and skills.

When team members self-select their areas of interest, they have a purpose. They start to exercise their autonomy so they can build more mastery. When managers assign people based on expertise, those managers reinforce the problem of resource efficiency.

Let the team members decide what features to work on and whom to work with. You will see better throughput and more of a chance at technical excellence. See *Creating Great Teams [MM15]* for more information.

If you have everyone on one campus, consider asking them to come to a large room. Explain the feature teams you expect: Admin, Diagnostics, Search, and so on. Label flip charts in different areas of the room with the names of the features. Ask people to stand near the flip chart they would like to work on.

Ask people to add their names to the flip chart. When the people are done moving around, see what you have. Ask each team to see if they are missing any capabilities on their team. Encourage the people around each flip chart to write down their capabilities and see where they are.

Facilitate organizing teams who have "too few" of any capabilities. In my experience, teams might be missing product owner, UI/UX, or testing capabilities.

If you can't get everyone in the same physical location, ask people to do the same exercise virtually. The virtual exercise works especially well if people want to work with a particular product owner. People may have worked with this person before, so the product owner attracts a team to work with him or her.

If your organization has optimized for resource efficiency (see *Managers Move from Resource-Efficiency to Flow-Efficiency Thinking*, on page 240), don't be surprised if you have teams that are not full-feature teams.

In that case, ask the team members to work in pairs (two people working together on one feature), and preferably as a mob (the entire team works together on one feature) so they can collaborate as a team. As they collaborate, they will learn—as a team—which other people they will need to create features. (See *Work as a Whole Team to Create the Product*, on page 131, for more information about pairing and mobbing.) Teams can start the hiring process, regardless of whether that means extending an invitation to someone inside the organization or hiring from outside.

In my experience, teams of four to six people are just about the right size. In agile terms, that's a couple of developers, a tester, and a product owner. Your experience might be different, so consider running experiments to see what the right team size is for different areas.

Facilitate the Team's Social Contract

Once the team has some people, it's time to help it create its agile culture. That culture helps the team members work together and deliver as a team. Edgar Schein, in *Organizational Culture and Leadership [Sch10]*, defines *organizational culture* as what people can say, how they treat each other, and what the organization rewards. (The team might reward differently than the organization, especially if your organization has just started its agile journey.)

One way to think about the team's culture is to think of the team as a social contract. Agile teams might be able to work with implicit contracts. I have found that because agile is so different than the team's previous ways of working, it helps the team to explicitly create its own social contract.

In turn, that social contract helps team members articulate how they are willing to work in the form of values and working agreements. Your team might realize that it says one thing and does another, which doesn't help anyone finish any work.

Ask the Team to Consider Its Values

Values are how people treat each other. Team members might explore how transparent they are with each other, what they focus on, and what they commit to. Instead of starting with a premade list of values, consider this activity, described by Dhaval Panchal,[1] to flesh out your team's values:

1. Ask everyone to meet for about 30 minutes.

2. Provide everyone with index cards and a large, dark marker. The team members will need to see each other's cards after writing them.

3. Ask each person to fill in this sentence: "I don't like it when some-one/people...." Each person might write down anywhere from two to five of these sentences.

4. Divide the team into pairs.

5. In pairs, select one card. Work with your partner to write down a statement that counters the negative statement. For example, if you said, "I don't like it when some people tell me what to do," you might write a statement that says, "I like it when people discuss our technical approach as a team." Continue until each pair addresses all its cards.

6. Ask the pairs to read each "I like it" card out loud. As the team members read the cards, capture what they say on a flip chart to post in the team area. (Note: the facilitator does not read the "I like it" statements. The team members read them.)

Now your team has described its values in a positive way. It's time to create the team's working agreements.

Ask the Team to Develop Working Agreements

Working agreements define the ways team members work together. These definitions might include what "done" means, ground rules of meetings, and team norms. For example, here are some working agreements to determine:

• Core hours—Does the team need to commit to core hours so everyone knows when members are available?

---

1. http://www.dhavalpanchal.com/sharing-values-a-team-building-exercise

- What "done" means—Does the team know what "done" means for a story? See the discussion in Chapter 11, *Know What "Done" Means*, on page 165.

- How the team treats meeting times—What will the team do if people are late to meetings or don't attend at all?

- What the team automates and when—It's not possible to automate all testing. On the other hand, it is possible to automate much of it. What does this team need to automate and when?

- How the team responds to urgent requests—If the team needs to respond to production support requests, it needs to know what those parameters are. So does the rest of the organization.

Consider Sustainable Pace as a Team Working Agreement

Sustainable pace means the team can work at this pace, day in, day out, week in, week out, month in, month out, year in, year out. If your team needs a break after several days, they are pushing to finish work. That's not sustainable over the long term.

When teams use the agile and lean principles, they often work together to finish work as a team. They work hard, together. If the team has also considered the lean pillars of respect and continuous improvement, they will discover that peaks and troughs of work don't create value.

In my experience, when teams adopt sustainable pace as an agreement, they realize some benefits: they choose to work together, as in pairing, swarming, or mobbing together. They work closely with the product owner to manage the story size. They choose practices to maintain their technical excellence.

Sustainable pace is not just about the team's throughput. It's about creating an environment inside the team that helps the team live the agile and lean principles to deliver value, day in and day out.

As the team members work together, they might realize they need working agreements in other areas. I have seen a number of teams decide that they need to timebox all their work, not just use timeboxes for an iteration. Your team might not need to do that. Working agreements make it easier for a team to collaborate to deliver.

Agile Teams Become Self-Organizing

Once the team starts to understand how to work together, it moves toward self-organization. In *Leading Teams: Setting the Stage for Great Performances* [Hac02], J. Richard Hackman includes a table that describes the differences between manager-led teams, self-managing teams, and self-governing teams.

No team moves from manager-led to self-management in a short time. Often, the organization does not allow a team enough leeway to manage itself the way it wants to. I have seen an intermediate state, set in italics in the table that follows, that shows what many agile teams can do as they learn to direct themselves.

Who Is Responsible For	Manager-Led Teams	*Self-Directed Teams*	Self-Managing Teams	Self-Governing Teams
Setting the overall direction	Manager	*Manager*	Manager	Team
Designing the team and its organizational context	Manager	*Manager*	Team	Team
Monitoring and managing work process and progress	Manager	*Team, with the exception of hiring and firing*	Team	Team
Executing team tasks	Team	*Team*	Team	Team

Table 3—Adaptation of Hackman's Type of Teams

Managers often create the team and set the overall direction. Agile teams take it from there. They direct their own work. They plan their work and deliver the work. The monitor their progress.

Too few agile teams are able to manage their own hiring and firing; however, agile teams must have the final decision about whom to hire. That's because the team manages its work. Managers sometimes believe they can make the hiring decision for a team. Instead, managers can facilitate the hiring process, making sure the team members know how to interview and make a decision as a team. See *Hiring Geeks That Fit [Rot13]* for details on how to hire.

If you are some sort of project manager, technical lead, manager, or other hierarchical position, your job is to serve the team. For example, the Scrum master role, as defined in the Scrum Guide,[2] explicitly says that the Scrum master's job is to serve the team. (For more information on how leaders serve the team, see *How Leaders Serve the Team*, on page 60.)

If your team is not managing its own work, consider the actions you can take that can help them do so. Create an agile culture of transparency and collaboration. The team will use that and deliver more finished work than you can imagine.

---

2. http://www.scrumguides.org/index.html

Keep Teams Together

Teams need time to learn how to work together. Many technical practices and interpersonal practices help teams learn how to work together. And this learning takes time.

People learn together by working together. Don't waste time on fake team-building activities such as anything physical. Those activities might be fun for some people, but they don't help people learn how to work together at work.

You might be familiar with Bruce Tuckman's forming–storming–norming–performing model of group development from *Stages of Small-Group Development Revisited [TJ77]* and illustrated by the following diagram.

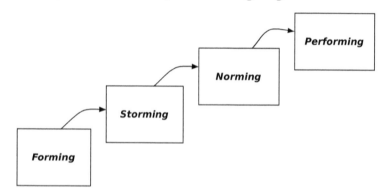

The team forms, whether the members select each other or someone decides they should work together. They are polite to each other and attempt to work together.

As they try to work together, they storm. One person doesn't like the way another person makes decisions. Or they disagree on the outcome. Whatever the issue, the team members learn how to work together.

After a while, they start to normalize. When developers work together, they often decide on a particular way of commenting code or how long a class or routine of some sort should be. When testers work together, they often decide how much to automate when. When the entire team works together, it learns who makes which kinds of mistakes—and how to look for those problems. The team learns who must have the last word. The team learns how to provide each other feedback and support.

Performing is where team members can learn to excel as a team. The team can be in flow together. They—almost instinctively—know who will react in which way. They can manage problems as a team, regardless of the kind of problems they have.

You want your teams to at least get to norming, and preferably to performing. It takes time for a team to learn how to norm and then perform. There is no substitute for working together on *their* work to move to norming and performing. That means it takes time for teams to learn how to be effective together. The more the team can work together, the faster they will norm and then perform. Your managers might be focused on utilization. See *Managers Move from Resource-Efficiency to Flow-Efficiency Thinking*, on page 240, to see how to help your managers create cross-functional feature teams.

Because teams take a while to learn to work together, keep the team together. In fact, consider making the team a *product* team, where the organization flows work through the team. (See *Managers Move from Resource-Efficiency to Flow-Efficiency Thinking*, on page 240, and *Manage Your Project Portfolio [Rot16a]* for more details.)

Recognize Team Traps

As you try to create collaborative cross-functional teams, you may encounter problems such as these:

- Your team is a component team.

- Everyone on your team is a narrow expert.

- The developers and testers don't work *together*, but rather in staggered iterations.

- The team's membership isn't stable, so the team has trouble learning to work together.

- The team pushes to finish work.

- The team cannot solve its own problems.

- Team members have a history and culture of individual work, not collective work.

You can work to overcome these traps. Here are ways that might work for you.

Trap: Your Teams Are Component Teams

You have a cross-functional team, but the team works across the layers of the architecture. Or you have a cross-functional team that is missing some scarce person, possibly a DBA or a UX person. These teams need help from other teams or other people to finish features. Whomever you are missing, your team cannot deliver a feature through the architecture.

Here's what you can do:

- Ask the person you are missing to join your team full-time for several weeks. While that person works with your team, pair or mob on everything that person touches. (See *Work as a Whole Team to Create the Product*, on page 131, for details on pairing and mobbing.) If you're like me, you might not become an expert in that person's area of expertise, but you will have more understanding. You might need that person less often. I have seen this work with UX and DBA positions.

- Explain to your management that you are missing a person with specific expertise. Your team doesn't have all the roles it needs. Maybe you can hire someone to join your team.

- It's possible you don't have enough people because your managers are stuck in resource-efficiency thinking. (See the discussion in *Managers Move from Resource-Efficiency to Flow-Efficiency Thinking*, on page 240). Create a kanban board showing cycle time, as illustrated in the diagram on page 186.

I do not recommend a relatively popular alternative: adding "visitors" to a team. Visitors interfere with the team's collaboration. The team will have to explain to each new visitor how it works. And the team will have to re-form as it learns how to work with other people. See *Keep Teams Together*, on page 32, for maximum teamwork and learning capability.

Trap: The Team Consists of Narrow Experts

For years, managers hired and rewarded people based on their ever-narrowing expertise. In agile, we need people with expertise in multiple areas, called generalizing specialists. Experts have one deep capability. Often, the more expertise, the deeper their capability in an ever-more-narrow area. Generalizing specialists have varying expertise in several areas, as illustrated by the following diagram.

People and Their Capabilities

Expert with One Deep Capability

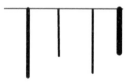

Generalizing Specialist with Several Capabilities

Everyone has preferences for what they like to do. When I was a developer, I preferred to work on the operating system (also known as the platform level) and algorithms, what we might call the middleware level in a several-tier architecture. I could work on the user interface, but I wasn't as comfortable there. I could test other people's code, but not mine—certainly not very well—at the system level.

I was a generalizing specialist with expertise in several areas. Did I have a preference? Of course. Was I willing to work with the entire team to complete a particular feature or set of features? Yes. Encourage that kind of thinking in your team. You might be able to have fewer people on the team.

Here are some ideas to encourage that kind of thinking.

- Make sure your managers and reward system recognize flow efficiency, not resource efficiency. See *Managers Move from Resource-Efficiency to Flow-Efficiency Thinking*, on page 240.

- Ask the team to limit its work in progress, so that the team has to work together to finish features. You can measure cumulative flow to see how much work in progress the team has for a given time and for the project.

- If you find it useful, consider lunch-and-learns. At a lunch meeting, one person at a time presents his or her area of deep expertise.

- Consider pairing or mobbing to avoid reinforcing expertise. (See *Work as a Whole Team to Create the Product*, on page 131, for details on pairing and mobbing.)

I have found it useful to make sure experts work with other people in some way.

Trap: Developers and Testers Work in Successive or Staggered Iterations

I've worked with and seen many teams where the developers and testers were not united in a single cross-functional team. The developers finish their work in the first two-week iteration. The testers might even start their testing in that iteration, but they don't finish in the same iteration. As illustrated by the diagram on page 36, the testers on this team were at least two weeks "behind."

Here's the problem. The iteration duration is the duration of development and testing, and whatever else you need to complete the work.

When developers finish first, they create WIP for the testers. They may also become interrupted when the testers find problems. That means the developers create WIP for themselves, which might be invisible WIP because it's not predictable.

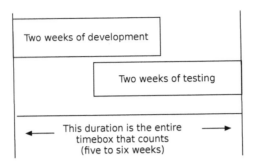

Sequential work based on expertise makes your iterations longer. What would it take for you to work as a team on stories and reduce the lag between the time the development is done and the testing is done?

Consider these possibilities to help create cross-functional feature teams:

- Create and use a kanban board to see where the work is waiting for people or specific skills/capabilities. Now you can see who you need.

- Measure the WIP to see how much work is waiting for which kinds of people or teams. Maybe that will encourage cross-functional team organization.

- If you have functional teams, see the suggestion in *Ask Teams to Organize Themselves*, on page 27.

Staggered development and testing is not agile or lean. It might be better than what you did before, but it's not an agile approach.

Trap: Team Membership Is Not Stable

Some managers are concerned that the team is not working at maximum output. Those managers ask team members to work on a couple of teams or on several projects. Those managers are stuck in resource-efficiency thinking. See the discussion in *Managers Move from Resource-Efficiency to Flow-Efficiency Thinking*, on page 240.

The more stable the team membership is, the easier it is for a team to become a norming or performing team. The team doesn't incur a cost of re-forming itself every time someone enters or leaves the team. The team members learn how to trust each other.

Every time a team changes membership, the team incurs a decrease in throughput. That's because the team starts back at forming again.

Keep stable teams together.

Trap: The Team Pushes Its Pace

Sometimes teams push themselves. Sometimes managers want to push the team into doing "more." Here's how you can tell if your team is working at an unsustainable pace:

- The team pushes to complete work just before a demo.

- The team wants a break between one chunk of work and the next. (In iteration-based agile approaches, teams want days or a week between iterations. In flow, the team members want a break between the work they complete and the next item on the board.)

- The team is working overtime all the time.

Developing great products requires everyone to be their best at all times. Don't expect or ask people to work overtime. In my experience, that's the fastest way to destroy technical excellence and creativity. Instead, ask people to collaborate at a sustainable pace.

Trap: The Team Requires Permission from Distant Managers to Solve Problems

Your organization might have powerful functional managers (development, quality assurance, and others) or a powerful PMO (project-management office). Those people dictate who works on your team and when, and what your team can do. Too often, those managers—while they mean well—do not understand the problems the team encounters.

The functional managers think about people as a "pool" of resources, as in the *"Shared Services" Often Aren't,* on page 242 approach to people. And too often, the PMO dictates the project documents or the approach to the project the team should take.

Too often, these folks want to dictate solutions for your team.

Consider this: these people want to do the right thing. Their experience shows them that the "right" thing is different from what an agile team needs. As a leader, you have at least these options:

- Ask these people to take a chance and allow the team to experiment with its process.

- Ask these people to empower you as the person who can facilitate the team's problem-solving process.

- Build your influencing and upward-coaching skills so you can work with these people over time to help them understand what agile approaches buy the team, them, and the organization.

And you always have the option of not using agile approaches. See *Manage It! [Rot07]* for a thorough discussion of life cycles that might be easier than using agile approaches. And read Chapter 16, *How Managers Help Agile Teams*, on page 237, for ways you can help your managers learn to think differently.

Trap: Team Members Are Wary of Collaboration

Each person has his or her own preferred culture and way of working. Sometimes you can see these cultural preferences, as covered in *Cultures and Organizations: Software of the Mind, Third Edition [HHM10]*. Some people enjoy working as part of a team. Some hate it.

Sometimes people hate being a part of a team because the corporate culture creates incentives around individual work. (See *Organizational Culture and Leadership [Sch10]* for guidance about corporate culture.)

Regardless of where the wariness arises, you cannot tell people, "Let's all be a team now!" Nothing you *say* will make a difference. On the other hand, there are things you can do:

- You can ask people to experiment in short timeboxes for how they can work together.

- If your organization still rewards people only for individual work, your attempts to use agile approaches are likely to fail. You have an impediment to an agile culture. Add this impediment (individual rewards) to your impediment list, and escalate that to management. See *Visualize Problems with a Board*, on page 121.

- Consider discussing the difference between flow efficiency and resource efficiency, as discussed in *Managers Move from Resource-Efficiency to Flow-Efficiency Thinking*, on page 240, with team members.

- Conduct one-on-ones to understand each person's concerns. Once you do, you can start to address those concerns.

Whatever you do, don't tell people they shouldn't feel a certain way. People own their feelings and beliefs. You might have a person or even a team that is not interested in agile approaches. Do not force agile approaches on them. Work with them for some reasonable amount of time. Help create a system of work that invites people into agile approaches. If that doesn't work, be honest. Are agile approaches for right this team now? Maybe not.

Now Try This

1. Assess your team. Does it have all the roles it requires to complete features? If you're not sure, ask the team.

2. If your team doesn't have enough people, what can you do to get the people you need on the team? Do you need to create different teams from several component teams?

3. Is your team larger than nine people? What warning signs would you notice to know if the team is not collaborating because of its size?

You have a cross-functional, collaborative feature team. Now let's see how teams learn to work together with interpersonal skills.

CHAPTER 3

Build Teamwork with Interpersonal Practices

One VP of R&D asked me this question: Why didn't his resources act like teams? He could see that they didn't trust each other much. He knew he wasn't getting the value he thought he paid for. He was confused.

Part of the problem was his thinking. He thought about people as "resources." Yes, what you call people matters. He didn't mind moving people off and onto projects at will. He also ranked people against each other. That made them want to collaborate less, not more.

The people on the team reflected his values. They treated each other as resources. They hated to ask for help. They knew they would be ranked against each other, so they competed, not collaborated.

Not surprisingly, they weren't a team.

Humans comprise the product-development team. Not resources, although the people are resourceful. I have found that when people stop talking about resources and start talking about humans, people in the organization start to change their mindset and, therefore, the culture.

Because agile is a human-centric, collaborative approach to product development, your team needs to build its ability to work as a team using interpersonal skills. In addition, managers need to change their language and the team culture. See Chapter 16, *How Managers Help Agile Teams*, on page 237, for an introduction to thinking about humans instead of "resources."

Many technical people didn't decide to work in technology because they had terrific interpersonal skills. They started their jobs because they liked solving problems. In organizations, many people realize they need to learn to build their interpersonal skills so they can collaborate on building the product. They build a little, get some feedback to inform the next part of the work, build a little more, and get some feedback. Successful agile teams use their agile mindset—that build, feedback, learn loop—for their interpersonal skills, too.

People work as team members and take risks when they are capable of providing feedback and coaching to each other. And leaders need to create safe environments for people to work as a team.

Interpersonal Skills Are Not "Soft"

Many people refer to interpersonal skills as "soft" skills. I don't recommend that. "Soft" has the connotation of "easy," or "not deep." On the contrary, interpersonal skills require deep skill: understanding, practice, and learning. Many of us discover that it's much easier to learn technical skills than to learn and practice interpersonal skills. Consider calling these skills "interpersonal," not soft.

Agile team members require at least two interpersonal skills: the ability to receive and provide feedback and coaching. When team members can provide each other feedback and coach each other, the team members can create a safe environment for the collaboration necessary for experimentation. Those abilities help the team members learn from their work, as individuals and as a team, and help the team learn to deliver small increments of value often.

First, let's think about what is similar about many agile team members.

How Agile Team Members Are Similar

Your agile team is unique. That said, successful agile team members tend to exhibit these interpersonal qualities:

- Team members collaborate with each other.
- Team members can ask each other for help.
- Team members are adaptable, willing to work on whatever is next and possibly outside of their expertise.

In addition, many agile team members exhibit these preferences:

- Do something good enough for now (as opposed to waiting for perfection).

- Create experiments to try something and receive feedback on the product or the team's process.

- Be willing to work outside their preferences as a generalizing specialist to help the entire team deliver.

When team members and teams exhibit these qualities and preferences, they are able to persevere. They have the courage to try something and to continue their work even when the work is quite difficult. They are able to set long-term goals and persevere to achieve them, one small step at a time.

Team Members Practice Continual Feedback

Too many people receive feedback once a year from their manager in the form of a performance evaluation. Too often, the data—if there is any—is too vague or late to be useful. And rarely do people on teams have a chance to practice feedback with each other or with their managers. Feedback seems to flow downhill, just as mud does.

Infrequent muddy feedback from people outside the team is useless. Frequent, data-based feedback from peers is helpful.

Learning How to Use Feedback Helped Us Release Faster
by: Gwen, Agile Project Manager

We had a team who was accustomed to waterfall, a sequenced approach to projects with one delivery at the end of the project. I knew we had to get good at releasing small deliveries to get feedback on our work, both on the product and how we worked together.

I explained to the team that I wanted us to know we could deliver useful chunks at least as often as every week. Were they willing to do that? Yes, they each said. I explained we would probably make mistakes along the way. Were they willing to provide feedback to each other? Not blaming, just the facts.

I explained how to provide feedback, especially how to agree on the data. One of the team members asked what happened if they didn't agree on the data.

I explained about "going meta"—starting at a higher level of abstraction—if they couldn't agree on the data. That seemed to help.

They practiced with each other in the meeting, to make sure they knew how to provide and receive feedback. They went back to working on the product.

It took them about a week of practicing every day, multiple times a day, to get comfortable with feedback. Once they did, though, wow. They were able to release value as often as we wanted. They took the idea of feedback and applied it to everything. Best thing I ever did.

Peer-based feedback helps team members collaborate, learn, and adapt to what the team needs to finish work now.

As defined in *What Did You Say? The Art of Giving and Receiving Feedback* *[Wei15]*, feedback is

> "Information about past behavior, delivered in the present, which may influence future behavior."

Consider using the peer-to-peer model of feedback, as explained in *Behind Closed Doors: Secrets of Great Management [RD05]*:

- Create an opening to deliver feedback.
- Describe the behavior or result in a way that the person can hear.
- State the impact using "I" language.
- Make a request for continued or changed behavior.

It doesn't matter if you want to ask someone to continue to do something great (reinforcing feedback) or to ask someone to change (change-focused feedback). This approach works.

Here's how feedback works in practice. Imagine you have a product that requires internationalization and localization to support multiple languages. A new tester, Dave, joins the team and discovers a problem in the English version. He checks the French and Spanish languages—and yes, the problem is there, too. He opens three defect reports, one for each language. Judy, the developer, has this conversation with him:

Judy: Hey, Dave, got a sec? I want to talk to you about these defects.

Dave: Oh, okay.

Judy: Okay, let's take this conference room. I'm not sure if you know about how we have reported internationalization problems in the past, but we report one problem against all the languages. You reported three problems that are the same. Did you realize that?

Dave: Uh, no. Is that a problem?

Judy: Well, it's not earth-shattering, but it's not how we work here. Can you make all these defects link to each other, and then only report one in the future?

Dave: Well, I can. But what about when I find three real problems?

Judy: Oh, report them! Don't worry. You know, if you're not sure, just ask me. I'll tell you if I think it's three problems. Actually, you can ask anyone on the team. You don't have to ask me, in particular.

Dave: That's okay? I thought I was responsible for quality.

Judy: Aha! Nope, we're all responsible for making sure the entire product works. Your job is to expose problems for us. You did. You just reported three instead of one. That's the only issue here. Okay?

Dave: Oh, okay. Thanks.

Dave had made a mistake. Judy explained with feedback and offered coaching on the tester's role. That's all.

Feedback is even more important when you have personal issues. Dirk had terrible body odor. Selma was supposed to pair with him and just couldn't take it. Here's how Selma handled the conversation.

Dirk: You ready to pair again, Selma?

Selma: Maybe. We have something more important to discuss. Please sit and let's talk.

Dirk: Now you're making me nervous.

Selma: Well, I'm kind of nervous bringing this up. Dirk, I have to tell you this. You have terrible body odor. I didn't want to tell you, but I'm having trouble working with you, sitting next to you.

Dirk: Oh, that's terrible. How long have you noticed this?

Selma: Since last month.

Dirk: You're only telling me now? Well, at least you're telling me now. Well, I did several things last month. I changed what I ate, I changed my deodorant, and I changed my laundry detergent. I don't think my clothes are that clean, and I can change back. Should I go home and fix this now or do you think we can pair?

Selma: I think you should take a couple of hours to get your old deodorant and take a shower and wash your clothes.

Dirk: Okay, I'll tell the boss.

You might think this is an extreme example. However, I have had to tell people their breath stank or that their body odor interfered with our ability to work together.

People on agile teams need the ability to provide and receive feedback about the work and the work environment. That includes us as humans. (For more information on the importance of feedback, also see "Building a Team Through Feedback."[1])

Meta Feedback Is About the Feedback

When people don't agree on anything, it's time to go "meta" and address the problems in the relationship, not the feedback. If you can't find a time to meet to provide feedback, that's a problem in the relationship. If no one agrees on the data, it might be time to verify the data with this question:

> What do you see or hear that leads you to that conclusion?

If necessary, ask about the other senses: smell, taste, and touch. We humans might interpret results or make meaning of the data and not provide specific data. Once each person has the data, they can continue.

There are any number of potential problems with feedback. Make sure you stick with the data, don't label people, and explain how this problem affects you personally. Then you'll be able to have the conversation about continuing, or change as necessary.

Whatever you do, separate change-focused feedback from reinforcing feedback. Often, team members need both kinds of feedback and they don't need the *Trap: The Feedback Sandwich*, on page 56.

Team Members Coach Each Other

In a cohesive agile team, you see feedback everywhere. Team members experiment together and separately, learning different areas of the product and learning how to make the product work. You'll hear things like this:

- "Did you know if you refactor like this, you can see that?" "Oh, no, I didn't. Show me more."

- "Hey, does anyone know why this test returned those results?" "Oh, we haven't fixed that part yet. Let's look at it together."

- Fist-bump. "Thanks for showing me how to do that."

Team members learn from one another and ask each other for feedback—not necessarily in the formal form. If you don't hear these kinds of conversations (or see in virtual conversations) you may have the *Trap: Not Enough Feedback*, on page 54.

That learning is where team members might coach each other. No one has an obligation to coach another, but the team members might offer coaching.

---

1. http://www.jrothman.com/articles/2012/10/building-a-team-through-feedback-2

Coaching is offering options with support. Not everyone wants coaching from everyone else, so coaches must have permission before they start to coach. Otherwise, the coach inflicts help on the other person. That doesn't help anyone. (See *Trap: Inflicting Help*, on page 55.)

Especially when coaching around new skills, I find it helpful to ask the other person to generate options. I don't want to be the know-it-all or default to teaching when coaching is so much more than that. When the other person can't generate more options, I might prompt with one option and then see if the other person can generate more. I use the Rule of Three as defined in *Behind Closed Doors: Secrets of Great Management [RD05]* to help people generate options before we evaluate possibilities.

In an agile project, the team members take responsibility for completing work together. They coach each other to help move the work across the board. When team members realize they don't know something about how to work or how to solve a problem, they may ask for more training or coaching. As a leader, you might be able to help. You might not.

Recognize When the Team Needs an External Coach

Software development is a collaborative effort. It is—so far—the most challenging type of work. (See Andy Hunt's *Pragmatic Thinking and Learning [Hun08]* for more information.)

When I want to improve my skills, I attend workshops where I can obtain guided practice. Sometimes I need more than a workshop can provide me, so I engage a coach for more help over time.

Coaches can help in any number of ways. Consider these possibilities adapted from *Choosing a Consulting Role: Principles and Dynamics of Matching Role to Situation [CKM90]* and outlined in the diagram on page 48.

What kind of a coach does the team need? Consider asking the team what kind of help it wants. Different coaches coach at different levels for different areas. Very few coaches can coach at the three levels: inside the team, for the team, and for the organization. Use the retrospective data to see where the team needs assistance first.

Teams new to collaborative work might need coaches who can help the team teach or facilitate or partner with some practices such as continuous integration, test-driven development (TDD), or even pairing. If the team is working well as a team but has internal impediments, the team (and you, as a servant leader) might need help seeing options for the team's process. If the team

Possible Consulting Roles

Counselor: "You do it; I will be your sounding board."	Coach: "You did well; what would you do differently next time?"	Partner: "We will do it together and learn from each other."
Facilitator: "You do it; I will attend to the process."	Teacher: "Here are some principles you can see to solve problems of this type."	Modeler: "I will do it; you watch so you can learn from me."
Reflective Observer: "You do it; I will watch and tell you what I see and hear."	Technical Advisor: "I will answer your questions as you go along."	Hands-on Expert: "I will do it for you; I will tell you what to do."

Responsibility for client's growth (vertical axis)

Responsibility for client's results

discovers that its impediments are from the culture or organizational processes, the team might need a coach at the organizational level. For more information about servant leadership, see *How Leaders Serve the Team,* on page 60.

Does the Team Need to Track Collaboration?

Feedback and coaching improve a team's collaboration capability. Team members don't *need* to track their collaboration. However, if explicit collaboration is a new practice for your team, they might want to track their collaboration.

Tracking collaboration helps if the team members don't collaborate to take stories together, or if they optimize in some other way for individuals and not the team. If the team wants to track collaboration, it might start with designing its own board, such as the example board shown in the figure on page 49.

The team on this board started to track with *A* (Ask for help) and *O* (Offer help). They decided different-colored stickies would be even better. Because this is data for the team and no one else, they could change their data collection at will. They found different colored stickies better than *A*s and *O*s. The stickies helped them see the distribution of asking and offering help more easily than the *A*s and *O*s did.

Encourage your team to find a way to track how well it collaborates as a team. The team members might decide to start with creating WIP limits to see how well they—as a team—move work across their board. I have worked with some teams that decided to track asks and offers for help as a way to encourage the team members to work together. Your team might need something else. You and your team might see other possibilities.

Possible Collaboration Board

Ask/Offer Help

Person	A/O	A/O	A/O	A/O	A/O	A/O	A/O	A/O	A/O	A/O
Tom	A	A,O	▨							
Dick	O	O, A								
Susan	O	A,O	▨							
Sally	O, A		▨▨							
Trina	O		▨▨							
Thelma	A		▨▨							

| Day | 1 | 2 | 3 | 4 | 5 | 6 | 7 | 8 | 9 | 10 |

Blue Is Ask ▨
Red Is Offer ▨

Help the Team Members Build Trust

Stable teams can learn to build trust when they work together. Team members who focus on the work, who learn how to give and receive feedback, who can coach each other and receive coaching, can create trusting relationships. In Chapter 9, *Create Technical Excellence*, on page 127, I'll talk about ways the team can focus on the work so they have a steady throughput.

If people are new to stable teams, they may never have worked at building trust with each other before. In *Building Trust in Business, Politics, Relationships, and Life [SF01]*, Robert C. Solomon suggests people are trustworthy when they do the following:

• Deliver what they promise to deliver
• Are consistent in their actions and reactions
• Make integrity a cornerstone of their work
• Are willing to discuss, influence, and negotiate
• Trust in themselves and their colleagues

Agile approaches help teams and team members see what they promise to deliver. Being able to give and receive feedback and coaching can help people manage small problems before those problems become large. When people use technical practices that support ongoing work, they can create work that has integrity.

Interpersonal skills, by themselves, won't guarantee the team can learn to trust each other. However, more team members can build trust when they have the interpersonal skills to manage their interactions.

Create a Team Environment of Safety

There's a bit of a chicken-and-egg problem with interpersonal skills. Teams need safety to build their skills. And building the skills helps the team members provide a safe environment for each other.

Amy C. Edmondson, in *Teaming: How Organizations Learn, Innovate, and Compete in the Knowledge Economy [Edm12]*, discusses the need for psychological safety in interdependent collaborative teams. Safety allows the team members to discuss, explore together, and learn.

What's the Big Deal About Safety?
by: Jim, VP, R&D

I initially pooh-poohed the idea of psychological safety. Then I realized that some of our teams had substantially more throughput than other teams. I had lunch with different team members and found a significant data point. Every single team with less throughput had at least one person as a "lead" of some sort.

I had created architectural leads, development leads, even test-architecture leads. I even called them my "indispensable" people. What a mistake. Those people imposed their agendas on the teams. No one else on the team felt safe to say something that disagreed with those leads. They were concerned about other peoples' possible negative perceptions of them.

I realized my mistake. I had one-on-ones with the leads and explained the problem. They agreed to each try experiments that removed them from the know-all position. One architect told me it was such a relief—he no longer had to know "everything." I explained the difference in how we thought about people. We created "communities of practice" and ways for these people to explore their influence on the business value of the architecture, automation, refactoring patterns, everything.

In addition, I focused on learning early. What small experiments could we run that would allow our teams to learn together, safely? That changed the culture over time. It took about six months before I saw a fight between an architect and a tester. I was thrilled. That meant these two people felt comfortable enough to disagree and still be able to work together.

As a by-product, I have many more "indispensable" people now, but I no longer have a bus factor of one. Our entire organization is more adaptable and flexible in the work they do and in what they understand.

I now understand the need for safety. People have to be able to ask questions, challenge assumptions, and find new ways of working together. I'm not big on the kumbaya nonsense. I want results in the best possible product as early as we can deliver it. Psychological safety allows the teams to do that.

In agile terms, safety allows the team to manage the ambiguity and uncertainty about anything: the stories, the architecture, the tests. Safety allows the team to learn early by creating small experiments. Safety helps people admit and look for mistakes.

We create safety when we

- encourage learning from small experiments,
- use clear and direct language,
- admit when we don't know,
- acknowledge when we fail, and
- set boundaries for what is a personal or team decision and what is not.

One of the best ways to create team safety is to create an environment in which team members feel safe to take risks.

Safety Helps the Team Evaluate and Recover from Risks

In more traditional projects, the project manager or the manager manages risks. That risk management often takes the form of "This could happen. How will we guard against it?" Sometimes the team learns (late) that it didn't manage a risk. Safe teams mistake-proof their work. Sometimes the leader leads the mistake-proofing. Sometimes team members do. It doesn't matter who leads it, as long as teams create ways to mistake-proof their work.

We Learned About Mistake-Proofing the Hard Way
by: Trevor, Technical Lead

We were rolling along, releasing features into the code base every two weeks. We high-fived each other at every retro, because we were so freaking awesome. I didn't realize that we each had specific roles in the release and we didn't know each other's roles.

Joe put together the release notes. He also did some manual checks, which I didn't realize. He went on vacation during the summer and we released as normal. We had Susie write the release notes.

The release notes were fine. The release didn't work. We had to back it out and we had egg on our face. It didn't matter that the previous 20 releases had gone well. This one didn't. I looked into what happened.

Joe had been doing manual checks for several items. He hadn't documented them. I hadn't realized and neither had Susie. We decided to re-create the manual checks with automation so we wouldn't make the same mistake again.

We didn't blame each other. We acted to make sure this problem didn't happen again for releasing. We took this opportunity to mistake-proof other areas in the team. We're so much more robust now. We have a side-benefit, too: we can release more often and faster.

In agile projects, team members are more likely to ask this question: "How can we recognize risks when they are small, and if they do occur, how can we recover from them?"

Those are two different attitudes about risks. More traditional projects want prediction and control. Agile projects provide resilience. You will find ways to build resilience into your projects. Consider these two ways to build resilience: the team's ability to manage its team membership and its ability to learn early.

Teams Manage Their Own Membership

Many organizations have a defined process for hiring: The manager fills out a requisition. The manager writes the job description. The manager phone-screens candidates. The manager decides who will interview the candidate. The manager decides who to hire.

If you want a collaborative, high-performing team, ask the manager to facilitate the hiring process, not manage it. Instead, ask the team to manage the hiring process. The more you want a collaborative team, the more the team has the ability to decide who is—and who is not—on the team. When managers decide, the team has less power to manage itself.

Teams who can manage their own membership help the team grow and deliver. They already know they want these people. The team is willing to invest time and energy into providing feedback and coaching to the team members.

Teams who don't have a say in their team membership might try to collaborate. However, I don't see these teams sustain their collaboration when team members don't fit.

Too often, we hire for technical skills and fire for interpersonal skills. See *Hiring Geeks That Fit [Rot13]* for more information about how to hire the for interpersonal skills your team needs.

Learn Early Instead of Failing Fast

One of the common phrases about agile is "fail fast." The problem with "failing" is that it is an emotionally loaded word. We have decades of experience in organizations that require us to *not* fail.

Instead of failing fast, consider learning early. I find that learning early creates a different mindset for me. I now create small, safe-to-fail experiments. I manage my ambiguity around the entire deliverable by creating small steps.

I might be unique with my concern about the "fail fast" metaphor. If your team members have trouble with the idea of failing, consider asking them what they can learn and how early they can learn it. When teams decide to learn early, they might select more small experiments to provide them information. That information builds resilience in the team.

Team collaboration and learning helps the team build safety and resilience. No one "bets the farm" on any one idea or one feature.

Safety Allows the Team to Build Respect

Feedback, coaching, and managing team membership helps the team create an environment in which people can work together, including experiment together, with safety.

One way to think about safety is to consider David Rock's SCARF model (*SCARF: A Brain-Based Model for Collaborating with and Influencing Others [Roc08]*). SCARF stands for Status, Certainty, Autonomy, Relatedness, and Fairness.

Here are some anti-collaboration patterns in terms of SCARF:

- When the team's *status* is uneven, such as when the manager is part of the team. People are reluctant to take a risk in front of their managers; see *Weird Ideas That Work: How to Build a Creative Company [Sut06]*.

- When the team feels *uncertain* about its next steps. The larger the feature is, or the more uncertainty around a feature, the less certainty a team has about how to do the next work.

- When the team has insufficient *autonomy* to work the way it wants to. The team might feel bound by decisions from outside the team.

- When the team doesn't know or can't manage its team membership—the team's *relatedness*. If managers pluck people from or add people to a team, the team members don't have the ability to develop their relationships.

- When the team members sense *unfairness* in how they are treated, as individual members or as a team. Agile approaches invite team recognition and rewards to address this potential unfairness.

It's not just management status that can reduce collaboration; it might be other hierarchy, such as technical architecture. Architects can help keep the codebase coherent. Good architecture practices can help with refactoring and improve the performance of the product. The problem arises when the architect is external to the team.

When the organization creates an architectural career path where the architects don't work on teams, the organization creates a hierarchy in the product-development organization. That creates safety issues and often code (or test) issues. Agile teams move fast, building just enough for now and verifying that what they built works. The team can't safely do that if they have to accommodate someone else's (well-meaning) architecture or design.

The reason architects exist is that they know a tremendous amount about how systems work. That expertise might be quite helpful to the team members. Consider building *communities of practice*, open to whoever is interested. You might need these to start:

- Architecture
- Test automation
- Technical practices that increase collaboration

Help your team increase its safety with equality on the team, certainty about its next steps by having small stories, autonomy for the team around its management and membership, and fairness in how the team members treat each other and how the organization treats them.

The more the team can provide each other feedback and coaching, and manage their membership, the freer the team will be to collaborate and build a safe environment for itself.

Recognize Interpersonal-Skills Traps

As people develop these skills, you might see some traps:

- The team members don't provide enough feedback to each other.
- Team members inflict help when they see a solution.
- Team members "sandwich" their feedback.

You can work to overcome these traps. Here are ways that might work for you.

Trap: Not Enough Feedback

Collaborative teams learn how to work with each other. They talk about the product and the process on a regular basis. Healthy teams have team members who feel safe enough to ask for help and to discuss what's going on for them. If you have ever encountered a problem where you got stuck and you asked for help, you used feedback.

For years, organizations recognized and rewarded people for *individual* work. That meant we had incentives to work alone, plug along, and solve the problem however we could. It also meant we worked alone for as long as possible, because the more difficult the problem, the more we might receive as recognition or reward.

That working-alone mindset is in stark opposition to a great agile team. Agile teams work together, to move work across the board, to help each other finish work, to work as generalizing specialists. Instead of being rewarded for individual work, we move to rewarding teams for team work.

That means even if people work alone on some chunk of work, we don't want team members to be stuck and not ask for help or feedback. If you see team members working alone and being stuck, consider offering these options to your team:

- Consider a team working agreement for how long people work alone without making progress. I like a timebox of no more than 15 minutes for being stuck. Then it's time to ask for help. The stuck person can explain what he/she has done up until now, and then ask for feedback and coaching.

- Talk to the Duck.[2] Rubber-duck debugging works even better when the stuck person pairs with someone else. (I explained my experiences talking to the duck in the article "Tell Your Problems to the Duck."[3])

- Suggest that the team pair or mob on the problem. Everyone has different expertise. Consider inviting the team to use its wisdom together. If several people get stuck on test-driven forms of development or how to create small stories, you know to consider a workshop or coaching. (See *Work as a Whole Team to Create the Product*, on page 131, for details on pairing and mobbing.)

If you don't hear a steady buzz, either in a team room or on some form of communication channel, consider asking your team members if they receive enough feedback from each other. Consider the feedback board in *Does the Team Need to Track Collaboration?*, on page 48, as a start to see what's going on.

Trap: Inflicting Help

Everyone on your team is smart. In fact, if your team members are like some of the teams I've worked with, some of those people are super-smart. They have a ton of experience. They're not afraid to help people, even if the people don't want the help.

---

2. https://en.wikipedia.org/wiki/Rubber_duck_debugging
3. http://www.jrothman.com/mpd/thinking/2016/06/tell-your-problems-to-the-duck

That's a trap. While people may offer feedback or coaching, no one has the right to coach without explicit permission from the other person.

You have several options if you see this:

- Provide feedback to the coach about what you see. That might be enough of a conversation.

- If the coach agrees with your feedback, ask, "Would you like some discussion of what else you might do?" If the coach agrees, remind the coach about the possible stances as outlined in the graphic on page 48. Together, you and the coach can discuss what might be a better alternative.

- Ask the person being coached if he or she would like some help. You don't want to inflict help either!

Make sure you have all the data if you think someone is inflicting help. You can try feedback to the people and then follow up with meta-coaching if they want you to do so.

Trap: The Feedback Sandwich

Feedback training isn't very common, so people think about feedback in a variety of ways. One way that people have encountered is the "feedback sandwich." That's where Person A provides reinforcing feedback, followed by change-focused feedback, followed by reinforcing feedback. When someone does this to me, I feel whiplash. I would rather receive all the changed-focused feedback at a different time than all the reinforcing feedback.

If you want to provide feedback to someone, and some is change-focused and some is reinforcing, consider these options:

- Ask yourself if the person really needs all this feedback. Maybe the feedback is about you, not the other person.

- Ask the person which feedback he or she would like to hear first: change-focused or reinforcing? Then, organize the feedback.

- Conduct separate meetings where you provide one kind of feedback. At a later date, provide the other feedback.

The best thing you and everyone else can do is to practice feedback. As with many agile ideas, the smaller the feedback, the easier it is for the other person to hear it and act on it.

Now Try This

1. Ask team members anonymously how comfortable they feel with feedback. Here's one way to collate the answers: On a piece of flipchart paper, label the x-axis from 1 to 5. 1 is not comfortable at all, and 5 is totally comfortable. Ask people to write their comfort-level number on a sticky note. Ask people to bring their stickies to the front of the room. (I turn my back so people can remain anonymous.) You post the stickies on the flipchart and then ask, "What do you make of this data?" Their answers will tell you what to do.

2. Ask the team members how they feel about coaching. You can use the same technique as above.

3. Ask team members how safe they feel. Use the same technique and then use the data to generate ideas about what to do.

Now that you know how the team can work together, think about the team's need for project leadership.

CHAPTER 4

Agile Requires Different Project Leadership

Every project needs some sort of project management. Not every project, especially agile projects, needs a project manager. In fact, if you have a cross-functional feature team and everyone in the organization has the agile mindset, you might not need any project leadership. However, I have yet to see this circumstance in organizations that are new to agile approaches.

When you first start using an agile approach, you may need a servant leader in the form of an agile project manager or a coach to help the team understand the process it needs. That servant leader might need to help the team recognize what to change about the team's process and how the team could change. You might need that person to protect the team from what I call "management mayhem" in *Avoid Management Mayhem*, on page 243. Agile project managers facilitate the team's process and remove impediments that prevent the team from delivering finished value.

You might be accustomed to more of a hierarchy in your project: the project manager took responsibility for the team's work and the team's process. Everyone reported to the project manager. Conversely, in agile approaches, team members report to each other. The team commits to and takes responsibility for its work and its process. That changes the kind of leadership a team needs.

Agile teams do not require anyone to control them. Agile teams don't need any hierarchy to work or to solve problems. In fact, hierarchy and control often prevent team members from feeling safe and collaborating, which many teams depend on for learning and experimenting. Agile teams require servant leadership—a different kind of project management.

Agile project-management activities facilitate the team's ability to work and to deliver value. In this chapter, I'll discuss what servant leaders are, the servant leaders you need, and the servant leaders you might consider for your team.

How Leaders Serve the Team

If you are accustomed to traditional project management, you might wonder who tells people what to do and when. The short answer is the team decides what to do as a team. The team takes its work in the way the team prefers. No one assigns work to anyone else.

When one person assigns work to another, that's called "command and control." It's inefficient and often leads to less-than-desired outcomes. Agile teams are in charge of their own deliverables and interactions. The product owner explains the results he or she wants. Then, the team decides how to perform the work.

Agile project managers, coaches, product owners, and even managers are all servant leaders. These people serve the team, not the other way around.

In *The Case for Servant Leadership [Kei08]*, Kent Keith defines seven practices of servant leaders:

1. They are self-aware.

2. They listen.

3. They serve the people who work "for" them. (Keith calls this "changing the pyramid.")

4. They help other people grow.

5. They coach people, not control them.

6. They unleash the energy and intelligence of others.

7. They work to develop their foresight so they can act, not react.

Servant leaders serve the team by facilitating the team's work.

I Serve the Team, Not Management
by: James, New Product Owner

I got training as a product owner, but it was nothing like what awaited me at work.

My team didn't have anyone in a position of leadership except for me. The functional managers thought it was just fine for them to add to any given person's backlog instead of telling me what they wanted.

I got fed up and called a meeting. I told them that adding more work to anyone's list of work was no longer acceptable. They would funnel requests through me or the team wouldn't do any of that work.

One of the managers asked, "Aren't you a servant leader?" I said I was. The manager then said, "Well, you need to serve us."

I saw red. I said, "No, I serve the team. You want me to serve you? Act like a team." I walked out.

After I took a walk around the block, I went back and knocked on my manager's door. I told him what I'd done. He said, "Good for you!" We discussed who served whom more and I was much happier about the entire situation. Oh, and we got someone to be the agile project manager so I didn't have to fight those battles.

Servant leaders are not wimps or pushovers. They serve the team, doing what the team needs them to do. Most people don't need to manage the management team. On the other hand, don't be afraid to do so. Your team will thank you for your service.

Agile Project Managers Facilitate to Serve

An agile project manager facilitates and serves the entire team. Agile project managers identify and manage risks that the team needs someone to manage.

Here is a list of what an agile project manager might do at the team level:

- Facilitate the team's process. New-to-agile teams don't have the agile mindset and culture baked into their DNA. Who will learn more about how they can make agile work for them? Who will schedule the demo and the retrospective and make sure the two meetings occur?

- Remove or enable removal of impediments the team members can't remove. Many impediments are at the organization level. The team isn't going to tackle them. The team "delegates" the impediment to the project manager.

- Assist the team in measuring the team's velocity, cycle time, and any other measurements. This might be as simple as creating the space for the team to measure as they walk the board.

- Assist the product owner in writing stories for the next iteration. New product owners may not understand how to write small-enough stories for iterations.

- Facilitate the team's workshopping of the project vision.

- Facilitate the team's workshopping of the release criteria.

- Facilitate the team's working agreements, including the team's definition of "done."

In addition, the team may need help in identifying and managing the team's risks. This can be many different things:

- Managing sponsor expectations. Too many senior managers think agile is a way to get "more, faster, cheaper" without realizing the team needs to learn—to learn how the product needs to work and to learn how to work as an agile team.

- Managing the project portfolio so the team has no context switching and is cross-functional and stable.

- Obtaining more funding if necessary.

- Making sure the long-lead-time items show up on time. This is especially helpful for projects with hardware or mechanical parts.

In addition, sometimes it makes sense for an agile project manager to represent the team and its status to more senior management. (See Chapter 14, *Report Your Project State*, on page 215, for what to report.)

This is not an exhaustive list. You might need other actions from your agile project manager.

If you use Scrum, you might say the agile project manager is a Scrum master. That is correct. I am not fond of "master" or "chief" names for roles. And if you use any other approach to agile, aside from Scrum, you can still use the term "agile project manager" for the role.

Servant Leadership Changed My Expectations of Myself
by: Sherry, New Agile Project Manager

I was accustomed to asking people what they would do and when we would see their deliverables. I didn't demand that people do anything, but I did ask for dates and status.

When we moved to agile, I had to change everything I did. It took me a while to figure it out.

I started to ask the product owner about the sequencing of the features in the roadmap and the backlog. I made sure he understood the difference between feature sets and features. We wanted features!

I had to educate my management about what they could expect from me and from the team. No more Gantt charts; they could see the roadmap. No velocity charts; we had product backlog burnup charts.

I did have to nudge—okay, push—my management to give us our own UX person. I had to explain about flow efficiency, which blew their minds.

I'm sure I did more. I think it took me about three months to change my expectations of myself. I was no longer the center of the team in terms of my deliverables. Instead, I made it possible for other people to deliver their work.

Project managers who act as servant leaders fulfill useful functions. Project managers can be especially helpful if managers don't understand the difference between resource efficiency and flow efficiency.

Controlling project managers? Not so helpful.

Here's what agile project managers do not do:

- The agile project manager does not assign work.

- The agile project manager does not estimate work on behalf of the team.

- The agile project manager does not commit to features, stories, or tasks on behalf of the team.

- The agile project manager does not agree to dates.

- The agile project manager does not agree to constraints on the project.

For many new-to-agile teams, this is a huge change. In serial life cycles, such as waterfall or phase-gate, there is no such role as the product owner. (In serial life cycles, the team works on all the requirements, then all the analysis, then all the design, and so on. Phase-gate life cycles have gates—checkpoints—after each phase before a team can proceed to the next phase.)

In the serial life cycle, the project manager assesses the requirements and decides what features/requirements/whatever the team should work on first, second, third, and so on. The project manager decides on the deliverables.

In agile approaches, the product owner decides the rank order of what the team will do, often using rolling-wave deliverable-based planning. Rolling-wave planning says to plan a little now—say up to four weeks of work—and as the team completes one week, add a week to the end. The team always has a four-week plan, a rolling wave. See *Manage It! [Rot07]* for a larger explanation and see *Create Rolling-Wave Roadmaps*, on page 96, for more details as to how to apply rolling-wave planning to agile projects.

The product owner decides which features (deliverables) the team needs to implement now, and what rank they are. The product owner decides when to replan. The agile project manager might assist/suggest/facilitate, but the deliverable-based planning is the product owner's job.

The product owner now performs some of the work a project manager might have done:

- The product owner (or the product manager) manages the "commitments" to external requests.

- The product owner defines deliverables for the team to focus on and deliver.

- The product owner defines the rolling-wave planning so the team can look ahead a bit.

This can be a large change for traditional project managers, who were accustomed to making their deliverable-based rolling-wave plan work. (Yes, you could make a waterfall project work with deliverable-based rolling-wave planning. It was difficult but possible.) Some project managers have a difficult time reconciling their role to be one of servant leader, facilitating the team's work rather than directing it.

This also means every team needs a product owner. If two teams work off the same backlog, it's possible those two teams can share a product owner. A product owner has the ability to decide about features in the moment, to define acceptance criteria, and to explain a story for the team at any time.

Beware of the *Trap: Your Team Has a Business Analyst Masquerading*, on page 69. Every team needs a product owner.

What Product Owners Do

Product owners represent the customer to the team. The product owner creates and ranks the product backlog for a team. Often, the product owner works with a product manager to create a coherent picture for the product (the roadmap) and this time period (the backlog).

The product owner takes input from the rest of the organization and creates and ranks the stories in the backlog. See Chapter 6, *Teams Deliver Features*, on page 85, for the details of how the product owner does that.

The product owner shepherds the business value of the roadmap and the team's backlog so the team always delivers the most valuable work.

How Roles Change in Agile Projects

Agile approaches demand changes in the project manager's role and the product owner's role. The team decides *how* to do its work. The agile project manager facilitates the team and its process. The product owner (a new role in agile) decides *what* to do and *when* the team should deliver that work.

These changes can lead to problems in expectations and in how the team works. I've seen expectation problems such as these:

- The product owner thinks the team doesn't need the stories broken down into something the team can complete each day (or more often).

- The product owner thinks the team cannot help write stories.

- The product owner thinks the team doesn't need to address the legacy problems it may have. (Instead, see *Trap: The Product Owner Has Feature-itis*, on page 101.)

When the product owners don't understand their roles, the agile project manager can help the product owner understand what to do and how to treat the team. The project manager can see if the team is struggling with too-large stories, and can facilitate the product owner creating smaller stories.

 Joe asks:

Does Every Team Need an Agile Coach?

Agile coaches are pervasive in the industry. Does your team need one?

Let's talk about the difference between knowing how to do something, such as automated testing, and how to do it *here*.

If your team doesn't know about some useful practices, it needs training. If the team doesn't see how to use those practices *here*, it needs coaching. As an example, if the team knows how to workshop stories or write automated tests at all levels, it doesn't need training. And if the team doesn't seem to be able to make time for story writing or automated test writing, it might need coaching.

Training helps people understand and, with any luck, practice a new skill. Coaching helps people see options as to how to use the skills they have. Or to realize they need more training because they are missing skills.

I often recommend a coach to help the agile transformation team. The agile transformation team often includes middle and senior managers. Those people rarely have experience with an agile mindset. Or if they know about agile mindset and culture, they may have trouble understanding why things aren't working *here*.

Consider coaching for your new-to-agile teams and the managers who want teams to use agile approaches.

Consider Your Team's Need for Management

For too long, project managers "herded," "managed," or "controlled" the team or its output. I have seen people attempt to exert their will on others. I was never successful with these approaches. I didn't like treating people like animals, or managing them like tasks, or controlling them as if they were robots.

Instead, I realized long ago I was much more successful if I treated people as if they were adults. If I respected them, helped them when they needed help, and explained the results I wanted, I more often than not got the results I wanted.

Your team might not need any form of "management." On the other hand, I have seen many teams that needed someone to help the team remove impediments and serve the team.

Recognize Leadership Traps

As a leader, you might not want to think about leadership traps. Aside from the obvious—acting in a controlling manner as opposed to a serving manner—many of the traps I've seen have been about product ownership. Here are the traps I'll highlight:

- When the team has several people who act as the product owner.
- When the team has no product owner.
- When the team has a business analyst who masquerades as a product owner.

These traps prevent team members from knowing what they need to do when.

Trap: One Team Has Several People Acting as Product Owner

I've encountered several organizations where the product manager "owns" a product, and negotiates for people to work on that product. Of course, that means begging, borrowing, stealing people from other projects, and lots of multitasking. It also means that specific people have very specific knowledge of products or pieces of products, and it's way scary for these product managers to consider allowing other people to work on their products.

This situation can devolve into several product managers working as product owners for one team. The team is supposed to work on Product Manager 1's project and Product Manager 2's project.

Sometimes the team splits into the different projects. That means the team needs to be large enough to split.

Sometimes the product managers collaborate on one joint backlog for the team and rank all the stories.

Sometimes they ignore the other product managers and assume the team works on just "their" stories.

It's a mess.

Instead of having multiple product managers talk to a team, ask one product owner to represent the rest of the organization. That product owner can make the stories small enough that the team can finish stories often. Even better, have the managers manage the project portfolio so that the product managers are not at odds with each other, competing for the same teams.

Trap: Your Team Has No Product Owner

What happens when you have no product owner at all? How does a team know what features to develop and in what order?

I've seen several patterns of "no" product owner:

- The team has a product manager who can work with the team up to a few hours every couple of weeks. That product manager assumes a full-time business analyst can fill in for the product manager. However, the product manager is the one person who can accept stories, and that person is not available on a regular basis. Too often, the business analyst does not have enough domain expertise or customer experience to decide for the product manager.

- The team's manager or a different manager in the organization acts as the product owner. That might work, but eventually the management work overwhelms the manager. The team no longer has a product owner. I've seen these other problems also: managers do not understand the real acceptance criteria; managers do not know the correct ranking of the stories; and, if the manager is a technical manager, the manager is too interested and involved in the *how* of the story instead of defining the *what* and *when* for the story. When managers work that closely with the team, they may well inhibit team safety by deciding for the team instead of with the team. (See *Weird Ideas That Work: How to Build a Creative Company* [Sut06] for more discussion.)

- The team shares a product owner with another team and that product owner doesn't quite understand what this team's feature set is.

Every team needs a full-time product owner. That product owner is a responsible person who can create and rank the backlog so the team knows the order of the work. Without that person, the team does not know what to do and when to deliver that value.

Without a product owner, the team loses something precious to agility: the customer collaboration as part of working with the customer or customer surrogate. The team loses the back-and-forth about the product that the customer or product owner helps the team understand. And there's no one who can rank the work the way a customer would.

Even when teams use managers instead of product owners, the manager is not the customer. The manager is not the person who can set the real acceptance criteria. The manager can see the demo, but the manager cannot say for sure that the team is developing the correct requirements in the correct order.

A team without a customer or product owner is not agile. The team might use iterative and incremental approaches, but it doesn't have an agile culture. Agile approaches separate who "owns" what. The customer or product owner owns the decisions about what problems the team should solve and when by creating roadmaps and ranked backlogs. The team owns the architecture and design decisions about how to solve these problems. A team without a customer or customer surrogate does not maintain that separation.

When the team manager gets involved, that allows the "business" to be unaccountable for developing the system. How do you know what is shippable product without the responsible person?

The problem is this: product development is a joint venture between the business people and the technical people. We need legal, marketing, sales, and anyone else on the "business" side of the house to help us with the what-and-when-to-build decisions. That's why we need a responsible person. In Scrum, that person is called a product owner. And we need a technical project team to deliver the value. We use agile as an approach and use the demo because it shows business value every iteration.

When the business is unaccountable, the agile ecosystem breaks down. We no longer have ideas coming into that funnel, as illustrated in the "general agile picture" on page 5, being evaluated by that responsible person. Sure, that responsible person has a lot to do. And that responsible person should develop product roadmaps and make the potential product direction transparent to the rest of the organization. That way, the next iteration or two is clear for the team, and everyone can discuss the product direction.

Feature teams cannot know the strategic intent for a given product. Feature teams tend not to discuss product strategy. Or the discussions go off in a different direction than the product needs to go. And that's a very bad thing.

Because when the discussions about product strategy don't occur, the technical group takes all the responsibility for the product: for what to build, when to build it, and how to build it. And that means we have let the rest of the business abdicate all of its responsibility for their part of the product. That's not the partnership or the transparency agile promises us.

You might be on the road to agile approaches if you have no product owner. If your team is better off, terrific. But don't fool yourself. If you want to become even better at delivering, you need a product owner who can represent what the organization needs now and later to define and rank the features. That person cannot also perform technical work for the project. Without a product owner, your team is missing a key cultural transformation that allows agile to succeed.

What if this is the best you can do? See Chapter 17, *Start Somewhere*, on page 247.

Trap: Your Team Has a Business Analyst Masquerading as a Product Owner

Many organizations have the problem of not enough product owners. The organization's managers think the business analysts can act as product owners, especially if the business analyst has the backup of a product owner.

I have yet to see this work. Inevitably, the product owner is not available—often because the product owner is the product manager, not the product owner. (The product manager is an external-facing position. The product manager visits with customers, gathering data about what should be in the product as a whole or in the next generation of the product. In contrast, the product owner is an internal position, a person who works with the team, providing details about the next stories and insight into the future.) Unfortunately, the team suffers the lack of a product owner.

Business analysts have a place, and that place is often with the product manager, understanding what the customers want and turning those desires into roadmap features. It's possible your business analyst can work with the product owner and create small stories. One of my clients defines a bazillion business rules for a given release. That client finds the business analyst can define the business rules and acceptance criteria to go along with the rules.

The worst part of this trap is when your management thinks the business analyst is sufficient for your team's needs. If you think you have a business analyst masquerading as a product owner, try these options:

- Count the number of times a story goes into a clarification wait state, such as "waiting for explanation," or "waiting for acceptance criteria." Your product owner is not clarifying the story.

- Look for causes of a relatively high number of fixes that don't stay fixed, as discussed in *Measure the Fault Feedback Ratio,* on page 192. One cause might be insufficient clarification of the feature.

- The product owner cannot lead the story-definition work. The product owner does not have the authority to define stories in any meeting, whether that meeting is a requirements workshop, the backlog refinement meeting, or the planning meeting.

Every agile team deserves one responsible person (and no more than one) to decide what to do and when.

Now Try This

1. Identify your product owner. Make sure that person is fully dedicated to your team and understands what the product owner does.

2. Does your team need an agile project manager (regardless of what your organization calls that person)? That person facilitates the team process.

3. Does your team need an agile coach to help people see their options for creating their agile mindset and delivering value?

You've got a cross-functional team with the servant leadership it needs. Start that project!

Part II

Design and Manage an Agile and Lean Project

CHAPTER 5

Start Your Agile Project Right

When it's time to go to work, do you drive in any given direction without a destination? When you have the time and flexibility you might decide to explore a new area, but when going to work? Probably not.

Projects need direction, too. Project teams—for all projects—need to know where they are headed and when they are done. This business of selecting the direction for a project and knowing when the project is done is part of starting the project right.

Let's talk about products for a minute. Every product has an introduction, several releases, and an end of life, when you retire the product. Every single one of those major events for a product is a *project*. When you introduce a product as "1.0," that's the introduction. You might have 1.5 as a minor release project and 2.0 as a major release project. Notice that I called them both projects.

Because the team can deliver value all the way through the project, sometimes people don't think they have projects in agile approaches. They do. Here's the key: when teams use agile approaches, you don't have to wait until the end of the release to see the value in the project. Your team might be able to release every day, or every couple of weeks, or every month. Those releases allow the customers to receive interim value for the project.

Also notice that I spoke about major and minor releases and our ability to release value. I am using the same word, *release*, in two different ways. That's part of the problem. Agile approaches allow us to release interim value as often as possible to our customers. And you still have projects you might call "Release 1.0," which is the project name for a *product*. Thinking about projects can be especially important if you have a product with hardware. You might have production stages at the end of the project. And you can still have an agile project with hardware and mechanical parts or products.

In this chapter, I'll discuss how you can start your project right, including understanding your context and risks. First, we'll examine why chartering a project is an important first step in starting a project right.

Charter Your Project

Every project needs a charter. Charters tell the team members why they are delivering this set of features (the vision) and how they know they are done with the project (the release criteria).

To start a project right, charter the project.

A project charter creates boundaries for the project and answers these questions: Why are we doing this project? When will we be done? The project charter provides the team a minimum set of data with which to start.

You might be accustomed to project charters that also address the risks, the test plan, the communication needs, and even more information. If you realize you need any of that information in your charter, add it. My question is this: Do you need that information to start?

I like to start a project with the project vision, the release criteria, and the first backlog. That's all. I have a question I ask of all parts of an agile project:

> How little can we do to satisfy our needs?

Notice that I do want to meet the organizational desires, and especially the customer needs. However, I want to make sure we are not delivering more than we need to for *this* project.

I apply this "how little" thinking to everything: the backlog, the feature sets, and especially any up-front work. I want to *see* the product evolve rather than *plan* for how the product will evolve.

I often ask the team to help write the charter, and I generally timebox this chartering effort to one hour. The team has a chance to coalesce around the project and learn a little about what it's like to work together.

The two parts I start with are the project vision and the release criteria.

Write the Project Vision

The project vision is a one-to-three-line statement of what the product manager wants the project to fulfill with this release. The vision guides the team and the product owner when they need to make decisions about what goes into this project and what doesn't.

I've certainly used project visions like this:

- Release 4.1 improves performance in these three scenarios by a minimum of 10%.

- Release 2.0 adds email functionality.

- Release 6.0 changes the UI across the product to our new standard.

Those visions are useful. They are not compelling. Here is another way to think about the project vision:

- Who is the main recipient of the project's outcome?
- What can the main recipient do with that outcome?
- What is the value to the main recipient?

When you think about the vision in this way, you might discover a compelling reason for the project.

Our Vision Describes a Higher Goal
by: Richard, Experienced Project Manager

I'd never thought about our users before. Oh, I thought about them during the project when we worked on the features, but I hadn't thought of them when it came time to create a project vision.

We had a project that was mandated by the government. Customers with retirement accounts over a certain age had to move to a new account by the end of the year. If they didn't, we would have regulatory problems. Our customers might lose some of their money, too.

When we wrote the vision first, it was something like, "Move from these kind of retirement accounts to those kind of accounts by October 15." Big yawn.

Then, we thought it might be, "Help all the retired people move their money by Sept. 30" or some such. It was fine, but not compelling.

Then one of the junior people on the team piped up and said, "Hey, what we're really doing is saving all the retired people's money from the tax man."

You should have seen the energy in the room. All of a sudden, we had a bunch of energized people. We had found our compelling vision: Save retired people's money. It wasn't about the bank. It was about our customers. We couldn't wait to start.

Thinking about the vision this way makes sense for customers outside the product-development team. What if you have a project for the product-development team? It's the same idea.

It's possible you're working on a legacy product. That product does not have enough test automation or the build is quite slow. Before you used agile approaches, it didn't matter, because you didn't build and test multiple times a day. Now it does. You have a project to address that problem.

Your vision might be something like this:

Increase our test automation so we can run unit tests in seconds after a build and system tests in minutes after a build.

or

Decrease the time for each build to no more than five minutes. This will save each of us at least 10 hours a week.

When you think about what your customers will be able to do with the outcome of your project, you may discover a quite compelling vision.

Develop the Release Criteria

Release criteria tell you what "done" means for the entire project. They tell you if you have met the project goals. (For a fuller discussion of release criteria, see *Manage It! [Rot07]*.) Agile projects release value during the project. Release criteria tell you not when you can release value, but when you can complete the project.

You might say, "We can end when there is no more value in the backlog." That might be correct. However, you don't need to "finish" this product in this project. Product managers and product owners often find that the customers receive more value when the customers can use the product and then provide more feedback to the organization.

Instead of focusing on having no more value in the backlog, define several criteria so you know when you have met the vision. The following table outlines examples of release criteria.

Type of Scenario	Example Description
Performance	For a given scenario (*describe it in some way*), the query returns results in a minimum of two seconds.
Reliability	The system maintains uptime under these conditions.
Scalability	The system is able to build up to 20,000 simultaneous connections and scale down to fewer than 1,000 connections.

Table 4—Possible Scenarios for Release Criteria

I have used preset or preloadable databases and other automation approaches to be able to verify the release criteria as the team works through the project. Sometimes the team achieves the release criteria earlier than you expected. You have enough functionality to stop this project and start another.

If you are accustomed to making decisions based on the "goodness" of the product, consider using release criteria instead. You may discover you can release earlier than you thought.

Defining Release Criteria with Managers Who Want "Everything"

Sometimes sponsors, customers, or other managers say, "I don't want to define release criteria. I want everything on the backlog, no ifs, ands, or buts about it."

These people may have good reasons for those feelings. One manager I know said those things because he had never seen a team deliver even 20% of what they thought they could deliver. When the team used an agile approach and demonstrated working product every two weeks, he changed his mind. He was willing to consider release criteria once he realized the team was able to deliver value on a regular basis. (See *Demonstrations Show Progress and Value*, on page 206, for more details.)

Agile approaches allow us to discover and take advantage of project advances. However, if the team doesn't know how to assess the end of the project, the team can't finish earlier than anyone expected. Release criteria helps everyone understand what the minimum for completion is.

Charter the Project as a Team

You might have created a project charter or project plans or architecture frameworks working alone in previous projects. Don't do that when you start an agile project. The team needs to own the project charter or plan and any experiments to understand the design and architecture.

You may have heard of "Iteration Zero" in your agile reading. That is supposed to be an iteration of project definition and product exploration. Don't do that either. Otherwise, you'll fall into the *Trap: Iteration Zero*, on page 82.

Instead, workshop the project charter with the team. If you're creating the vision and release criteria, timebox that workshop to one hour. Yes, I called it a workshop, not a meeting. You are creating value, and not leaving any action items for the future, so it's a workshop.

If you need to explore the architecture before you start the project, ask the team to swarm around several features. That helps the team learn to work together and provides you with completed features. Sure, you might have to refactor them later, and that's fine.

Identify Your Product Type

Projects allow you to organize a team of people around managing the risks to create and release the product. I am using the word *product* purposefully here. You may be accustomed to using the words *release* or *system* or *application*. Those words describe how the customers will use the product. However, if you have customers and you want to use an agile approach, consider thinking about *products*. That word will help you think in an agile way about everything.

Products have customers. Products are the result of a product-development team's work. You will release products. You can decide if there is more value in releasing a product now or waiting until later based on what the company wants and the customers need.

Beware of Initiatives

 I know of some organizations that use the word *initiative* instead of project. Many of them forgot that they had to release the project. They were great at starting, not so good at finishing. Remember that projects finish. They either release or they stop. But they don't wander around in the desert, looking for the promised land.

Product is a useful word, especially in the context of agile approaches. Thinking about "product" helps you focus on who will use your product and how you will help those customers receive the product.

How often *could* you release your product? Thinking about how the organization releases the product helps the team start with the end in mind.

Every decision would be easier if there were just two kinds of products: those that released continuously, as in software as a service, and those that released infrequently, as in hardware. However, you might be in an organization where —for any number of reasons—it's difficult and/or costly to release often. There's a continuum of release frequency, as illustrated by the following diagram.

Potential for Release Frequency

Digital-Only Product Such as Software as a Service	Boxed Software	Product with Firmware	Software with Hardware or Mechanical Components
Continuous	Intermittent		Less Frequently
Continuous Deployment: As often as several times a day	Often: But the cost of release is still high	Less Often: The cost of release is high	Infrequently: Every release might be a major release

If your product is totally digital or software as a service, you could release continuously because the cost of release is low—or could be low. That's because if you can get to frictionless releasing, you only have to worry if there is a business decision for releasing.

If your product has hardware or mechanical components for the product, the cost of release is high. You would not release as often as several times a day. I doubt you would release the entire product even monthly. You might release internally often—and use release criteria to know when the cost of release is worth it to the organization.

You might find that you have a better idea about the overall project risks when you consider how the product could release, not necessarily how it releases now.

Our Customers Can't Take the Product Often
by: Janie, VP, R&D

Our customers are in a regulated industry. They need to do their checks on our product. Sometimes they integrate our product with other vendors in their environment.

They only want the product once a year. Of course, they want fixes to problems ASAP. For the product, it feels like "hurry up and wait." For the fixes, I get a call from my CEO and their CEO and other people if we don't release a fix in a day or so.

We use agile so we can release whenever we want. That includes fixes.

It took us a while—about eight months—to get to the point where we could release a fix in a day. The team—whichever team it is—swarms on the problem. We have enough test automation and our builds are fast enough that the team can iterate on possibilities and test them to know they will satisfy our customers. Or the team can involve the customer with up to three potential fixes.

I made the deliberate decision to invest in our capabilities, the build and test automation, so we could release what we want, whenever we want. We now have frictionless releasing. We release the product once a year, down from 18 months. I suspect we'll get down to six months in the next year. And we release fixes whenever we want.

Assess Your Project's Risks

Projects have risks. That's because you cannot manage the work with a checklist. Your project is more complex than a checklist. Your project will have risks with how the team thinks about the domain and solves the problems: technical risks. In addition, your team might have other risks, especially in the areas of scope, cost, people, and schedule.

Every project, including agile projects, has risks. I use the following pyramid to consider the risks for my project. I find that there are inside-the-project risks and outside-the-project risks.

Project Pyramid: Tradeoffs and Potential Risks for Projects

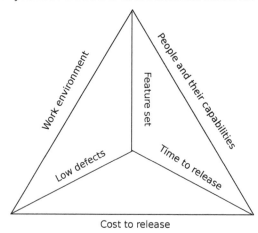

Cost to release

When projects start, management often wants to fix the outside of the pyramid: the project cost, the project environment, and the people and their capabilities. Inside those constraints, the project can deliver some number of features, with some expected defect levels in some time.

In reality, the project team can change almost any of these. I bet you've seen projects where management decided it was okay to spend more money to deliver more features. I bet you've also seen projects where you started with not quite enough people and you managed to get more people on the project.

Since we expect to change the feature set with agile approaches, you may have more flexibility than you realize with the feature set and the date. I've seen agile projects end much earlier than anyone expected because they had completed enough features for now and had no WIP.

You might have risks from *Avoid Management Mayhem*, on page 243. One way to assess your potential risks is to conduct a retrospective for work or a project these team members just completed. Their experiences (and yours) will help the team think about risks they want to review and manage.

Consider asking the team how it wants to manage risks. Sometimes creating a board of the top 10 risks and managing those risks during problem-solving meetings or planning meetings might be enough. Consider a board of risks, impediments, and concerns that the team evaluates on a regular cadence. See *Visualize Problems with a Board*, on page 121.

> \\//
> ‿ᑴ **Joe asks:**
> # Is Budget a Risk for Your Project?
>
> Some managers want to see a budget for a project. An agile project has an easy budget:
> the run rate for the expected amount of time plus the capital equipment costs.
>
> An agile budget is easy because the team members remain on this (and only this)
> project for the entire project. If you need to, you can estimate the "entire" project, as
> covered in *Create Approximate Estimates for Management*, on page 156. Do remind the
> managers who need an up-front budget that you expect the product backlog to change
> and you might be done earlier.
>
> If you need to provide and manage a budget, make sure the entire team is dedicated
> to your project and no one attempts to multitask. When people leave or join a team,
> the team incurs a cost of delay while they learn to work together. The more important
> the budget is, the more you need a stable team.
>
> If you do need to monitor a project's budget, add that to your reports, as detailed in
> Chapter 14, *Report Your Project State*, on page 215.

Start Architecture Thinking

You and your team might be accustomed to defining the architecture at the
beginning of a project. In fact, there's an acronym for that: BDUF, Big Design
Up Front.

In agile approaches, we expect to evolve the architecture as the product proceeds. The team will add features, iterating over the feature set. The team
builds, increments, and refactors the code and tests as it proceeds. Those
activities help the team evolve the architecture. However, your team—and
any architects your team might want to consult—can and should start
thinking about the architecture.

There are several reasons to avoid having an architect hand down architecture
for a project:

- Architects need to be part of the collaborative team. Just as we still need
  project management for agile projects, we still need architectural thinking.
  Agile projects do not need an architect who is not part of the team.

- If the architect is not part of the team, the project will evolve and the
  architect will not understand the changes should the team require
  architectural assistance in the future.

- I have yet to see a project where the architecture didn't change as the
  team finished features.

Having architectural expertise on your team helps a team finish work faster. Architects can be servant leaders, coaching people to think about the effects of decisions. Architects can pair or mob with a team to show how to think about architectural qualities such as performance and reliability. (See *Work as a Whole Team to Create the Product*, on page 131, for details on pairing and mobbing.) I particularly like architectural spikes (not longer than one day) to experiment, scout, or wayfind in the problem domain.

When I work with people who are accustomed to starting with architecture, I ask them to draw a low-fidelity picture of the architecture they think will work. I ask them to update the image of the architecture as the team progresses.

If I work with an architect who needs to define the architecture at the beginning, I ask that person to explain three things that might go wrong with the architecture. I have found that architects who cannot think of three (or more) things that can go wrong don't understand the entire problem well enough. They are not sufficient for my team.

I have been able to remove those insufficient architects from my teams. If you have a manager who wants to impose an architect on your team, remind that manager that *Teams Manage Their Own Membership*, on page 52.

Recognize Project-Startup Traps

As a leader, you have direct control over avoiding these traps:

- The team starts with Iteration Zero to define the project.
- The organization wants detailed planning for the entire project before it starts.

As the team starts the project, be aware of these traps and avoid them.

Trap: Iteration Zero

Some teams learned or thought they needed an entire iteration of planning or architecture or estimation for the entire project. I've actually seen teams fall into "Iteration Minus One," "Iteration Minus Two," "Iteration Minus Three," and so on.

For example, one team had trouble starting because it had always defined the architecture at the beginning. The team was faced with a new product and management wanted an estimate. The team spent Iteration Zero developing an architecture, and Iteration Minus One developing an estimate. That changed the architecture so the team spent Iteration Minus Two redoing the original architecture. The team was ready to estimate again.

A manager familiar with agile approaches stopped by and asked to see the team's walking skeleton. When she realized the team had been planning and estimating, she asked it to create one specific feature for her to see the next day.

The team did and was surprised by three things: it needed to change the architecture again, it could complete a feature in one day, and the estimates it had prepared had no relationship to reality.

The manager helped the team realize it had fallen into Big Design Up Front and a phased approach to the project. The team continued to work on one feature at a time at the start of the project to see what the team could deliver and to have some idea of the accuracy of the team's estimate.

Instead, consider these possibilities:

- Spend up to half a day creating a list of experiments so the team knows where to explore.

- Determine the hardware or other resources the team requires and start that effort. Ask the team if it can start on anything without those resources.

- If the team wants to use iterations and has no idea how to estimate together, consider a one-week timebox so the team can learn to work together. Use that week to define several small stories and see how the team jells.

- If the team has no stories ready, consider a one-day workshop to generate stories small enough that the team can work on them and the product owner can generate more stories.

Ask yourself the "how little" question applied to starting: How little can we do as a team to get ready so we start delivering value?

Trap: Your Organization Wants Detailed Project Plans

In waterfall (and some other kinds of projects), organizations try to optimize everyone's "efficiency." (See *Managers Move from Resource-Efficiency to Flow-Efficiency Thinking*, on page 240.) To organize the project and to utilize everyone, "efficient" projects need detailed plans: communication plans and often Gantt charts.

You don't need those plans when you use agile approaches. When organizations use agile and lean thinking, the project has a fully formed cross-functional, collaborative team able to deliver value on a regular basis. That team doesn't need a communication plan.

The team might have to provide status in some way to others in the organization. I have suggestions for that in Chapter 14, *Report Your Project State*, on page 215. However, you don't need many other plans.

The *team* doesn't need Gantt charts. Gantts mean nothing to an agile team. What people need to see is the initial product roadmap and the rolling-wave deliverables as the team completes the work. See Chapter 6, *Teams Deliver Features*, on page 85.

If your organization wants detailed project plans, ask about the value it receives for these deliverables. Instead of writing plans, show demos of the product. If your organization wants detailed plans for milestones, show the product roadmap.

If managers in your organization send you mixed messages, such as "Give us all the old measures and work in an agile way," you have major impediments to a successful agile transformation. Consider how you will help people see the new measurements that provide value. You might have to meet people where they are. See Chapter 16, *How Managers Help Agile Teams*, on page 237, for ideas.

Now Try This

1. Gather all the information you have for this project as preparation for a project charter. Gather the team and workshop the vision and release criteria.

2. Decide if you need more planning to start. If so, ask the team to plan with you.

3. Review risks from previous projects. Ask the team to help plan to mitigate those risks.

You have just enough to start the project now. Next, let's see how to describe what the team delivers.

CHAPTER 6

Teams Deliver Features

In the past, you might have worked on a team that received a gigantic product-requirements document from a product manager. You worked on that project for months—maybe longer—and invited the product manager in to see the work you finished. That product manager might have had any of these reactions:

- You gave me what I asked for. It's not what I need.
- The market changed. I don't want this now. I want something else, yesterday.
- This isn't what I wanted. You read what I wrote, but that's not what I meant.

Or your team was working on all the features, and halfway through the project a product manager or a Very Important Manager came to your team and said, "We need to ship tomorrow. What do you have?" Since the team worked across the architecture rather than through the layers of the architecture, the team had nothing to release. The team had many features in progress, but nothing was done.

Maybe you had a different experience, and it still wasn't good. You needed more collaboration with the business, or to deliver something more often, or to finish some work to release early.

Agile approaches address all those problems. That's because agile teams deliver finished features on a regular basis. Agile teams use feature-driven development (FDD), regardless of whether they use an FDD approach (see *Java Modeling in Color with UML: Enterprise Components and Process [CdL99]*) or some other plan-and-implement-by-feature approach.

When a team delivers features, everyone can see the shape of the product from the beginning as it evolves. That's what we'll discuss in this chapter:

what features are, how to think about planning features, how to plan and replan, and how to understand the difference between features and waste.

First, let's talk about what we can plan.

Plan at Several Levels

How much certainty do you have about what your customers want? You might have certainty about some of the requirements *for now*. Most of the organizations I work with have some certainty about the next month or two, less certainty about the next couple of quarters, and not much certainty for the next few years. Agile and lean approaches help when you don't have a lot of certainty about the requirements or the technical approach(es) that might work.

You might work in a different environment, where you have total certainty for the next several years. If so, you don't need agile approaches for the requirements feedback. You might want to use agile approaches for seeing product progress and the team's ability to release regularly.

Sometimes when you're starting a new product or offering, you understand the strategic value of the features, but your certainty past the next week or two is quite low. You're using agile and lean approaches to deliver value fast and be able to change as often as possible to respond to feedback.

We plan and replan at various levels when we use agile approaches. The organization can plan the project portfolio, the mixture of projects that will define the organization's strategy. (For more about the project portfolio, see *Manage Your Project Portfolio, Second Edition [Rot16a]*.)

Product managers (often with product owners) plan the product roadmap: what the product people want when. I often see six-quarter roadmaps that look like the top figure on page 87. This roadmap doesn't have much detail, but it does show an external release every quarter. Some teams, when they start to use agile approaches, have trouble releasing even once a quarter.

While senior management and product management might be able to talk to customers about expected or hoped-for timing, a six-month roadmap (shown in the next figure on page 87) can show much more detail.

The six-month roadmap shows you the months, the external releases, the internal releases, and the feature sets the product management team *hopes* will be in the release. Roadmaps are hopes, not commitments.

Don't worry if you can only create a one- or two-month detailed roadmap. When people try to plan in great detail, they tend to overplan. That creates

Agile Roadmap for a Product: Six-Quarter View

Q1	Q2	Q3	Q4	Q5	Q6
External Release Tulip	External Release Daisy	External Release Rose	External Release Carnation	...	
Feature Sets/ Themes	Feature Sets/ Themes	Feature Sets/ Themes	Feature Sets/ Themes		
Feature Sets/ Themes	Feature Sets/ Themes	Feature Sets/ Themes	Feature Sets/ Themes	...	
Feature Sets/ Themes	Feature Sets/ Themes	Feature Sets/ Themes	Feature Sets/ Themes		

Agile Roadmap for a Product: Six-Month View

M1	M2	M3	M4	M5	M6
External Release Tulip			External Release Daisy		
Internal Release 1	Internal Release 2	Internal Release 3	Internal Release 4	Internal Release 5	Internal Release 6
Feature Sets/ Themes	Feature Sets/ Themes	Feature Sets/ Themes	Feature Sets/ Themes	Feature Sets/ Themes	Feature Sets/ Themes
Feature Sets/ Themes	Feature Sets/ Themes	Feature Sets/ Themes	Feature Sets/ Themes	Feature Sets/ Themes	Feature Sets/ Themes
Feature Sets/ Themes	Feature Sets/ Themes	Feature Sets/ Themes	Feature Sets/ Themes	Feature Sets/ Themes	Feature Sets/ Themes

waste. I run my business on an six-month big-picture roadmap and a one-month detailed roadmap. I update these roadmaps on a two-week rolling wave. (See *Create Rolling-Wave Roadmaps*, on page 96, for more details.)

Release for Learning, Feedback, and Value

These roadmaps show quarterly external releases and monthly internal releases. For many teams starting with agile, a quarterly release might be as fast as they can have anything of value to release. Here's a question you might find useful to help with thinking and small stories: when do you need to learn about what?

The more often your team can release internally or externally, the more the team learns about what it takes for the *team* to release. When teams start to use agile approaches, they discover they don't have enough tests at any level. The team might discover builds take too long or require some manual intervention.

The more often your team practices releasing, the easier releasing becomes. Add to that the idea of releasing into the organization, and the more the team can receive feedback from others across the organization. The more often the team can release externally, the faster the team will receive customer feedback.

We Learned About Releasing the Hard Way
by: Stuart, Software Director

Before I became a director, I was a project manager. One of the other projects had finished, so I facilitated their retrospective. That project was almost six months late. The company needed the revenue from that release. Now that the product was out, everyone felt relieved. They were happy to think about what they had done.

As part of setting the stage for the retrospective, the VP of engineering said, "Our goal was to release these features by that date. Let's see why we released, but late." One of the engineers said, "Is that all you wanted? We could have had that six months ago. But releasing is such a pain we didn't release it."

We learned how to release more often after that retrospective.

Releasing is not just to deliver value to your customers. Releasing creates an environment of feedback for the team about its deliverables. The team can learn if the deliverables meet the customers' needs for functionality and performance.

The more often your team can release, the more opportunities your team has for feedback. At first, your team might have trouble releasing as often as once every two weeks. Your customers might not be able to take your product even once a quarter now. However, the more often you can release, the better the team will become at releasing and the more likelihood you can get feedback.

The more often you release, the more often everyone learns.

When teams release often, they get feedback. And teams have to release value, not architectural or technical bits of work, to receive that feedback. Let's explore what value is.

Deliver Value Through the Architecture

You may be accustomed to teams working across the architecture, as in the GUI person does the GUI for several features, and the platform people develop platform libraries. You see this when people work in "front end" or "back end" teams. Agile teams deliver through the architecture. Author Bill Wake originated the term "slice of cake" to explain how teams implement in vertical slices.[1]

Your team might have a front-end person and a back-end person on the team. As shown in the figure that follows, the team might have a middleware person and an app-layer person. The team works as a *team* to deliver value by implementing by feature through the architecture. In this figure, the squiggly lines indicate a small and complete story through the architecture, one slice.

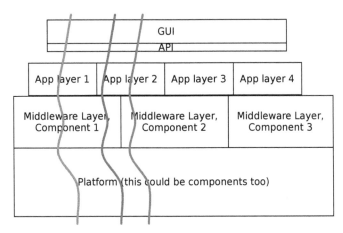

When teams deliver value through the architecture, one small slice at a time, they get feedback early. They rarely deliver a large feature set that doesn't meet someone's needs. Teams that deliver slices can release *something* when they want to. Teams that deliver slices learn early what their product owner or customer wants.

Remember that the more narrow the slice, the more often the team can release.

While your team might start with back-end, middleware, and front-end people, encourage the team members to become generalizing specialists. That will avoid the *Trap: The Team Consists of Narrow Experts*, on page 34.

---

1. http://xp123.com/articles/invest-in-good-stories-and-smart-tasks

Create a Walking Skeleton

When people start to talk about what the product might do, they often jump to a vision of the entire product. That means we see all the requirements, the big picture of the product.

It's tempting to think we need to deliver all of those features. Instead, think about how little you can do to create a walking skeleton of the product, and add more features as the features have value.

Suppose you have a product with a variety of reports: sales by geography, kind of product, aggregated by several customers. It's tempting to try to create the database schema that would support all those reports. It's also tempting to create the entire login/security process at once.

Instead, if you create a walking skeleton, you might say this:

- Let's have one of each kind of user be able to log in, and we already know their usernames and passwords. That allows you to create a flat file of four entries and still see what the different reports might produce.

- Let's have each user create just one kind of report: a report by one kind of product for one customer. That also allows you to create a flat file of data to use as input, and maybe not even a pretty report-based format.

I might do this in two ways: to create a paper prototype of the flow of information and as a way to see the user's flow. As the team and the product owner learn about the product and what the product owner wants next, the team refactors to add more login capability and more report capability.

Deliver Value to Someone by Using Features

We hear a lot about stories, epics, and themes in agile. You might have other terms for your requirements, too. Let me explain some of these terms:

Story
> The smallest possible value to a specific user. It might not be sufficient to release *by itself*.

Theme
> Related group of stories. I call this a "feature set." You can deliver any of the related stories and realize value.

Epic
> A compound story that's not easy to tease apart. I find that epics often contain feature sets.

You might have other words for these terms, especially if you're using a tool for your board. I encourage you to think about stories and feature sets. That will simplify your planning and delivery.

Here's an example that might help. Assume you have an administration interface for your product. Different kinds of users (customers, internal sales people, external sales people, and company management) all want to run reports of some sort. Because there are different kinds of users, you'll need some form of secure login. Each kind of person will have access to different data to run reports.

There are several login stories, all part of a feature set:

- Existing user login
- Ability to register as a new user
- Ability to change a password
- Ability to block a current user
- Ability to change a user's privileges
- And many more

I can imagine several report stories: Report on sales by geography, by kind of product, aggregated by several customers for the internal people, and much more. Assuming each report type has more than one story, I would use the term "feature set" to describe each kind of report.

For the purposes of this book, I'm going to discuss stories and feature sets. I find that people too often lose the idea of stories when they start talking about epics and themes. The larger the chunk of work, the longer it takes to get feed-back. That's why I talk about stories and feature sets. Feature sets help people realize there are several deliverables. A story is one of those features.

Stories are small; epics and themes are not.

The story—a feature for a specific user that provides value to that user—is the unit of requirement in agile. If your thing—regardless of what you call it—does not deliver value to some user, it's not a story.

Some teams work on what they call "technical stories." Those are "stories" that allow the team to explore architecture or database schemas, or some form of design. Those are not true stories.

It's possible your team needs to experiment to understand a feature more. That's great. Create a user story, a real feature the team could release if it chose to, as an experiment. When teams understand who the feature is for, they are more likely to experiment in a shorter time and receive results they understand better.

Joe asks:

Can I Use Tasks or Technical Stories Instead of User Stories?

You may have seen story advice that tells the team to break the work into tasks, such as setting up a database, or creating tests, or some other function-based work.

Don't fall for that advice. Don't create tasks or technical stories. The story is too large if you need to create tasks or technical stories.

Teams create tasks because they don't understand the story's user—who the value is for—or if the story is quite large and the first item of value is not clear to the team. The team thinks it will save time by creating what it calls technical stories or tasks.

In reality, the team wastes time because it doesn't need the database or the UI or those tests *yet*. (The team might never need the technical story, once the team starts delivering value.) The first piece of value is much smaller than the task.

You don't need to use user stories as your only definition of a story. However, I don't recommend tasks or technical stories.

If you're worried about making sure you have tests for a given feature, don't make "testing" a task. Instead, limit the team's WIP and/or ask the team to pair, swarm, or mob on the story. (See *Work as a Whole Team to Create the Product*, on page 131, for details on pairing and mobbing.) When the developers and testers work together, they often create a better story, with the supporting tests happening faster.

Define Stories So You Can See the Value

Stories often follow this format:

> As a (particular kind of user), I want (some sort of action) to (provide me some achievement, value, or result).

Not all stories arise from humans interacting with the product. Sometimes the product monitors its health and takes autonomous (non–human-initiated) or asynchronous actions. In that case, consider this format from FDD as an alternative.[2]

> Some action — the result — some object

I've contrasted these two story types in the table on page 93.

Know who the story is for. That way you know why you're implementing it.

---

2. https://dzone.com/articles/introduction-feature-driven

User Story	FDD Alternative
As a system, monitor race conditions so I can reboot the master processor.	Reboot the master when I discover a race condition between processors two and three.
As a buyer, I want to cancel a sale within three days of buying the car. (Note: some states require that a buyer can cancel a sale and return the car.)	Cancel a sale.
As a machine-learning system, generate a list of possibilities for the future so I can examine them later.	Generate list of possibilities and log them for future consideration.

Table 5—Contrasting Story Types

Here's what I mean by a story:

> As (an already registered user), I want to (download my bank statement) so (I can see if my budget is on track).

This story assumes several pieces of other stories:

- There is some sort of security and login. That's the point of "an already registered user." We are not talking about creating new users in this story. Creating new users is another story.

- The action, to download, assumes some sort of secure connection with sufficient performance. We haven't talked about acceptance criteria yet, so look for performance in the acceptance criteria.

- The value, to check actuals against the budget, assumes that the download arrives in some format, which we have not yet discussed. Again, we'll discuss this in the acceptance criteria.

Creating user-based small stories makes the value transparent to the product-development team.

You might be thinking there are boundary conditions and other stories that are not part of this one story. You are correct. Here is a possible feature set that might include this story:

- Allow related users, where you would need to create a relationship between bank account holders, to download the statement.

- Allow downloads in several formats: spreadsheet, tab-separated text, comma-separated text, and PDF.

- Allow downloads into several different money-management tools.

All of these might be the "Download statement" feature set.

Note that each of these stories provides value. You might need to experiment with different facets of the story or the feature set to understand how to proceed in your product. That's the point of a minimum viable experiment (MVE).

Manage Work Other than Features

You might be wondering: how do you manage the list of defects you have in addition to the features? You might even have a list of technical debt and unfinished work, work you didn't do before releasing a feature.

Consider these ways to manage defects:

- Write user stories to explain the acceptance criteria for a defect.
- Gather several related defects together and write a user story to explain them.
- Add the defects to the backlog for a given iteration as part of what the team will deliver.

Experiment and Spike to Explore

We rarely know exactly how a feature will turn out. We have ideas, but until we've implemented the story, we don't exactly know how it will work. That's why we don't do Big Design Up Front in agile. Instead, we think of the smallest possible experiment or prototype that we can learn from.

It's easy to create waste without trying. Here are some ways I've seen teams create waste without meaning to do so:

- The team or an architect spent weeks defining an architecture up front and then the requirements changed.

- The team or members of the team said, "While I'm in there..." and implemented more of a feature set than the product owner needed now.

- The stories were so large the team spent considerable time in estimation.

- The stories were so large the team took a long time implementing anything. By then, the customers had left for another vendor.

I bet you've seen other examples of waste in projects.

Teams can avoid many of these problems if they experiment to try something, prototype something for feedback, and spike to see what this "story" will really take. Teams reduce waste as a side benefit of experiments, spikes, and prototypes.

What Are Spikes?

 Spikes are timeboxed prototypes that provide the team information about the rest of the feature or the feature set.

It's even better when the team and the product owner write small stories. The smaller the story, the less work a team has in estimating the story or in writing the story or the necessary tests to support that story. The smaller the story, the faster the team can release it. And the smaller the story, the easier it is to experiment and understand if the customers want this feature or feature set.

Small stories allow a team to experiment with its ability to do everything. Keep your stories small.

Write Small Stories

Just as short iterations provide you more frequent opportunity for feedback, small stories—as in one-day stories—provide you more possibility to see your progress and adjust.

Consider creating small stories that are one day or less in duration. Stories that short help the team see its progress and learning. The product owner can see the team's progress and provide feedback frequently. The shorter the story, the faster the throughput.

Here's a tip for creating small stories: Write the story on a 3x5 index card. You might have a tool that you're supposed to use to keep the requirements in. While you build your agile mindset and learn how to work as an agile team, use index cards.

On the front of the card, write down the story. On the back of the card, write down the acceptance criteria. If your story and the acceptance criteria do not fit on one index card, the story is too big. Remember, stories are a promise for a conversation. The card does not have to have absolutely everything on it.

Is it difficult to create small stories? Of course it is. It's worth it. Think about a specific user and think about the flow of his or her work. See these books for guidance as to how to create better stories: *User Stories Applied [Coh04]*, *User Story Mapping: Discover the Whole Story, Build the Right Product [Pat14]*, and *Fifty Quick Ideas to Improve Your User Stories [AE14]*.

Create Rolling-Wave Roadmaps

Agile approaches invite change. The more often a team completes one small feature, the more often the product owner and team can change what the team delivers next. I like to show these possibilities with rolling-wave roadmaps.

There are at least two reasons to use rolling-wave planning:

- We might get far enough into a feature set and realize we don't need to do any more, either at all or for this project.

- Agile approaches invite change. With rolling-wave roadmaps, we can show people how things might change.

This figure that follows shows a possible one-quarter rolling-wave roadmap.

Rolling Wave Example: One-Quarter Agile Roadmap

Internal Release 1		Internal Release 2		Internal Release 3	
Secure Login, Part 1	Secure Login, Part 2	Secure Login, New ID	Text Transfer, Part 1	Text Transfer, Part 2	Secure Login, Part 3
Admin, Part 1	Diagnostics, Part 1	Admin, Part 2	Admin, Part 2	Admin, Part 3	Admin, Part 3
File Transfer, Part 1	File Transfer, Part 1	Engine, Part 1	Engine, Part 1	Engine, Part 2	Engine, Part 2

Secure Login 1, 2, 3	Secure Login 7, 8, 9	Secure Login 10, 11
Secure Login 4, 5, 6	Diagnostics 1, 2, 3	Admin 3, 4
Admin 1, 2	File Transfer 2, 3, 4	Engine 1, 2, 3
File Transfer 1		

...   .

MVP for release   MVP for release   MVP for release

This roadmap shows an internal cross-organizational release every month. In addition, the team releases formally to itself and the product owner on a cadence of every two weeks. That's why you see the "MVP for release" at the end of the iteration/cadence.

I've only specified a few stories for each two-week time. Your team might define fewer stories if it's in flow, or more stories with timeboxes.

I've color-coded the two-week chunks of work. The left-most chunk is clear, either what the team has completed or what is currently in the backlog. The next three are somewhat gray and the last two are grayed out. The next three are our plan, and the grayed boxes are what we think the plan is. We can see the uncertainty by seeing how much is grayed. The six shaded boxes on the bottom are the actual stories in each feature set.

Many teams discover they need to accommodate more change and learning than a three-month rolling wave provides. Consider a maximum of a two-month rolling wave, as shown in the next figure.

Example: One-Month Agile Roadmap & Rolling-Wave Plan for Next Month

Internal Release 1		Internal Release 2	
Secure Login, Part 1	Secure Login, Part 1	Secure Login, New ID	Text Transfer, Part 1
Admin, Part 1	Diagnostics, Part 1	Admin, Part 2	Admin, Part 2
File Transfer, Part 1	File Transfer, Part 1	Engine, Part 1	Engine, Part 1

Secure Login 1, 2, 3
Secure Login 4, 5, 6
Admin 1, 2
File Transfer 1

Secure Login 7, 8, 9
Diagnostics 1, 2, 3
File Transfer 2, 3, 4

Secure Login 10, 11
Admin 3, 4
Engine 1, 2, 3

...

MVP for release

MVP for release

MVP for release

When product owners and teams use roadmaps like these, they have the option of changing the next bits of value. Starting with the two-month rolling wave, this product owner changed the value, as shown in the next roadmap on page 98.

The product owner decided there was more value in starting Text Transfer and Diagnostics rather than the original plan.

Rolling-Wave Roadmaps and Parking Lots Worked Better than the Big Roadmap

by: Michelle, Product Management Director

We're a typical big company. We have six-quarter roadmaps for products and even bigger roadmaps for other initiatives. To be honest, our roadmaps got in our way once we wanted to use agile approaches. Everyone thought the roadmaps were set in stone.

For our agile projects, instead of the six-quarter roadmap, we used a two-month rolling wave and a parking lot. The parking lot told us what we *thought* the value was as we discussed the feature or feature set. The more we delivered finished work, the more we could use relatively short rolling-wave roadmaps and parking lots as a way to discuss our features.

Original Sequence: Two Months

Internal Release 1		Internal Release 2	
Secure Login, Part 1	Secure Login, Part 1	Secure Login, New ID	Text Transfer, Part 1
Admin, Part 1	Diagnostics, Part 1	Admin, Part 2	Admin, Part 2
File Transfer, Part 1	File Transfer, Part 1	Engine, Part 1	Engine, Part 1

Changed Sequence After One Iteration/Cadence: Plan for Remainder of Time

Internal Release 1		Internal Release 2	
Secure Login, Part 1	Secure Login, Part 1	Text Transfer, Part 1	Secure Login, New ID
Admin, Part 1	Diagnostics, Part 1	Diagnostics, Part 2	Admin, Part 2
File Transfer, Part 1	File Transfer, Part 1	Engine, Part 1	Engine, Part 1

Use a Feature Parking Lot to See Possibilities

Some projects have a potential roadmap a mile or two long. Instead of trying to slot everything into quarters, consider using a visible parking lot, like the one shown in the following table.

Idea	Date Added	Value to Us	Why
Engine automation at scale	January 12	Might be able to capture the vertical we keep talking about	No one else does this
Cloud-based search	February 2	??	Danny, CTO, wants us to do this
Calendar integration	June 15	Need to integrate calendar and email at some point	Customers have been requesting this

Table 6—Possible-Feature Parking Lot

The parking lot helps separate "what we do now" from "what we want to do later." It might help your organization see the uncertainty you have in the roadmap.

Consider ways you can show uncertainty in the roadmap, and be able to change what the team delivers on a frequent basis. As long as you have small stories, creating and using rolling-wave roadmaps will help the team and the sponsors see your lack of certainty and the possibilities.

Consider Minimum Viable Products and Experiments

Each of the preceding roadmaps has something called "MVP for release." MVP means *minimum viable product*. Some feature sets are quite small. The team can deliver the entire feature set of multiple stories in one small chunk of time, such as an iteration or within a short cadence.

I see many feature sets that require more than one planning cadence or iteration to complete. And in the case of these roadmaps, you can see that the product owner wants the team to make progress across multiple feature sets in one planning iteration.

How can you show progress? With an MVP or maybe an MVE. A minimum viable product has enough functionality for the customer to use, even if it's not the full functionality. A minimum viable experiment provides feedback for the team and the product owner.

In *The Lean Startup [Rie11]*, Eric Ries suggests the Build-Measure-Learn feedback loop, shown in the following figure. The concept is that you build the smallest possible piece of your idea in the form of a product. When you release that product (the MVP), you can measure its success by gathering data. You can then learn, which helps you create the next batch of ideas.

Eric Ries's Build-Measure-Learn Feedback Loop

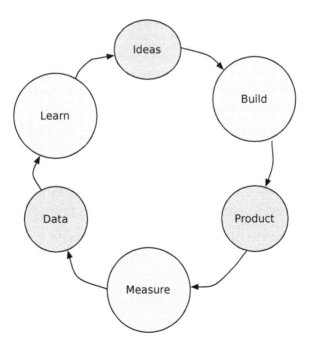

When product owners create MVPs to test out the minimum features, they can use the Build-Measure-Learn loop.

Sometimes we want to see something even smaller than a useful feature or feature set. That's an MVE. With an MVE, the product owner might think it's worth considering a feature set. But the product owner wants more data. That's why you create an MVE, something even smaller.

An MVE Saved Us a Ton of Money

by: Cindy, Product Owner

We have an embedded system. That means everything takes longer. It takes longer to develop, to test, and to release. I had this idea for a new vertical market, but I wondered if the boot speed was fast enough.

I checked with a great client. I got my product manager to visit the client and ask a bunch of questions about the vertical market and whether they needed something like what we were thinking. Yes, they were interested.

It turns out they were quite concerned about boot speed *and* application processing speed. Okay, that's fine. The product manager asked them if they were willing to work with us to test an MVE, not an MVP. We might not deliver a full product, and were they okay with that?

They agreed and we all signed pages of nondisclosures.

I selected four very small performance enhancements, happy path only. No error paths. The team took three days to develop and test the work. Then we all went to visit the customer to watch what the client did.

The team and I were surprised. Turns out boot speed was irrelevant (well, within certain parameters). What made the difference was one particular path through the application. The other three were irrelevant for this specific customer.

That gave us a ton of data. We spent a team-week altogether, on the development in the office, the travel, and watching the customer use the MVE. It looks like a ton of money, but I learned what a "necessary" feature was and wasn't.

If you develop digital products, you might find that you don't need nearly this amount of work for an MVE or even an MVP.

Sometimes you have a complex product and you can't find a customer willing to experiment with you. The potential customers might think it's too much work, or too complex to work on an MVE. Consider these possibilities:

- Identify the smallest MVE you can. What can you do to release that MVE as something a potential customer will try?

- Consider a simulation you can show potential customers. Maybe they can provide feedback on the simulation, not a product.

- Revisit your strategy to see if it demands this project now. (See *Manage Your Project Portfolio [Rot16a]* for more details.)

The less work you do before you release, the more valuable the work the team completes is. That's because the team can receive feedback on what it's done so far.

Recognize Value Traps

As the team works on defining and delivering value, see if it encounters these traps:

- The product owner has feature-itis.
- People in the organization want detailed schedules, such as Gantt charts.
- People are unsure about an MVP or an MVE, so they think they can't recognize any value until "all" of the work is done.

You have options for managing these traps.

Trap: The Product Owner Has Feature-itis

Product owners have feature-itis when they say things like this: "Gimme features. I don't care about no stinkin' framework. I don't care about no technical debt. I don't care that it's going to make your work harder later. I only care about now. I'm short-sighted, focused on today, or this iteration, and that's all I care about. Show me the features, baby. Show me the features!"

Now, I bet that you have never heard a product owner or customer say those precise words. But you have heard words like them. If you have, you are witnessing feature-itis. And you have some options.

1. Explain to the product owner that you are a professional team. Make sure that all your estimates include the necessary architectural, refactoring, and testing work—whatever your team needs to deliver finished value.

2. Explain the cost of not looking at the architecture, or at least the local design as you proceed, to the product owner. Explain that *Technical Debt Is Not Unfinished Work*, on page 139. The more you have unfinished work—incomplete refactoring to patterns, build or test automation—the more expensive it is to finish that work later. The team runs the risk of implementing Conway's Law, where the design of the system reflects the organizational design.

3. Track velocity in a burnup chart. You will see if you start finishing fewer features over time.

You can placate the product owner, swallow your pride and your professionalism, and just do what the product owner asked for. Sometimes this is the right answer. But it's often the wrong answer.

Feature-itis is a seductive disease common among relatively new product owners. For the first time in their careers, they actually see features coming out of the technical teams. It's a heady feeling. No wonder they fall prey to the dark side.

But with that feeling of excitement must come a feeling of responsibility. Not only is the product owner responsible for the product features; the product owner is responsible for the business value of the product and knowing that the team is able to continue to develop the product. Without architecture, tests, and all of the necessary engineering practices that good software requires, a technical team cannot deliver.

Trap: Your Organization Wants Detailed Schedules, Such as Gantt Charts

I said before that agile approaches change the culture of the project. In addition, they change the organization's culture. However, not everyone changes at the same time. If your managers are used to assessing project progress with detailed schedules or Gantt charts, they might want to continue seeing those artifacts.

I have had good results when I've offered people the different pictures of the roadmaps: the longer roadmaps covered in *Plan at Several Levels*, on page 86, and the shorter, more detailed roadmaps discussed in *Create Rolling-Wave Roadmaps*, on page 96. In addition, consider the tips in Chapter 14, *Report Your Project State*, on page 215.

What do you do if someone really wants a Gantt chart? Do what you think you must. I don't advocate placating those people. I recommend you help them learn how to read the other measurements.

Trap: It's Not Done Until Everything Is Done

Some people are concerned that they can't release anything until "everything" is done. They say things such as this:

- "While I'm in there, I'll do this, too."
- "It will take longer to do it later. I'll just finish it now."
- "But no one can use it like this. I (or we) need to finish everything before we can release anything."

There are several possibilities here:

- People are concerned they will look incompetent if they don't finish "everything."

- People might worry they can't get to the rest of the value if they don't do it now.

- People don't understand what an MVP or an MVE is.

You might, as an organizational leader, show by example that it's okay to release interim, not-yet-totally-finished work; that might help people see that you don't suffer any ramifications. You can do this with code, tests, a project charter—anything.

These people might have managers who want them to finish "everything" for some reason. A manager who doesn't understand agile thinks people should receive performance evaluations based on "their" features. See *Managers Help with Team-Based Recognition*, on page 242.

It's possible a product owner or team member doesn't understand how to slice and dice features so a team can release interim value. Review the MVP and MVE discussion.

Help people see that adding more work that's not on the board (doing work while in a certain place in the code or tests) adds to the WIP and increases cycle time. That means the team has less idea of its estimates and when it might complete work.

Have a one-on-one with the team member or, if the team has sufficient safety, address this in a team meeting, such as a retrospective. You might also find that a backlog planning or refinement session is a good place to raise the issue.

Now Try This

1. Does your project have a product owner—a full-time product owner—who can work with the team to create stories, accept those stories, and refine them based on feedback? If not, that's a huge impediment and I recommend you work on that first.

2. Ask the product owner and the team to think about sets of features and how to tease the features apart so the product owner can rank them.

3. Help everyone think "how little" instead of "how much" by working with the product owner or asking the product owner to create the smallest stories that still have value to some person.

Now that you know how to create stories, it's time to learn how to order them.

CHAPTER 7

Rank the Work

Think back to the last time you had a list of chores you needed to finish on a weekend. How did you decide what to do first? Maybe you attacked the one that would take the least amount of time, just so you could cross something off your list. (Finishing something can also impress a family member. You score points.)

Maybe something was no longer valuable if you didn't finish it in time for a family member visit. If you're supposed to finish hanging pictures because Aunt Martha is coming to visit and you don't finish, is it really worth hanging the pictures after she's gone? You might choose other work to do.

Maybe you decided you had a large project that you needed to explore a little first. In my house, home-improvement projects that involve painting are like that. The painter paints a swatch of paint and I get to look at it in different light.

Maybe you wanted to timebox some of the work to see how long the rest of the work would take. I hate cleaning my office because I could be doing other work that I find much more enjoyable instead. I'll tackle that work by time-boxing the cleaning up to 30 minutes or an hour just to see where I am at the end of that time. If I think I can finish in a short period, I might do it. Otherwise, I get to do work I prefer doing next.

If I think something is risky, I might try to do something small to learn more about it. For example, if I think writing a specific book might be a good idea, I might try writing a blog post or an article first, before committing to a book. I haven't expended much time and I have the value of the post or article.

You can rank work in these ways and more. If you don't like these alternatives for ranking features in a project, consider the alternatives in *Manage Your Project Portfolio [Rot16a]*. There are additional options there that, even though they are for ranking projects in a project portfolio, will work for features also.

Rank the Shortest Work First

Don Reinertsen in *The Principles of Product Development Flow: Second Generation Lean Product Development [Rei09]* suggested that we consider delivering work that takes little time to do, as a way to rank the work. That's called Shortest Job First. Since we're talking about knowledge work, I'm going to use "work" instead of "job."

It's a terrific idea, as long as you really have short work. And it's a great idea if you have different lengths of work. That's because you can push through some of the short work and get feedback before you attack the longer work.

Doing the shortest work first provides you quick wins. You might be able show people a walking skeleton, as described in *Create a Walking Skeleton*, on page 90, and ask for feedback. If they don't like the skeleton, you haven't invested too much time. And you can see finished work even if the work is not full feature sets.

The shortest-work-first approach works, as long as the time is short. By that, I mean *not* more than a couple of days in duration. I prefer no more than one day in duration. If the work takes more time, or if you have a ton of work that is all short and *must* be done now, consider using cost of delay to rank the work.

Use Cost of Delay to See Value

One way to define the value for the work is to make sure the work is still valuable. Use the ideas from cost of delay to define the value now and in the future.

You may understand cost of delay without having known the name for it. Cost of delay, as illustrated by the diagram on page 107, is the cost you incur from not releasing the work when you want to, and the implications of that delay on future revenue.

There are four potential costs when you delay work:

- The company misses the potential sales from the introduction delay.
- The delay introduces lower maximum sales.
- The delayed introduction creates less overall demand, so the feature has less value in total.
- With less demand, the end of life might be earlier with a delay. Often, this is a function of not being able to capture the market at the optimum time. Since you don't have the customers, you have an earlier end of life.

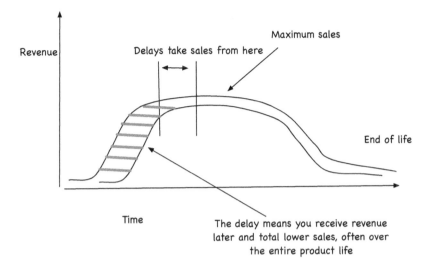

Here's a quick example. Imagine you're working at a game company. Game companies make most of their money when people buy presents for Christmas. When you release a game before October, you make the maximum amount of revenue, because your game is available when the buyers want it. If you release the game in October, you may have lost some buyers, because some people buy their holiday presents before then. If you release the game in November, you will still capture some buyers, but some—even many—of the potential buyers have already bought their presents. If you don't release until December, you'll have lost most of the buyers. If you release in January, no one will care. And if this is your first product release, you might have to end-of-life the product in January because no one cares enough to buy a follow-on release.

The real question is this: When is the "best" time to release this feature (and, by extension, the project)?

Estimation often assumes that the feature has the same value over time. However, if you miss a specific time, the feature often has a decreasing value over time.

Thinking about when the feature no longer has value is one way of articulating value via cost of delay: When does this feature no longer have any value? When does it have maximum value to us? The diagram on page 108 shows how you might graph the value over time when a feature (or release) no longer has value.

In this case, the release has the maximum value anytime through September. Once we get to October, the release loses at least half its value. By December, there's almost no value.

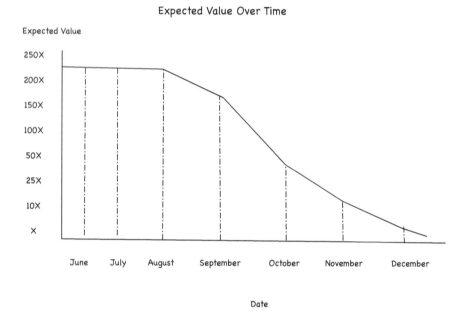

Although I've discussed the value of a *release*, you can use the same idea for features. Does your product need a way to send and receive email *now*? If so, you might not need to forward email or cc email immediately, but sending and receiving is something you need to do *now*.

When you start to break apart a feature set into features and use the value-over-time idea to rank the stories in a feature set, the product owner and the team can have a rational conversation. The product owner no longer says, "I need everything or it has no value."

Too often, product owners (or other manager-type people) say, "You have to do everything by next Friday or it has no value." I've seen very few situations where the maximum-value date was that close in and the team had to have finished *all* of the work. But even if that's true for you, here are the benefits of ranking by value over time:

- The product owner might not even start work on this feature or feature set if the team can't finish it when the feature runs out of value.

- The team can deliver the most valuable work and not have to start work that's no longer valuable.

- The product owner might be able to have a conversation about which story is first, second, and third. That helps the product owner and the team break apart feature sets into smaller features.

> **Joe asks:**
> ## What If We Still Need "Everything" Now?
>
> One of the ways agile approaches challenge people is in the idea of keeping things small. That "how little" thinking challenges many of us, especially if we can envision the entire product in all its beauty.
>
> You might need to draw something like the "Expected Value Over Time" graph on page 108 for every feature in a feature set. You might discover some features lose value over time. Some features might gain value over time. Some might lose value soon and gain value later.
>
> When people think there is value in "everything" now, they aren't thinking about the value at all. They might be thinking about the pressure other people have put on them to deliver the "final, complete, finished" product.
>
> Very few feature sets need to *all* be done right now. See if you can have a reasonable discussion with the people who rank the work.

While I like the idea of ranking by seeing the value increase (or decrease) over time, that's not the only way to rank. Sometimes interim learning is most valuable for everyone.

Rank by Valuing the Learning

Sometimes it's worth learning more about a feature before you decide how to manage the roadmap or rank the entire feature set. In that case, consider these three approaches:

- Instead of valuing an entire feature set, decide what you want to learn from an MVP or an MVE.

- Spike the work to understand the feature set.

- Try something quite risky to understand the risks more.

Learn from an MVP or an MVE

Back in *Consider Minimum Viable Products and Experiments*, on page 99, I suggested you might want to consider what was the minimum requirement for products and experiments. Especially if you are thinking about creating small MVPs or experiments, you might value some of those features higher than others.

If you know what you want to measure and learn, you can create small experiments that provide you value. I'm not suggesting you work on an entire feature set, one small experiment at a time. I suggest you consider the smallest experiment you can to try to create some data that will help you learn what to do next.

Spikes Can Help Everyone Understand the Value

Sometimes you need to value something you've never done before. You can't know how long it will take, so you can't use Shortest Job First. You might not even be sure of what the entire feature set is.

In that case, you might consider timeboxing a little work to understand what the entire feature set is. You might even learn enough to be able to estimate it. That timebox is a spike.

Back in *Experiment and Spike to Explore*, on page 94, you learned about how to use spikes. Consider timeboxing your spikes to not more than one day. Your team might want to make it several hours instead of an entire day. I encourage the entire team to work on the spike, swarming or mobbing to complete the work. At the end of that timebox, the team can see what it completed and what is left to complete for an MVP. (See *Predicting the Unpredictable [Rot15]* for more details.)

Use Risk to Assess Value

Sometimes you want to try something that's quite risky, because you can learn more about the risks. In that case, consider taking one story from a feature set, or create an MVE to try. Rank that story or experiment high because the learning from finishing that one story will help inform the team and the product owner about the rest of that work.

Recognize Ranking Traps

Ranking the work by value challenges many people. Watch for these traps:

- Using estimation—and only estimation—to rank the work.
- Someone else pressuring the product owner to change the ranking to accommodate another person's desires.
- Ranking *all* the work for months or a release at the beginning of a project.

You have options for managing these traps.

Trap: Rank Only by Estimation

Some teams try to use estimation to rank their work. If we had perfect knowledge, we might be able to use estimation. However, we rarely have perfect knowledge about the work or the estimate.

If you *know* you have a one-day or shorter story, you can *Rank the Shortest Work First*, on page 106. However, teams often have less knowledge than they need about the story size. Or the story is much larger than one day. In that case, using estimation to rank often doesn't work.

Trap: Someone Else Pressures the Product Owner

You may have heard of the HiPPO (Highest Paid Person in the Office). I would love to say that agile approaches make HiPPOs go away. Not so. However, agile approaches make it clear that the HiPPO exists.

If you have a HiPPO who declares, "Everything must be done!" or "Do this first!" or the like, use your influence and collaboration skills to help that person realize the team will progress faster if it limits its WIP and works on one thing at a time, in a way that makes sense for the product.

Sometimes it helps to ask that person about his or her goals or measurements. Sometimes people act in a way that satisfies the people measuring them.

Trap: We Must Rank All of It

Even if you consider rolling-wave planning, as discussed in *Create Rolling-Wave Roadmaps*, on page 96, someone might want to rank "all of it." That's a trap because as the team finishes small stories, the product owner wants the ability to change which stories the team should do when.

Here are some ways of managing this "all of it" thinking:

- Consider ranking up to three iterations worth of work, or enough to fill a cycle time of about six weeks.

- Consider creating a parking lot, as discussed in *Use a Feature Parking Lot to See Possibilities*, on page 98, as a way to manage the not-yet items.

- See if clarifying the product vision and the release criteria helps the product owner and the team manage the requests for "all of it" now, as opposed to later.

It's tempting for people to want to do "all" of anything. See how you can help people move to "how little" thinking as opposed to the "how much" they traditionally had.

Now Try This

1. Select a ranking approach aside from Shortest Work First. I'll discuss estimation in Chapter 10, *Agile Estimation:*, on page 147. Too often, the team can't tell which story is shortest, so it's a good idea to try other ranking approaches.

2. Try that ranking method either for an iteration or as the product owner updates a board. Discuss the ranking in the retrospective to see if the team thought it had delivered the highest-value work.

3. Articulate the value of the work under discussion. Sometimes the value changes over time. Sometimes the value is about quick learning. The more everyone can bring the discussion back to value, the easier it will be to rank the work.

Now that you know how to rank the work for the team, it's time to show the team members their ranked work. That's the point of the board—to help the team to visualize its work.

CHAPTER 8

Visualize Your Work with a Board

If you've worked on any project, people have asked you these kinds of questions: When will you start this thing? When will you be done? Who's working on this? You may have pointed people to a project dashboard, or shown them some other graphical representation of the status data.

I used yellow-sticky, rolling-wave, deliverable-based scheduling in my projects before I knew about agile approaches. I found it helpful to be able to show people the current view of the schedule. (See *Manage It! [Rot07]* for more information.)

In agile approaches, we have multiple tools for explaining the project's plans and current state. (See *Plan at Several Levels*, on page 86.) The big-picture roadmap helps people see a larger view of the proposed deliverables, the larger plan. The rolling wave–style, shorter roadmaps help people see what the product owner has planned for the near term. The project board helps the team and other people see what's happening now—the current state.

Boards help teams visualize their work, their bottlenecks, and their delays. The idea is that the team members can see—at a glance—where they are with all the work on the board. At the very least, the board tracks the state of the work: is it ready, is it in some sort of progress state, or is it done?

Your team board helps the entire team see what's going on. First, let's discuss how to start creating your board.

Start with a Paper Board

It's tempting to select an electronic tool when you start with an agile approach. Electronic tools provide you places to put your planned and in-progress work. You're probably accustomed to electronic project-management tools. And electronic boards make it easy to calculate cycle time or velocity.

However, paper boards have several benefits electronic boards don't have:

- The team members can pass around a card or sticky to review, add/subtract, or rephrase. That's how people on the same team build the same mental model of the story or feature set.

- People don't move something to some sort of in-progress column without actually standing up from their desk, walking over to the board and moving it. Electronic tools make it too easy for the team members to say, "Yes, I'm done with that" or "I'm working on it" when neither state is true.

- Electronic tools can hide the details of the card. Often, the box is too small to see the story details or the acceptance criteria at a glance.

- Paper helps you create smaller stories, because the paper (cards or stickies) is small.

- When you start with paper, you can see which columns you need on your board and easily add or subtract them.

- Paper helps you limit the team's overall WIP. Paper creates a physical limit for what everyone sees, considers, and works on.

If you're worried about how a distributed team can see a paper board, see *Create Visible Boards for Geographically Distributed Teams*, on page 122, for more details.

Teams that start with electronic tools fall into many traps. These traps are not the tools' fault. The problem is that the tools don't help the team create new, agile habits. The team reinforces old habits. I've seen these problems when teams started with a tool:

- The team's stories are too large to complete in an iteration, never mind in one or two days.

- The team creates architecture-based work or tasks, instead of stories.

- People tend to create tasks around the story to break it apart instead of swarming around the feature.

- People tend to say, "I'm an expert there, for that story. Assign it to me." Aside from the fact that no one should assign anyone work, reinforcing the expert problem creates bottlenecks and reduces team learning and feedback. Paper boards don't have a need to assign anyone to the story when the team creates the story.

One of my clients used a whiteboard with index cards. Each person on the team had one magnet. Because each person had only one magnet, each person had limited WIP.

Another client had index cards on corkboard. They used pushpins with people's faces on them to push the index cards onto the correct column. They had three pushpins for each person on the team. When I asked them how it was to have people be on three cards at the same time, the director said, "We know that having people assigned to multiple items is not helping our throughput. However, we can *see* what people are working on."

Start with paper on your board. Paper invites collaboration and the agile mindset. Paper will help you see what you're doing and not doing, as individuals and teams.

Don't start with an electronic board. Start with paper of some variety.

Iteration-Based Boards Show Team Commitments

You might have seen a typical Scrum board, similar to the one shown here:

Scrum Board

In Scrum and other iteration-based agile approaches, the team estimates what it can commit to for its iteration. The team takes that work and puts it in the Ready column in rank order.

The Ready column does not change during the iteration. This is important. The team, along with the product owner, commits to what the team will do during the iteration. This is one reason why an iteration is different from a cadence. (See *Distinguish Between Cadence and Iteration*, on page 11.)

If a team has to manage interruptions, such as support requests, the team leaves room in the iteration for support work. See *Estimate Support Work*, on page 157, for more specifics.

The team decides how it will work. The team decides the flow, and the flow is not explicit *unless the team decides to make it explicit*.

Teams own their own boards. If your team wants to separate support requests from the entire backlog, or add a column labeled "Today," it should do so. The board exists to help the team members see and finish their work.

Teams that use iterations might even decide to map their flow on their board. As soon as they create WIP limits, the board is technically a kanban board. Does that matter? No, except to the team.

One Scrum team decided that it liked the idea of iterations for cadence, but the members needed to see their flow. As shown in the following figure, they also wanted to have a "Today" and an "Urgent" queue for work. They created a board that looks a lot like a kanban board, which they call their "ScrumFlow" board. (Yes, they made that name up.)

"ScrumFlow" Board

Ready	Today	Develop and Unit Test	Dev-Done	System Test	PO Accept	Done
	2	2		2		

| Urgent | | | | | | |

Teams decide what goes on their board. Teams manage their boards. Teams can name their boards. As long as your team's board provides the team members the data they need to manage themselves, it doesn't matter what they call the board or what the board shows.

Kanban Boards Show Team Flow and Bottlenecks

Kanban boards are each unique to their teams. That's because each team has its own unique flow.

The following kanban board has WIP limits on all major columns, including the Ready column. The WIP limits exist to make sure the team sees its flow and possible bottlenecks.

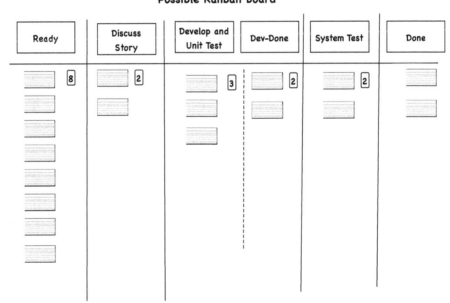

Possible Kanban Board

The Ready column has a WIP limit because the product owner can change what's in the Ready column. This particular team has a step called "Discuss Story" in its flow. That column also has a WIP limit so the team doesn't get too far ahead of itself.

Notice that this team has a WIP limit on the number of stories in Dev-Done. You can think of the Dev-Done column as a buffer for the System Test column.

Each of the columns with WIP limits is full, which means this board is full. If the team respects its WIP limits, the team can't start a new story, nor can it take a story into Develop and Unit Test. This team has to move a story from System Test to Done before anything else on this board can move.

When the team has a full board, the members look at the board from *right to left*, to see what is closest to done. The team has a responsibility to move whatever is in System Test to Done before pulling any more work. (See *Walk the Board*, on page 199, for more specifics.)

One team discovered that its board looked like the (overloaded) Scrum board shown in the following figure.

(Overloaded) Scrum Board

The team had started with a Scrum board. They had many items in the "In Progress" column. The developers noticed they were always "ahead" of the testers. They decided to create the kanban board on page 119 to see where the problems were. With a kanban board, the team was able to see the problem. The testers were behind on creating test automation, and had to test too much manually.

The developers and testers paired on the work in System Test until the team created sufficient test automation for the team. Because they saw the bottlenecks, they could discuss the problems and fix them as a team.

Once they cleared the System Test bottleneck, they could move to the next leftmost column and see why they had bottlenecks there. Once they cleared their bottlenecks, they create WIP limits to manage where they had work in progress.

Overloaded/Full Kanban Board

Ready	Discuss Story	Develop and Unit Test	Dev-Done	System Test	Done

Joe asks:
Do We Need to Create and Respect WIP Limits?

The short answer is yes. A resounding yes.

When people limit their work in progress, they make it possible to finish work. When people finish work, they feel a sense of accomplishment. That sense of accomplishment allows them to finish more work. (See *The Progress Principle: Using Small Wins to Ignite Joy, Engagement, and Creativity at Work [AK11]* for more specifics.)

When a team respects its WIP limits, it commits itself to addressing only the work it can. The members will work as a team to finish the work on its board. Creating and respecting WIP limits is a form of team commitment and agreement on how the team will work.

One of the reasons I suggest you *Start with a Paper Board*, on page 113, is that paper has natural WIP limits. If you can't fit any more paper on the board, the team has its WIP limits.

For example, if your team has interruptions from support, you might need an Urgent queue on your board. The board in the image on page 120 has one urgent item. That means that, depending on the agreement with the people who put items in the Urgent queue, the team might stop working on one of the items it's working on now and have more WIP. The additional WIP is the work the team stops plus the new work.

Possible Kanban Board

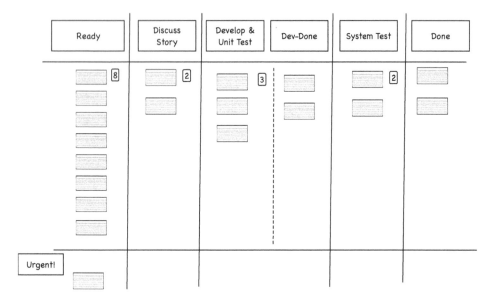

Every team has a different meaning for "Urgent." Some teams use Urgent as "Stop what you're doing right now and start this." Some teams use Urgent as "Take this next." If you use an Urgent queue, decide if the team can override WIP limits to take on new work. Almost any decisions your team makes are fine, as long as it makes a decision about what Urgent means and if and when the team can override its WIP limits.

If you do use an Urgent queue, consider defining response time in the working-agreements part of chartering the team. See *Ask the Team to Develop Working Agreements*, on page 29.

Make Your Own Board

Teams are responsible for their own boards. It doesn't matter if you use an iteration-based agile approach or a flow-based agile approach; create a board that matches your needs.

If you have several projects underway and your team is supposed to make progress on all of them, consider a kanban board with WIP limits. You will need to see how many items you can have in progress for your team. If your team addresses production support issues, consider adding an urgent queue to your board.

If your team has people in many time zones, you might need to see where the work is to see the state of everything in progress. I recommend your team use a kanban board with WIP limits, so no one gets too far ahead or behind.

As you start to use an agile approach, notice the kind of work you have and what flows easily through your team. Especially notice if you have bottlenecks and adjust your board to make those bottlenecks visible.

Visualize Problems with a Board

Your team might want to note problems (impediments, risks, other obstacles) on its board. I prefer to separate the problems from the work. That's because a servant leader (not the team) may take the lead on addressing these problems. One team uses a board like the one shown in the following figure.

Risk/Problem/Obstacle Board

Concern with Date Added	Ready	In Progress	Waiting for External Decision	Waiting for Team Action	Done

The team wants to track the date it added a problem to this board. If the team doesn't address risks early enough, the risks turn into problems. But visibility doesn't mean the team has to start working on it yet. When it's time for someone to work on the item in the Concern column, the team promotes that item into the Ready column. This team has a WIP limit of seven items in progress to make sure it continues to review and address its problems. Whoever works on the item can move it into a Waiting state too—waiting for an external or team decision. Once the person or team resolves the item, the item is moved to Done.

I've been vague about who would work these problems. Often a servant leader manages these problems. Sometimes team members do. There is no One

Right Way to address risks, impediments, or other problems. Make the work visible and work it. Your team might want to track items from a retrospective parking lot on this board, especially if it has trouble starting the work on that parking lot. (See *Use a Parking Lot for the Improvement List*, on page 198.)

Create Visible Boards for Geographically Distributed Teams

You might be working on a geographically distributed team. You can still use a paper board to start instead of an electronic tool.

The team creates the board as described in *Make Your Own Board*, on page 120, in one physical location. Someone takes a picture of it and posts it on the team's project space. Now the team has at least two choices. The team can ask one person in that physical location to please move the cards as people take and finish stories. Or the team can replicate the board in each physical location. Each person can move his or her own cards, take a picture, and let the entire team know which card moved and where.

The team creates a team norm about how to move cards. When a team member moves a card, the team member notifies everyone according to the team norm.

When the team practices with its board, and gets feedback from how the board works and how its process works, the team might decide to move to an electronic board. However, stay in paper as long as possible. You will find that your stories are smaller and that your feedback is faster.

Beware of Board Tyranny

When people take stories alone, the standup or walking of the board tends to focus on the person. Too often I hear, "Why didn't you finish this work?" (See *Standups Create Recommitment and Collaboration*, on page 200, to see how to use standups.)

Instead, ask the team to focus on moving work across the board. It might be easier for your team to use flow to do this. The WIP limits help people focus on moving work across the board, rather than on what individuals are "responsible" for. See Steve Reid, Prateek Singh, and Daniel Vacanti's experience report, "Ultimate Kanban: Scaling Agile Without Frameworks at Ultimate Software."[a]

Never blame people for not doing "their" work. All the work belongs to the team, not one person.

---

a. https://www.infoq.com/articles/kanban-scaling-agile-ultimate

Paper helps a team see its real flow, not what it thinks its flow should be. "Well, once a dev is done, a tester *should* just take it." Are the testers in the same room, or at least on the same floor as the developers? Did the testers participate in story creation or refinement? I've seen time zones and insufficient understanding prevent the testers from "just" taking a story. The longer a team stays in paper, the more it is apt to create a board that reflects its real flow of work.

What if your management mandates a board in the form of a tool? That's the *Trap: Management Mandates Your Boards*, on page 123.

Recognize Visualization Traps

Not every team gets its board right the very first time. And defining a board that works for your team might be even more difficult if your team encounters these traps:

- Management mandates your boards.
- Every person takes his or her own story.
- Waterfall masquerades as kanban.
- The team works in iterations of waterfalls.

You have options for managing these traps.

Trap: Management Mandates Your Boards

Your management says, "Do Scrum!" or "Do Kanban!" Your management has an idea of what it wants to see for your board and your output.

Don't fight with your management—at least, not yet. Instead, use the project frame that they request. If they request Scrum, use two-week iterations.

Use the board you want. If you have a ton of interruptions, use a kanban board to make that work visible. Use the board to measure cumulative flow and cycle time. I would not even bother measuring velocity. With all those interruptions, cycle time and cumulative flow are better predictors of your capacity. See *Cumulative Flow Shows Where the Work Is*, on page 183, and *Cycle Time Shows How Long Work Takes*, on page 185, for information about these measurements.

Trap: Everyone Takes His or Her Own Story

Sometimes when teams are new to an iteration-based agile approach, they fall into the trap of dividing the work by the number of people. "We'll each take our own story. We'll make tons of progress." Or someone, such as a manager or product owner, asks or demands that everyone takes his or her own story. (When people demand that experts work on "their" stories, it's the *Trap: Experts Take Their Own Stories*, on page 160.)

It sounds like it should work. If we divide up the work, we can get done faster, right?

Well, no. Knowledge work is interdependent work and requires learning. That means we need other people to deliver a feature and we will learn as we deliver. I have yet to see one-person features. Every feature requires at least a person who creates the feature and a person who checks the feature. Most features I see require more people.

If you have noticed this trap, consider these options:

- Move to a kanban board and create WIP limits. This will help everyone see where the work is and if the team has bottlenecks.

- Ask the team to *Swarm on the Work*, on page 134, or *Mob on the Work*, on page 135, on every single feature. When people work together, they will finish the features faster.

- At a minimum, ask the team members to pair on every single story.

Maybe you can see more options for your team. The team will make much more progress when people collaborate on stories than when each person takes his or her own story.

Trap: Waterfall Masquerades as Kanban

Just because you have a kanban board does not mean you are agile.

I've seen at least two kinds of flow that were not agile at all. In one, the team used a waterfall approach and its board had these headings: Analysis, Architecture, Design Specs, Functional Specs, Coding, and Testing, in that order.

Those headings might be okay, but here's how they worked: The "product owner" supplied a large document full of functional and nonfunctional requirements. The product owner then put all those requirements into the Analysis column. The requirements were not in the form of stories with acceptance criteria. The architect developed an architecture based on those requirements and handed off work to the senior developer. The senior developer wrote design specs and many functional specs. The other developers finally joined the project and wrote their functional specs. Finally, the developers wrote code that tested their earlier assumptions. The testers joined the team just in time to start working on requirements in the testing column. They had code and documentation to use to guide their testing. Except the documentation didn't match the code.

The team had a tremendous amount of WIP, lots of up-front documentation that didn't reflect the final reality, and little collaboration.

Its flow was not agile. And because the team had no WIP limits, it didn't use any of the agile or lean principles to collaborate and finish work. The board itself is not bad. If the team collaborates on everything, uses WIP limits, and eliminates up-front documentation, this kind of a board might work to help a team move to an agile approach.

I've also seen a team where the architect was outside the team and told the team how to do the work. That team had these columns on the board: Receive Specs, Coding, Testing, and Rework. Yes, the board actually had a Rework column. That's because that team's experience was like many other teams': its up-front design was often wrong.

Both of these teams felt as if they were wearing straitjackets. No one had any fun.

I can't guarantee agile projects are fun. However, as the team defines its own workflow and its work, many agile teams appear to have more fun more often.

Trap: You Have Iterations of Waterfalls

Some people who start with an iteration-based agile approach have a two-week iteration that looks like this:

- Day 1: Commit to work. Start development.

- Days 2-6: Continue development. The testers are bored because they have nothing to do yet.

- Days 7-10: Test and send back work to developers.

- Day 10: Realize the team didn't finish half of what it committed to finishing. Or the developers "finished" but the testers didn't.

The team doesn't finish the work it thought it could. Often, the team discovers (or, worse, the testers discover) that the developers created a number of defects along with the feature. And sometimes the team doesn't realize that it let defects escape into the next iteration. The team has a ton of WIP during the iteration that might be invisible to the team.

The real problem is that the *team* doesn't take the responsibility to complete the work. Instead of a collaborative approach to starting and completing work, the team uses a waterfall approach inside iterations. Maybe you have board tyranny, as discussed in *Beware of Board Tyranny*, on page 122.

You don't have to work this way. You have at least these options: *Swarm on the Work*, on page 134, or *Mob on the Work*, on page 135; use a kanban board and measure your WIP; or make your iterations half the duration of what they were.

The way to *see* if your team is doing this is to use a kanban board. See *Kanban Boards Show Team Flow and Bottlenecks*, on page 117. Make sure the team re-creates its flow on the board. Once the team sees its flow, consider asking it to create WIP limits, so people can see what they start and when.

If the team uses iterations, it can still use kanban to see the flow of work. However, it might be time to reduce the iteration duration to see what's going on. In *Keep Your Iteration Duration Short*, on page 14, I said to make your iterations short enough that if you had to throw away everything you had done, you could. If your iteration is four weeks, divide it by two and use a two-week iteration. If your iteration is two weeks, make it a one-week iteration.

When the team halves the time, it puts pressure on itself to commit to less work. When the team commits to fewer features in less time, it reduces the batch size. That has the effect of increasing throughput.

If you are already using one-week iterations, consider this question: What would you have to do to get one feature done? Maybe the problem is your feature (story) size.

Now Try This

1. Decide if you will use iterations, a cadence, or flow. That will help you decide which kind of a board to use and when to update it.

2. Consider using kanban to map your team's flow of work, whether you use iterations or not.

3. Add WIP limits to your board to see how much work in progress you have. That will help your measurements.

Now that your team members can visualize their work, it's time to see how to move the work across the board, incorporating technical practices to help the team deliver.

CHAPTER 9

Create Technical Excellence

Do you like to practice some form of craft or hobby, such as cooking, woodworking, or knitting? When we practice our crafts, how do we go fast? Part of it is experience with our craft. Part of it is how we create and maintain our environment.

I'm going to use cooking as an example. We need to know what we want to accomplish: is it making dinner or a grand dessert? The plans (recipes) for each are different. We need our tools, such as good knives and pots and pans. We often need interim deliverables, because things need to melt and then cool for desserts. Or we need to sauté vegetables and put them aside for later combination.

Above all, I have noticed that when I am pressed for time I do these things: I read the recipe through a few times so I know what I'm going to do and when. I gather my ingredients so I know I have everything at hand. And I clean the kitchen as I proceed, so I can see my workspace at a glance.

We do something similar with code. We discuss the stories with the product owner so we know what we need to do. We review the code and tests already there to see what exists and what might need to change. And we create tests at a variety of levels to keep the code clean as we proceed.

I'm not saying that producing software products or any other kind of knowledge work is as easy as cooking. However, when we practice our craft, we often need to think about what we will do and how we might do it, and then keep our workspace clean as we proceed.

For software (and hardware and mechanical) products, we spend far more time discussing what we should do (defining and refining the requirements) and reading the existing code and tests than we spend writing new code and tests.

That means we need to consider these ideas to go fast:

- Optimize for reading the code and tests. That often means we need to refactor (simplify) as we proceed.

- Optimize for early delivery to see how we're proceeding. That often means small stories and continuous integration as we proceed.

- Optimize for creating technical excellence as we proceed. That means we need to test at a variety of levels as we proceed.

Although I've written this book for agile software teams, I've thought about other possible readers. If you are not a software person, please translate these ideas for your kind of product. Do you read and reread previous plans, schematics, or some other artifact to discover what you need to consider next? How can you iterate on the requirements to refine the work as you proceed? How can you test as you proceed so you know you have a valuable product while you develop, not just at the very end?

How Much "Quality" Does Your Product Need?

Not every product needs excellence in order to be released. Consider Geoffrey Moore's technology adoption life cycle (see *Crossing the Chasm [Moo91]*) as a way to think about product quality. I added the part about what customers want at different times in the following diagram.

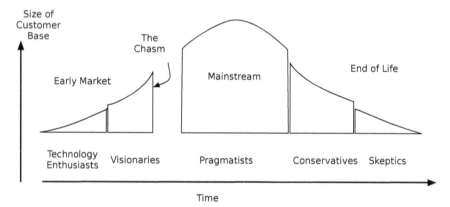

What Customers Care About at Different Times:

Enthusiasts:	Visionaries:	Pragmatists:	Conservatives:	Skeptics:
1. Time to Release 2. Low Defects 3. More Features	1. Time to Release 2. More Features 3. Low Defects	1. Low Defects 2. Time to Release 3. More Features	1. Low Defects 2. More Features 3. Time to Release	1. Low Defects 2. More Features 3. Time to Release

If you are in the early part of the life cycle, with enthusiasts and visionaries, your job is to release small increments of value fast. Those customers will provide you the ability to learn. (For more information, see *The Lean Startup* [Rie11].) That means your batch size, the size of your stories, must be small—and yes, you can take shortcuts to achieve a fast delivery.

However, once your customers pass the chasm, when your product achieves mainstream status, you now have to focus on low defects: preventing and fixing defects so your customers can use the system.

The product owner, possibly via the product manager, might ask the customers what quality means to them. Sometimes the answers surprise everyone.

Too often, managers encourage teams to take "shortcuts" to shave time off the schedule. Gerald Weinberg in *Quality Software Management: Volume 1, Systems Thinking [Wei92]* names the Zeroth Law of Software Quality: "If you don't care about quality, you can make any other requirement," including schedule.

Shortcuts create cruft and a mess.[1]

Our project speed is a function of the code and tests that already exist, the technical excellence of the code and tests, the clarity of what we want to do next, and the complexity of what we need to do next.

You might think of the team paying attention to the feedback, the learning, from the early part of the chasm. As the team learns, it now has to pay attention to the quality of the code and the tests. The team has options to create a high-quality product. That's what this chapter is about.

As a leader, you look for results from your team: a continuous flow of running, tested features. Your team can achieve these results by thinking about how it can do the following:

- Integrate often to see progress
- Keep the code and tests clean
- Work together to maintain throughput and focus
- Test at all levels so the team has support for frequent change

In this chapter, I'll discuss specifics your team might use to achieve those results.

---

1. http://docondev.com/blog/2010/10/technical-debt-versus-cruft

Integrate as Often as Possible

If you are accustomed to large, multiday or multiweek chunks of work, you might not be familiar with continuous integration. Continuous integration means the developers (and testers) work on some small chunk of value, check that value in the version-control system, make a build, check that build, and, as long as everything works, they're done with that piece. When I think of continuous integration, I think of people checking in *at least* twice a day. I check in my work every hour or two. I recommend a smaller time frame rather than a larger one.

Here's the value of continuous integration:

- You can see what you're done with and what's still in progress.
- Developers can check to see if they broke the build.
- Automated smoke tests can check that the product's performance or reliability still works the way everyone expects.
- Other people can use what you finished.

Other people here might be developers or testers. Developers across the project might be waiting for another developer's code, even if that code is an MVE. Testers can start testing the real code as soon as they have it available.

Continuous integration provides a team the support it needs to move fast. When developers write a little code and write some unit tests to go along with that code, they know the code works. It's the same way with tests: when testers write small tests and verify those tests work, everyone knows the code works. And the team can see its progress because the team gets to move a card across the board.

The more often the team integrates the code, the more they see how the product works. They get immediate feedback about their thinking and coding or testing.

They learn fast.

If you want faster product development, create small stories and use continuous integration.

Consider Continuous Delivery

Back in on page 78, I showed you the potential for release frequency for different kinds of products. If you have a totally digital product, you can have continuous delivery. See *Continuous Delivery [HF10]* and *Unblock! A Guide to the New Continuous Agile [Sin14]* for ways you could organize your company to deliver multiple times a day and mistake-proof the delivery.

Even if you can't use continuous delivery, consider how often you can release internally to learn what it takes your team to release. (See *Release for Learning, Feedback, and Value*, on page 88.)

Refactor Every Time You Touch Code or Tests

I said earlier in this chapter that we want to keep the code and tests clean. You may have worked on a large product that had some automated tests. And eventually those tests didn't work anymore. No one refactored those tests as the code changed.

Even worse, you may have seen projects where "all of a sudden" the build didn't work. Often, the suddenness arises from lack of integration. But part of the problem is also that no one updated and simplified the code or the build scripts.

I've seen code bases where the code had several ways to get data and several ways to output data. They didn't all work the same way. By the time a new team worked that code base, it needed to redesign the code, not refactor. I'm not suggesting that you never have to redesign, but refactoring simplifies and makes everything clear as you proceed. You are less likely to need to redesign.

Refactoring is simplification. It's not redesign. It's not rearchitecture. Refactoring —by itself—does not add features to a product. It's entirely possible that when you add a feature you first add functionality. Then, you refactor to simplify.

Refactoring works for both code and tests.

Work as a Whole Team to Create the Product

I talked about the interpersonal skills agile teams need to work together in Chapter 3, *Build Teamwork with*, on page 41. The payoff for the team building its safety and trust comes when the team members collaborate to build the product.

You've seen that agile approaches are about team collaboration to deliver value. Your team might take the collaboration to another level with pairing, swarming, or mobbing.

Pairing
Two people work together on one story, on one machine with one keyboard. Developers might pair-program. A developer and a tester might pair

together to review performance. Two testers might pair-test. Any two people working together are a pair. See *Pairing Creates an Environment of Continuous Review*, on page 133.

Swarming

The team works together on one story, but each person contributes based on his or her expertise. The platform developer works on the platform, the middleware developer works on the middle ware, the UI developer creates the UI. In addition, the tester develops tests. When each person is done with "their" part, that person offers his or her assistance as a pair to whomever is still working. See *Swarm on the Work*, on page 134.

Mobbing

The entire team works together on one keyboard. Think of mobbing as team-pairing. See *Mob on the Work*, on page 135.

Here's the value of pairing, swarming, or mobbing:

- The team limits its WIP, which helps it focus on getting work done.

- The team can learn together in swarming and does learn together in mobbing.

- The team collaborates, so it reinforces its teamwork. Team members learn how each other person works. They also learn who has expertise now, who might need which expertise, and how each of their colleagues learn.

- The team has multiple eyes on small chunks of work, so it gets the benefit of continuous review.

Managers who are unsure of flow efficiency may wonder about the "cost" of pairing, swarming, or mobbing.

I Used to Think Pairing Was Expensive
by: John, VP, R&D

Early in our agile transformation, I thought pairing was expensive. I was paying two people to do the work of one person. What were these people doing?

Then we had a cascading problem. It started off in the Admin part of the code. The Admin guy fixed it. Then, a new problem popped up in the Engine. The Engine guy fixed that, and broke Payments and Search.

First, the Engine guy started to work with the Search guy. The Payments woman overheard what they were doing and said, "That won't work!" I think they had a knockdown, drag-out fight. It was a little ugly.

The manager for the team asked this question: "What if you all worked together on this problem, so you can all explain what's going on to each other?" The team agreed to do so.

I was not happy. Now I was paying five people to do one person's job. We'd already spent two weeks on this problem.

They finished the fix the next day. One area in the code had made assumptions that another area hadn't. They would have taken forever to find this working alone.

If they could be so fast and fix—really fix—the problem, what would they be able to do when they wrote new code?

In an agile approach, we want the team to take responsibility for its work. We want throughput as opposed to busyness. Pairing, swarming, and mobbing all use the ideas of flow efficiency to finish the team's work.

The more the team feels as if it has collective code ownership, the less the team reinforces resource efficiency and the more it reinforces flow efficiency.

Here are some references for pairing, if you would like to read more: *Pair Programming Illuminated [WK02], Beyond Legacy Code [Ber15], Remote Pairing [Kut13]*, and *Agile in a Flash [LO11]*

Pairing Creates an Environment of Continuous Review

You might think pairing is about working on something where one person doesn't understand it. Pairing works then. Pairing is even better when people learn and deliver together as a pair. Pairing works and takes less time than any one person working alone. That's because the pair focuses together. Each person acts as a check on the other person.

When team members pair in person, they work on one item—on one machine, with one keyboard. The pair trades off who types and who looks. The person typing is called the driver. The person looking is the navigator.

Often, the two people change places every 15 minutes. That gives both people a chance to see the small picture (what the driver sees) and the big picture (what the navigator sees).

With the real-time review that pairing provides, we can avoid the number and severity of defects that either person might produce alone. Pairing saves the team time and therefore money.

I have found another benefit to pairing: Each person learns about this domain from the other person's perspective. I often ask what I consider stupid questions when I am the navigator. Sometimes the questions aren't stupid—they prompt us as a pair to understand the story better. I find that when I pair, I learn a ton about the domain.

Swarm on the Work

Swarming is another way to collaborate as a team. The entire team works on just one story at a time. The team's WIP limit is 1.

In swarming, the team members work alone or maybe in pairs, according to their expertise and desire. They often start off the work with a short standup where people will say, "Here's what I will do."

The swarming team discusses the story. Then the team members work as they choose (solo, pairs, triads) in a short timebox of one hour to work on their own. After that timebox, the team returns to check in with each other and see how the work is going for everyone. They might need to resolve issues in the code or the tests, so they decide what to do next. They then repeat the work and check in until the team finishes the work. The team has a cadence: work for an hour, check in with each other, scatter to work for an hour, check in, repeat until the item is done.

If one person is done before the others, that person offers his or her services—possibly as a reviewer—to the rest of the team.

Swarming helps the entire team understand the feature under development. Because the entire team works together, the team has no interruptions. No one multitasks. The team can reduce its cycle time for a given feature.

If your team has a difficult time making the stories small, swarming is one way to deliver larger stories faster.

Here's how this might work in practice:

Team 1 gets together as a team and discusses the item with the product owner to make sure everyone knows what they will do. They talk among themselves for a couple of minutes to decide on their "plan of attack" (their words) and then scatter. The testers develop the automated tests and take notes on the exploratory tests. The developers work on the code.

Team 1 has an agreement to return every 25 minutes to check in with each other. They do this with this kind of a report: "I'm done with this piece. I need help for this next piece. Who's available?" Or "I'm as done as I can be for now. Anyone need another pair of eyes?" This team chose 25 minutes because it has smallish stories and wanted to make sure it maintained a reasonable pace/momentum.

As people finish their work, they help other people in whatever way they can. Early in Team 1's agile days, it had a ton of automated test "technical debt." (I would call it insufficient test automation, but whatever term you like is fine.) The developers often are able to finish their code first and then help the testers bootstrap their test automation.

You can swarm in any number of ways. On Team 2, the UI, platform, and middleware developers get together to discuss for a couple of minutes and then write code together, each on their own computer. They have a team room, so they can see each other.

On Team 3, the platform and middleware developers pair, on one keyboard for all the code-writing work. The UI person works alone, checking in when she is done. Everyone checks their work into the code base as they complete it.

There is no right or wrong way to swarm. The only problem with an agile team is if someone is stuck and no one knows and that person does not ask for help.

Mob on the Work

When a team mobs on the work,[2] it combines swarming with some of the pairing ideas. The team has a WIP limit of 1. And the team mobs around one keyboard and large screen, so everyone can see what the driver is typing at all times.

The team changes drivers on a frequent basis, say, every 10 minutes. Many teams use a very large television as a monitor or hook up the computer to a projector. Whatever you do, make sure the team is comfortable: everyone has chairs that work for them. Many teams who mob also use hand sanitizer as a matter of course.

Team 2 mobs. The entire team sits around a table with one keyboard. The monitor output goes to a projector so everyone can see what the person typing is doing. This team has a guideline that it trades off "driving" (the person at the keyboard) every 10 minutes. Sometimes the tester leads, developing automated tests. Sometimes the developer leads. This team often uses test-driven development, so the tests guide their development.

Team 2 checks in at least as often as they change drivers. They use continuous integration. They find that the change of drivers with the check-ins helps them see if they break anything or if they need to refactor next.

The nice thing about mobbing is that everyone checks everyone's work as the team proceeds. Everyone learns about the code and tests.

Years ago, I was part of a "tiger team" that had to find and fix a problem a Very Important Customer discovered. We mobbed on discovering the problem,

---

2.   http://mobprogramming.org/mob-programming-time-lapse-video-a-day-of-mob-programming

all looking at the area(s) of the code that seemed to be the problem. Once we had a couple of hypotheses, we swarmed—each of us using our expertise to contribute to solving the problem. We met every couple of hours to check in with each other.

We worked on that one problem, reviewing our progress and reviewing our code and tests as we proceeded. For some of the challenging code, we pair-developed and pair develop-tested, so we had multiple eyes on the code and the tests. We wanted to make sure we found and fixed this problem. You may have had the same experience. At the time, we did not call it pairing or swarming or mobbing. We called it "finding and fixing the problem as a tiger team."

Test at All Levels So Change Is Easy

Think about the kinds of testing your team might do:

- Automated unit testing for the code to know that we can refactor easily.

- Automated and exploratory story testing (acceptance testing) for a story to know that we have satisfied the story's criteria.

- Automated feature testing for feature sets to know that the feature set looks and feels as if we have a coherent view of it.

- Automated smoke testing for a build to know if the build is any good.

- Automated system testing for the entire system, from the API so we have the ability to quickly know if we broke anything.

- System testing from the GUI, possibly with some automation, so we know the first interaction the user has works.

- Exploratory testing at the system level so we find the interactions and potential problems we didn't or couldn't find with automation.

It sounds like a lot of testing, doesn't it? However, the more tests the team has—and the more automated they can make those tests—the faster the team can test. A nice effect of all this testing is that the tests support changing the code when the requirements change.

One of the problems with all this testing is that the team might not know how to do it. If the team thinks about automating as it proceeds and building tests even before developing the product, it will find this testing much easier.

Automate as You Proceed

The more the team can automate, the easier it will be for everyone to complete their work. Aside from build and smoke-test automation, do consider asking the testers to automate little tests as they proceed.

Perfect Test Automation Doesn't Exist

by: Sherry, QA Manager in a New-to-Agile Organization

We were trying to find the "best" or "perfect" test automation tool. In the meantime, all the testers tested manually.

Well, it didn't take too long before we realized the testers were the bottleneck in finishing features. We had so much testing to do—new and regression testing—that we almost fell into the trap of staggered iterations.

I stopped looking for the perfect test automation tool. Instead, I made a list of reasonable tools and asked people to experiment. Their job wasn't to find the best tool. Their job was to test as quickly as possible to provide feedback to the developers.

Once they started automating, they actually found more problems. I hadn't expected that. And problems that cropped up again and again? The testers gave the developers their tests. The developers were happy to use the testers' tests to understand where they had gone wrong.

We decided to refactor our tests as we proceeded. That worked. Every few months, we need to assess our tests and look for duplicate tests—yes, we still have duplicates. But we have an organization and naming system that works for us. We don't need the "best" test automation tool. We can refactor our way into good enough.

Use Testing to Drive Product Development

In the agile community, we have advocates for a variety of approaches for using testing to drive product development:

- Test-driven development (TDD) is when a developer writes a test that fails (red), creates just enough code to make it pass (green), and, when it's time to add to that code, refactors to clean any messes.

- Behavior-driven development (BDD) is for specification by example, where *given* a certain context, *when* the user behaves in a certain way, *then* we can expect certain results. See *Define Acceptance Criteria for Each Story*, on page 166, for more details.

- Acceptance test–driven development (ATDD) helps us create tests by thinking of the acceptance tests for the product.

Each serves a different purpose. While you can use all three kinds of testing to think about the product, teams often use TDD for developing and refactoring with unit tests as they proceed, BDD for feature or feature-set testing with examples of behavior, and ATDD for system testing with examples of how the user might use the system.

When the entire team collaborates to write stories with acceptance criteria, as discussed in *Create or Refine the Stories as Preparation for Future Work*, on page 208, the team can create examples that guide its testing. Often, the testers will see devious, strange, and horrible possibilities for the story. When the entire team starts to think about "what can go wrong," the product owner might see ways to create several stories.

Why test first? When we think about the tests first, and what would make a test pass or fail, we think about more possibilities for the product's design and use. Our thinking is richer. That means we can question and refine the requirements.

For many years, requirements problems have caused problems in the code and the product (see *Estimating Software Costs [Jon98]*). Anything that helps teams clarify and refine requirements will have a payoff in the future of the project. (See *Measure Your Cost to Fix a Defect*, on page 190.)

Here's the real value of all this testing: one of the big problems with changes to requirements is knowing whether or how the changes will affect the rest of the product. Tests provide support for changes. The team has much more confidence in its code and the changes to that code when using tests as support. The team can know what "done" means at several levels: a given story, the entire feature set, and the project.

When the product owner realizes the team needs to change a feature or a feature set, the team and the product owner can have a deep conversation. When the team members ask for examples for ATDD and BDD kinds of testing, the product owner clarifies the new actions the product owner expects.

I use a form of ATDD and BDD development to write my articles and books. I find using those approaches clarifies my thinking and therefore my delivery.

Beware of Technical Debt and Cruft

If you work on a legacy application, you probably have a code base that is not clean, with all kinds of supporting tests. Let me address what you have and how you might fix it.

We hear a lot about technical debt. I have consciously made the decision to meet a trade show deadline or to meet a demo date for a Very Important Customer. We scripted the demonstrations of those products and told the people running the demos not to stray off the very straight and narrow path.

We didn't add in all the alternative paths. We didn't do input-checking for bad input. We didn't work on performance. We did the bare minimum and it wasn't pretty. We made the deadlines. We had code for a specific, limited application. We didn't have enough time to do "all" of it and we were willing to trade off time to make something we could show. That's a conscious decision to take on technical debt.

Here's an alternative scenario: You realize after you wrote the code that there is a better way to make that code work. That's not technical debt. That's learning. And if you need to address performance or reliability in that code later, that's a good time to change how the code works.

However, too much of the code I see is a mess. The developer(s) didn't think about how to structure it. The developers didn't test it, or didn't test it well. The testers never got a real chance to test it, or the tests are insufficient for the code. That's taking a shortcut and it's not technical debt. That's a mess—cruft.

Technical Debt Is Not Unfinished Work

Too often, we discuss unfinished work: insufficient refactoring, insufficient test automation, anything that we didn't complete, as "technical debt." That's not debt. Debt is something you plan for.

If you, as a team, decide to take on technical debt, that's fine. It's a team decision that you will not address this root problem in the code or tests. You make that decision consciously.

However, if you don't make the decision consciously, you "just" don't finish the work —you don't have debt. You have cruft, bloat, and possibly unneeded complexity, unfinished work.

One way to help the team avoid technical debt is to create automated tests for release criteria, as described in *Develop the Release Criteria*, on page 76. Sometimes thinking about ATDD and BDD tests and automating them (as much as reasonable) can help the team see how to write good code and keep it clean.

Work at a Sustainable Pace

Too often, teams feel pressure from someone outside the team to "do more!" That's often accompanied by the depressing "with less!" I don't know of a way to do more with less. I understand how to do less with less. Much of that less is thinking.

I said at the beginning of the chapter we should optimize for reading the code, since team members tend to read a lot more code (and tests) than they write. Why? Because people are looking to see if someone has already done this thing somewhere. Or this piece of functionality looks more like an octopus, with tentacles dangling into multiple places in the code or tests.

When people read code, they think. When people discuss what to do in the form of a small story and how to do it in the form of design, they are also thinking. Sometimes they think collaboratively with other people when they define stories or acceptance criteria. Sometimes they think alone. However, they think.

Software development—in fact, most of knowledge work—is about the thinking ability of the people developing the product. That means the people need space and time to think.

Some people can manage being inside a team room and still think. Some people can't think there—they need a private place to think. For me, even more important than having space to think is having time.

When managers or product owners pressure a team to deliver instead of think, the team creates defects. We see this effect when we multitask. We see this effect when people take shortcuts when they shouldn't. Artificial deadlines don't make it easy for people to deliver.

Small stories make it easy to deliver. If you need high-quality code, the technical practices, especially around review and testing, make it easy to deliver. Pressure does not.

I have never seen teams deliver under sustained pressure. I have seen teams deliver with very brief pressure, a break, and then back to normal time at work. That means if you want sustained delivery of features, you should create a project that has a sustainable pace. People work together for a six-to-eight-hour day, five days a week. Some teams understand how to do ten-hour days. Some teams actually take time off in the summer, working four eight-hour days.[3]

---

3.   https://m.signalvnoise.com

If your team pairs or mobs, they will be exhausted at the end of somewhere around six to seven hours a day. They have finished what they can. Encourage them to go home and recharge.

I have seen many teams improve their throughput when they stopped working overtime. (I wrote about those circumstances in *Manage It! [Rot07]*.) I have seen too many teams, agile or otherwise, lose momentum and create problems for themselves when they pushed to work more hours than they could sustain. If you want your team members to do "more," make sure they aren't spending time in unnecessary meetings, that they aren't multitasking, that they work on the highest-value work, and that the work is small.

Use Technical Excellence to Speed Development

I said at the beginning of the chapter that project speed is a function of the code and tests that already exist, the technical excellence of those code and tests, the clarity of what we want to do next, and the complexity of what we need to do next.

As a leader, I recommend you invite your team to consider these possibilities for increasing and maintaining the technical excellence of your code base. When I teach, I ask the teams to swarm for an hour on a small story to see how close they can get to finishing a story in one hour. Many teams finish the story in one hour, including automated unit and system tests. They are thrilled with their progress and start to see how to use these approaches to work in a way that is fast and fun.

Your team might have to use shortcuts for a limited time, for a specific reason, such as a trade show or a demo for a Very Important Customer. But shortcuts, over time, will slow your product development. You will have more escaped defects, the cost to fix a defect will be high, the team's cycle time will increase, and your team will find it ever more difficult to estimate.

There are many books and many online resources for creating technical excellence in the code. Here are some I particularly like:

- *The Pragmatic Programmer [HT99]*
- *Clean Code: A Handbook of Agile Software Craftsmanship [Mar08]*
- *Practices of an Agile Developer [SH06]*
- *Working Effectively with Legacy Code [Fea04]*

One of the problems with craftsmanship is that too often people think about software-development craftsmanship. In my experience, testing requires just as much—if not more—craftsmanship. Consider these books for learning about a variety of testing practices:

- *Agile Testing: A Practical Guide for Testers and Agile Teams [CG08]*
- *More Agile Testing: Learning Journeys for the Whole Team [CG14]*
- *Test Driven Development [Bec10]*
- *Beyond Legacy Code [Ber15]*

There are plenty of other books and online resources about how to develop your team's capabilities with more testing support. I encourage you and your team to discover them.

Your team members might have other books they like. Ask them. See *Create Learning Opportunities*, on page 211, for some possibilities.

Recognize Excellence Traps

The technical excellence traps are about thinking you can get speed by not doing the necessary cleanup as you proceed.

- Thinking the team can proceed faster without refactoring code and tests
- Waiting for other teams to test the team's work
- Feeling like no matter what you do, the defects multiply—or they never seem to decrease

You have options for managing these traps.

Trap: We Can Go Faster Without Clean Code and Tests

I have met people who want to postpone refactoring of code and tests because they think the team will proceed faster. Or they don't want code review or some other way to get multiple eyes on the code, such as pairing or mobbing.

You can't go faster when you avoid technical excellence.

Sure, your team might be able to finish a demo or make a trade show. That product is not going to work in production environments without problems.

Don't trade speed of delivery for excellence in production code. Your team will create technical debt and cruft. (See *Beware of Technical Debt and Cruft*, on page 138.) Technical excellence creates speed.

Trap: Waiting for Other People or Teams to Test

Some teams don't have all the skills and capabilities they need. Often, they don't have enough tester capability. When a team doesn't have enough capability to test at all levels, it ends up waiting for another team to test its work. That increases the cycle time and creates WIP. Too often, the team receives feedback about earlier work. That feedback is an interruption, a cause of multitasking.

Consider how you can make this problem and its results visible:

- Add an insufficient number or type of testers to your impediment board, as discussed in *Visualize Problems with a Board*, on page 121.

- Measure the cycle time, as discussed in *Visualize Your Project's Delays*, on page 220.

- Consider creating a table, as in Table 12, *Number of Multitasking Requests for Individuals or the Team*, on page 218.

The more a team has to wait for other teams, the longer the project will take. The cost of delay will rise rapidly. Or if a HiPPO says, "release it anyway," the customers might not like the quality. Do what you can to create an environment of technical excellence.

Trap: Defects Prevent the Team's Progress

Teams discover many causes for their defects. If they don't practice keeping the code and tests clean, the code and tests can become so complex that it's impossible to make progress. (Joe Rainsberger has an excellent talk called "7 minutes, 26 seconds, and the Fundamental Theorem of Agile Software Development" about this problem.[4])

If your team's cycle time increases, or if the fault feedback ratio becomes too high, consider the following possibilities:

- Identify the root cause(s) of the last six to ten defects. With any luck, they will share root causes. Here are some possibilities I've seen: fixing one defect uncovered more; cascading defects, where one defect causes several more; and the code is so complex that finishing anything is akin to climbing Mt. Everest.

- If the team understands the root cause(s), see if there is a handful of defects—which, when the team fixes them, will help it proceed faster. Sometimes the team needs to fix only a few things before it can make progress.

- Ask the team if it's collaborating and refactoring as it proceeds. Maybe it needs a practice radar chart to see if its practices lead to clean code.

---

4. https://vimeo.com/79106557

For example, one team started to chart several practices when it started its agile adoption, as illustrated in the radar chart that follows. The team experimented with these practices, under the assumption that if it practiced these ideas, it would have better throughput with fewer defects and a lower fault feedback ratio.

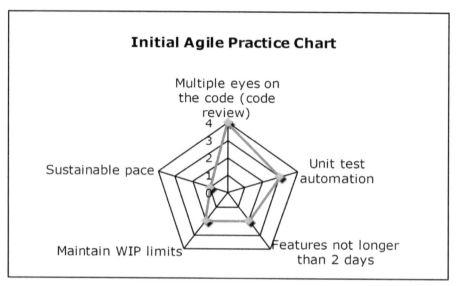

The team worked on its technical practices to see if the practices helped the team's throughput and defects. After three months, the team's chart looked like this one:

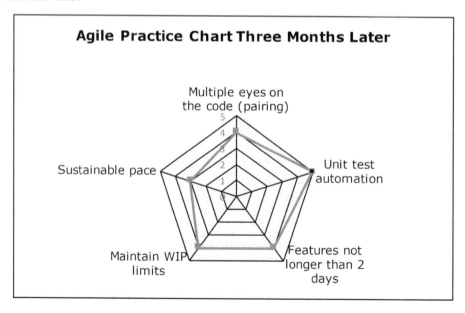

The team wasn't perfect in its adoption of its chosen practices. However, it had many fewer defects, its throughput was up, its stories were smaller, and it was seeing the end of overtime. The team had started with code review and moved to pairing. The team was thinking about TDD or BDD as a way to help its unit test and system test automation. It used its practice chart as a way to help the team think about its improvement.

You, as a leader, might need to work with the product owner to make sure the team has the opportunity to fix problems—even problems not related to the features the team is working on now—to move toward a clean code base. Those problems might be code. More often, I see insufficient testing. Your team might have both problems.

Now Try This

1. What would it take for your team to use continuous integration? I often see teams move to smaller stories and support those stories with a wide variety of tests.

2. Ask the team what it can automate that will make it easy for the team to succeed. Does it need more test automation, build automation, or anything else?

3. Ask the team to note where it has unnecessary complexity or cruft in the code. Create stories for that work and add them to the product owner's list of work.

Now that the team knows what to do for stories and what it might want to use for technical practices, it's time think about estimation.

CHAPTER 10

Agile Estimation:
The Good, The Bad, and The Ugly

Estimation is about setting expectations. When I drive somewhere, I want to know how long I should *expect* that drive to take. You might say, "It will take me about 30 minutes to get from Point A to Point B." That's because you know from experience that it should only take you 20 minutes. And depending on road and weather conditions, it might take you closer to 40 minutes. You split the difference and call it 30 minutes.

That's a gross estimate, an order-of-magnitude estimate. That's the kind of estimate your managers want when they ask you for an estimate. Those estimates are accurate, but not necessarily precise.

The team might need estimates, too. If people work alone, not pairing, swarming, or mobbing on the work, the project team needs to understand when this part of the work will be done so that each team member knows when to expect the work. That's a more precise estimate.

Every team estimates differently from every other team. There are good reasons for that. Sometimes the team members are not stable, so the team has no idea who will work on the story. The team doesn't know if it will have the necessary expertise to fly through the story or if it will be a slow slog.

Sometimes the team timeboxes an experiment (an MVE or a spike) and after that experiment, the team will know more about the feature set so it can assess the complexity of it.

Sometimes the team doesn't know about the complexity of the code base. While the feature seems straightforward, the last time someone touched this code was years ago and that person has since moved to Fiji and is enjoying an umbrella drink on the beach.

Teams can provide an accurate estimate if they understand their current reality (what the code looks like), their typical speed (velocity and/or cycle time), and how much work they think this feature will take. If any one of those things is unknown, their estimates will not be accurate. In addition, if the team members are supposed to multitask on features or projects, their estimates cannot be accurate.

In this chapter, I'll discuss using velocity as a way to guide relative estimation, using cycle time to create rule-of-thumb estimates, and what a team could do if it chose not to estimate at all, the #NoEstimates movement.

Understand Velocity

First, understand the definition of velocity in agile approaches. *Velocity* is a rate of change coupled with a direction. Velocity is not acceleration.

Imagine you're driving to an appointment 10 miles away. You drive the posted speed on the side streets, one velocity. As you enter a highway, you accelerate to achieve highway speed. As you continue to drive, you achieve a stable state: You get into a lane and maintain a constant speed, with any luck. You stay stable with respect to the road and your direction. Your velocity stays the same—especially if you use your cruise control. The more steady the traffic and the more you use your cruise control, the more your velocity stays the same. You arrive at your destination at the time you expect to.

Now imagine these scenarios: the highway is gridlocked. You are not going to achieve your expected highway velocity. You will be late. Or imagine that it has just snowed three feet and it takes you more than twice the time you estimated just to get to the highway. You will not make your appointment on time.

That's the problem with using velocity as a way to estimate. A team's velocity depends on achieving a stable rate of completion, which often depends on a stable relative size of story and the context in which the team works on that story. If the team is trying to estimate something inside crufty code, even if the story is straightforward, the work will take the team longer. The team will have to create enough tests and possibly try some experiments before it can say it has solved the problem.

> ## Story Size Changes What Velocity Means
>
> In "Velocity—A Squishy Measure,"[a] Kathy Iberle provides the insight that we think about velocity as a change in speed where the units are the same. Regardless of the activity: driving, bicycling, hiking, we *know* that the distance measures don't change. A mile is still a mile. What changes is how long it takes us to finish that mile.
>
> When we use stories of varying size in velocity calculations, we no longer have a standard distance measure. We are not measuring the same thing over time. Yet we use the word *velocity* to describe this measure. No wonder people want to compare teams based on velocity.
>
> I've suggested and continue to suggest that you write and deliver one-day stories. When you do, you can use velocity as a measurement of capacity and have confidence in your measure. The more your story size varies, the more difficult it is to use velocity as any kind of a predictive measure for what your team can finish.
>
> _____
>
> a.   http://kiberle.com/2017/06/29/velocity-a-squishy-measure

You can use velocity as a basis for estimation. Some teams are successful using velocity as a way to estimate, once they have achieved a stable rate of completion. That stable rate often takes six or seven iterations to achieve.

Think of velocity as capacity. Your team can, *on average*, deliver some number of stories, some number of fixes, maybe something else. Velocity is not acceleration.

Learn to Estimate with Relative Sizing

If you have a new team or a team new to agile approaches, no one has any data about what they can do as a team. You may have been in this position before as a leader in your organization. Your managers may have asked you to estimate on behalf of the team.

Don't estimate for the team or even think about committing it to any deliverables in an agile environment. The team is in charge of its own work. The team manages its work. The team manages its estimation.

However, there is something you can do. You can help the team estimate its work with relative sizing, even if the team members have never worked together and have no historical data.

Relative sizing uses two ideas to improve estimates: the team compares story sizes (points) against what it's accomplished in the past (the relative part), and it estimates using the wisdom of the team as a form of Wideband Delphi estimation. As everyone comments on the story and as people suggest a relative size, the team gathers better data and can therefore develop a better estimate.

A Short Explanation of Wideband Delphi Estimation

Wideband Delphi is a team-based estimation approach. Before agile approaches, some teams used Wideband Delphi to create an entire project estimate. The person(s) who wrote the requirements explained all the requirements to the team members. The team disbanded and the members created *their* estimates for their part of the work.

The team members then met to discuss their estimates and where their understanding of either the requirement or the complexity occurred. Teams might have met up to four times to review and re-estimate. (I provided a more detailed explanation and how to use Wideband Delphi in *Manage It! [Rot07]*.)

To effectively use relative sizing, first ask the product owner to create stories that are as small as the product owner can create. Make sure these stories are real user stories so the team can understand who will see the value in each story.

Ask the team to group the stories by size, from the smallest to the largest. Keep similar-size stories together. The entire team decides how large the stories are.

Assess the story sizes. Using the Fibonacci sequence (1, 2, 3, 5, 8, 13, and so on), assign all the smallest stories to the size 1 bucket. The next-sized stories are a 2 and the next are a 3. Continue until the team agrees on the relative sizes of the stories. (See *Agile Estimating and Planning [Coh05]*.)

Once the team agrees on the relative size, take the stories estimated as 2. Do all the 2 stories look like they're about the same size? If so, now estimate the duration for the 2 stories.

If the team thinks all the 2 stories will take about 10 person-hours, you now know how long the 1 stories will take. Divide the duration for the 2 stories by 2 to derive the duration for the 1 stories. In this example, our 1 stories would take five hours. Ask yourself whether that makes sense. If so, you now have the factor to use to multiply against all the other relative sizings.

If you see you have stories larger than an 8, size up to 13 and then use 20, or 40 for very large efforts. (The reality is that no one understands the size of anything past 13, but we can use these numbers in a different way later.)

If you have stories larger than say, 8, the team has plenty of unknowns, or thinks those stories are highly complex. Consider a spike first to break the task into smaller pieces. (See *Spikes Can Help Everyone Understand the Value*, on page 110, for more information.)

Here are some guidelines that have helped teams in the past:

- If a "1" is larger than a team-day, see if the team either has too-large stories or the team isn't a feature team.

- If the team regularly sizes stories as larger than 5, there could be several problems: the stories are too large; the team doesn't understand the stories; there is no defined MVP; or the code is in terrible shape. Ask the team to discuss and address the root cause of larger stories.

- Ask the entire team to workshop the stories with the product owner and to see what it takes to get to a size of 1.

When teams create stories of size 1 (where 1 is a team-day or less time), the team knows several things:

- The team can count the stories for the next estimation period and have confidence about what it can deliver.

- The team can deliver at least one story every day.

- The team has more confidence in its estimate, which reduces overall project risk.

Your Small Stories Might Be Larger than Mine

As you've seen, I like very small stories. However, you might find that "small" for you is a little larger than for me.

One product owner I know says, "As long as the team can collaborate on the story and finish it inside of two days, that's small enough for me." Me too. One agile coach I know says, "We don't want stories smaller than a 3 because it's not worth breaking them down and then people don't work together on a story."

I'm still going to talk about one-day stories—for a team, not a person. As long as your *team* releases a story every day, or every other day, that might be small enough. You might find it worthwhile to ask the team what it thinks is small enough. I'm sticking with my one-day stories.

The larger the number for the story, the greater the uncertainty the team has for the estimate. See *Predicting the Unpredictable [Rot15]* for more details about estimation.

Use Relative Estimation for Iteration-Based Estimates

If you use an iteration-based agile approach, your team will want to estimate what it can deliver for the next iteration. It can commit to what it can fit into an iteration.

To use relative estimation for iteration-based estimates, the product owner first creates the ranked backlog as described in *Plan the Backlog*, on page 207. The team then estimates each story as a team. Some teams use planning poker cards. Those cards have the Fibonacci series of 1, 2, 3, 5, 8, 13, and whatever larger numbers the team needs to estimate its work.

 Joe asks:

How Do I Use Planning Poker?

When teams create or use the Fibonacci sequence (or any other relative sizing technique), they can use planning poker.

Every person has a deck of cards with the sizes on the cards. If you use Fibonacci, every person would have eight cards, one each with 1, 2, 3, 5, 8, 13, 20, and 40. When the team estimates, someone, often the product owner, holds up a story and asks, "What's your estimate for this story?" Each person takes his or her card showing the relative estimate of each story.

Planning poker is a Wideband Delphi estimation technique. It surfaces concerns and issues about a story so the team can resolve those issues or concerns, or know that the story might be troublesome. Planning poker is especially useful when team members disagree on the story's relative size. Teams decide what to do: go with a larger estimate or a smaller one—or break the story down into smaller chunks of value.

If you have stories of size 1, planning poker is easy. You ask, "Does anyone think this is larger than a 1?" If so, the team has other choices: spike the story to timebox the work to one day to understand what else to do, or break up this story, which is really a feature set, into other stories.

Here's the problem with relative estimation and deciding what a team can pull into an iteration: the larger the stories are (larger than a 1), the more uncertainty the team has about the work it can commit to for an iteration. Instead of more discussion around estimation, consider a workshop to create smaller stories or an additional backlog refinement meeting. See *Create or Refine the Stories as Preparation for Future Work*, on page 208.

Large relative story sizes provide qualitative data: it's possible the story is complex; the code might be cruft or this story might be an entire feature set. The team might need to explore if it can create a more accurate estimate. See what you can do to help the product owner create stories of size 1 before the team has to estimate the story.

Count Stories Instead of Points

If you use an iteration-based agile approach, you will need some idea of how much work the team can commit to for an iteration. Some teams count story points and estimate the number of points they can deliver in an iteration.

Here's a wild and crazy idea: instead of spending time estimating larger work, consider breaking apart those large stories into small, one-day stories. Here's why: your customers buy and use features or feature sets. Your team releases features or feature sets. Why not estimate by feature?

One of the problems with large stories is that a team creates tasks to break apart the story. Too often, the team says, "We need a front end of this many points, a back end of this many points, and testing of that many points."

That kind of estimation is task-based estimation. Agile allows us to deliver features, which allows us to perform deliverable-based estimation, a different kind of estimation.

When we estimate deliverables, we often realize that what we are thinking about—the deliverable—is too large. We have a one-, two- or even a three-week deliverable. In *Predicting the Unpredictable [Rot15]*, I said that the estimate can be off by the unit of estimation. That is, if you have a one-week estimate, you might be off by one week. That's because you are not estimating the deliverable; you're estimating work that gets you to the deliverable.

Story points can help a team learn what it can do in a certain amount of time. And I have seen teams try to convert story points to hours or days, and then fill in the tasks. Instead of deliverable-based estimation (the story), the team uses task-based estimation, interim work that might or might not be useful.

Instead of counting story points, count features or stories. Workshop the stories to be one-day stories, or decide to pair, swarm, or mob on large stories so the team maintains a high throughput and can count its stories. If your stories are larger than one day, use your cycle time for a feature to see how large the stories are.

Consider Cycle Time to Create More Accurate Estimates

I recommend that teams in transition to agile approaches measure their cycle time as described in *Cycle Time Shows How Long Work Takes*, on page 185. Here's why:

- Cycle time helps a team see how large its stories really are.

- Cycle time provides a team a rough rule of thumb for quickly estimating a large number of stories.

- Cycle time helps people see whether they tend to be optimistic or pessimistic estimators.

Here's how you use cycle time for estimation:

1. Decide on a time period for your measurement. I recommend you consider two to four weeks for your initial measurement period. That time might provide you enough information for your average cycle time.

2. As the team completes stories in this period, count the number of stories and measure how long each story took. You will have something like the following table.

Story	Story Start Day	Story End Day	Story Duration
1	Day 1	Day 3	2 days
2	Day 3	Day 4	1 day
3	Day 4	Day 6	3 days
4	Day 7	Day 8	2 days
5	Day 8	Day 10	2 days
Totals:			
5 Stories	10 days	Average Cycle Time:	2.4 Days

Table 7—How to Use Cycle Time for Estimation

The average cycle time helps you know the *average* duration of a story. Some of the stories will take longer and some will take less time. You can count the stories, multiply by the average cycle time, and have a reasonable estimate.

What if you see a cycle-time variance as shown in the table on page 155?

The average cycle time is 3.6 days, but the maximum is 8 days. Can you use cycle time for estimation? You can, but your confidence will be lower if you do.

Story	Story Start Day	Story End Day	Story Duration
1	Day 1	Day 3	2 days
2	Day 3	Day 7	4 days
3	Day 7	Day 15	8 days
4	Day 15	Day 16	1 day
5	Day 16	Day 19	3 days
Totals:			
5 Stories	19 days	Average Cycle Time:	3.6 Days

Table 8—One Team's Varying Cycle Time

Know the Purpose of Your Estimation

In agile approaches, we can use the team's wisdom to create accurate estimates, up to a point. For me, the question is this: Who wants what kind of an estimate?

Your managers might need gross estimates to understand roughly when they could plan on having a feature set available, or when the project might end.

Your team might want to predict its capacity to understand how much it can bring into an iteration. If you use flow, you might not need to estimate anything. You might have to work with the product owner to explain how large you think a specific story is so the product owner can understand if the team's historical cycle time is valid for this story.

If your team is willing to create stories of roughly the same size, you don't need to estimate anything at all. You count the stories. Counting works even better when you have one-day stories.

I'm not talking about tasks. I'm talking about stories, value to a user of the product. In my experience, when a team starts counting stories, it realizes several beneficial side effects:

- The team creates and accepts stories of roughly the same size.
- The team creates stories that tend to become smaller over time, approaching one day or even less.
- The entire team understands stories across the product.

Consider counting stories for your estimates.

Create Approximate Estimates for Management

Many managers are accustomed to thinking about when "all" the features will be done. That's because they could not see the value from the project before the end. In agile projects, we can deliver value before the end of the project. As a project leader, consider how you can help your management see value before the end of the project. And ask what kind of an estimate your managers need.

If your managers want to know when it will "all" be done, check to see if they mean when they can start to release value to the customers. They might want to know when they can capitalize the software. They might want to know when they can recognize revenue from sales or support. Show them the roadmap and explain how often the product owner will update the roadmap and when the team will know better.

If they still want to know when it will "all" be done, use the information you have to create an estimate with a percent confidence. (See *Predicting the Unpredictable [Rot15]* for more estimation options.)

Here's how to estimate "all" the features:

1. Ask the team to take all the details they know about the features in the roadmap.

2. Use whatever relative sizing approach you prefer.

3. Walk through the roadmap, estimating as you proceed. In addition, count the larger features. The larger the features, the more uncertainty you have in your estimate.

4. Add up your relative estimate (either points or cycle time). Add up the large features so you understand your confidence level.

Here's how one team did this. It had three feature sets for which it had good detail on the stories. The team had two more feature sets for which it had almost no detail on the stories. Management wanted the team's best estimate in two days. The table on page 157 shows how it estimated.

This team had about a day for a one-point story, so it thought it might be 354 team-days. The team had an uncertainty of "Medium." Here's how it framed that to its managers:

> "If we do 'all' of this work and nothing horrible happens, we think it will take us roughly 70 weeks and we only have about 50% confidence in that number. However, we can deliver interim value starting in the next two weeks. We will be able to update the estimate and the uncertainty at least as often as every couple of weeks. When would you like to know more?"

Feature Set	# Stories	Relative Estimate for Stories	Total Story Estimate	Confidence Level
1	16	2 or 3 for each story	40	High
2	8	1	8	High
3	12	2 or 3 for each story	30	High
4	15	5 or 8?	120	Medium
5	12	13?	156	Low
Totals:				
5 Feature Sets	63 Stories	Unclear	354 points	Medium

Table 9—One Team's Project Estimate

This team could have used cycle time instead of story points. See *Consider Cycle Time to Create More Accurate Estimates*, on page 154.

Instead of using relative estimation, consider counting stories.

Estimate Support Work

Many teams provide support work for the product they're working on now, or even for other products they worked on in the past. That means they have to manage interruptions. And if they work in iterations, they need to somehow estimate or leave room for support work.

Here's one way to estimate support work:

- For the next three iterations, measure the amount of support work the team does. Track the cycle time for the support work, regardless of what kind of a board you use.

- At the end of three iterations, see if the cycle time clusters around some average or mean. You might have two different means: the relatively easy support items and the much more difficult items.

- Now, leave room in the iteration for the number and type of support items you see from your history.

You might discover that support takes close to half the time in your iteration. If so, do some root-cause analysis. Does the team need to fix cruft in the code as it proceeds? Does the team need to add tests because it has insufficient tests due to having taken shortcuts?

One question I like to ask is: Do we need to fix this problem now or is it possible to package up several fixes and do them all at one time? Sometimes the answer is yes. If so, gather the problems and spend some team time fixing those areas of the code and tests so the team has more confidence in those areas.

Use Previous Data to Inform Your Next Estimate

All the way through this book, I've suggested the team create and refine stories so each story is a team-day or less. When the team can manage that, it discovers that its throughput is high, and estimating the work is as simple as counting stories. However, your team might be learning how to create smaller stories or learning how to avoid multitasking. Your team's stories take longer than one day.

If your team has stories larger than one team-day in duration, consider using previous data to inform your next estimates.

Here's how to use the team's current velocity to feed that information forward to your next estimate:

- Measure velocity for several iterations. Teams new to agile approaches often need six or seven iterations to discover their true capacity, their velocity.

- Does your team have an upper and lower bound? If your team measures in story points, it may discover that it can do 37 points in one iteration, 54 points in the next, and 24 in the third. That team's velocity is not stable. It might need to count feature story points separately from defect points, separately from changes. See *Iteration Contents Show What the Team Completed*, on page 180.

- Once the team's velocity settles down to +/- 10% in either features or story points, the team can check its current estimate against what it "typically" can do. In addition, if the team needs to estimate past the next iteration, it can use its average velocity to create a gross estimate.

In the same way a team can use velocity as a check against a future estimate, the team can use cycle time. See *Cycle Time Shows How Long Work Takes*, on page 185.

Multitasking Is a Barrier to Great Estimation

 Multitasking slows all throughput. It doesn't matter if a person multitasks or if a team multitasks. The more work any one person attempts to do at the "same time," the lower the throughput. To create great estimates, stop any multitasking.

Aside from multitasking, avoid estimating too far into the future. Instead of estimation, agile approaches allow a team to provide a demonstration and ask if the project is done enough.

Consider the Value of #NoEstimates in Your Organization

It's not clear that estimation is very helpful to many teams. Too often, the product owner wants to change the stories to provide more value. Or the team realizes that the story it thought was small is not small. Or the team gets into the code and realizes the code is a mess.

The consequence is that all the estimation the team did is useless. The team will work in a different order, or the estimates are off.

What if you worked without estimating, and instead worked by value? That's the promise of the #NoEstimates philosophy.

Sometimes there's value in estimates. You can provide a ballpark, an order of magnitude about how long this project or feature set will take. However, if you are working in an agile way and you have a team that is able to maintain a steady throughput of value, you might not need to estimate at all.

Imagine this scenario: the product owner creates stories either alone or with the team that take one day or less for the team to complete. The team swarms or mobs on the stories, so everyone knows what they need to do and when. The team has no or very little WIP because it releases stories as they are finished.

In that case, what is the value of estimation? You might need to count the stories and see how many remain so you can see how many days are left in that feature set.

In a serial life cycle, the team only releases value at the end of the project. With any luck, your team releases value *at least* every two weeks. The value of estimation changes when the team releases value that often.

You might no longer need estimates to provide the same service to your management.

Recognize Estimation Traps

Watch for these schedule games or estimation traps:

- The team thinks experts who "sign up" for their own stories will help the team's throughput.

- Managers misunderstand the idea of velocity and use it as a target for the team to achieve.

- Sometimes the team thinks it can do more—with no data behind that thinking.

- Your organization wants your team to estimate the entire project before it starts delivering value.

You have options for managing these traps.

Trap: Experts Take Their Own Stories

Especially when teams start with agile approaches, they realize that they have specific expertise. Janet knows about the database schema; Dan knows about the middleware; Sharon knows the UI; and Steve can test anything you throw at him. The team finds it tempting to estimate as individuals and then to assign stories based on expertise.

When experts work alone, the team creates WIP, often substantial WIP. Instead of the team collaborating, swarming around one story at a time, each person tries to make progress alone. However, the people on the team need each other to make progress.

The problem is that the team can't release *features* unless people collaborate. At the very least, a developer and a tester need to collaborate to finish a feature. Many teams have barely enough testers, so when experts take their own story, the team creates queues of work, delaying all the stories.

Consider these options:

- Ask the team to estimate as a team, not only for each individual's part. Possibly show the team the difference between resource efficiency and flow efficiency, as described in *Managers Move from Resource-Efficiency to Flow-Efficiency Thinking*, on page 240.

- Ask the team to work as a team, as discussed in *Swarm on the Work*, on page 134, or *Mob on the Work*, on page 135. If it's possible for the team to work (swarming or mobbing) for a two-week timebox without an estimate, it will have a better idea about how the team works together for the next estimate.

- If the team members insist on reinforcing their expertise, make any delays visible, as discussed in *Visualize Your Project's Delays*, on page 220. Make sure to raise your concern at a retrospective.

When experts take their own story, they optimize for a single person and busyness. When team members take stories together, they optimize for working as a team and delivering results.

Trap: Double Your Velocity

This trap arises when someone—often a manager or project manager who doesn't understand agile—wants to improve the team's output. This is a classic misuse of velocity as a measurement.

Velocity is a way for teams to use their historic information to predict what they might be able to do for the next iteration. This is a way for teams to avoid a total SWAG (scientific wild tush guess) for their prediction.

Velocity is not a productivity metric for the team—or worse—for the individual. See *Velocity Is a Capacity Measurement*, on page 188.

Here's cynical answer #1: If you want to increase your velocity, the fastest and easiest way is to double the number of points you assign to your stories; that will double your velocity. It doesn't change how many stories you actually finish in an iteration, but it will look like you've doubled your velocity.

Cynical answer #2: If you want to alleviate the pressure from someone, you can play this game, too. You can divide the stories into two parts: Story Part 1 and Story Part 2. With any luck, you are dividing your stories along reasonable lines so that you see business value from each part. If not, well, the stories are still small enough that you finish them quickly. You can also double the points for each part. You can recurse on this trick almost indefinitely.

Of course, when you randomly split stories like this you're not splitting your stories so they help you deliver business value more often, which is what you really want to do when you split stories. But you are playing schedule games.

Now, here's the real answer: To break this trap, ask your manager this question: "What result do you want? Is there something you are looking for aside from completing the project as quickly as possible?"

Explain that in agile approaches, you ask the team to work at a sustainable pace, providing business value frequently to stakeholders and asking for feedback. The team works at the best pace for it. The team doesn't move slowly by design—the team works hard. The team might encounter spaghetti code, or code and tests that haven't been refactored, or code that appears to have side effects with no supporting tests. The team isn't going slowly on purpose—it's working at a pace that allows it to proceed without making big mistakes. What is the manager looking for?

In addition, remind the manager that team velocity is personal to a team, as hair color or eye color is to a person. As soon as you change team members, the velocity is likely to change. If you change the product domain, the velocity could change. It's a measure of past behavior that is likely to predict future behavior. It's not a guarantee.

Instead of showing anyone velocity, consider showing any of the measurements in Chapter 14, *Report Your Project State*, on page 215.

Trap: We Can Do More

The team has created a stable velocity of 35 points per iteration. In some iterations it can finish 37 points. In other iterations, it finishes 32 points. But as an average over the past six months, it finishes 35 points.

Someone thinks the team can and should do more. The team needs a "stretch" goal or some such nonsense.

Stretch goals don't belong in estimates. They don't belong on agile teams, because the team's velocity is based on a sustainable pace.

When teams create accurate estimates and *meet* those estimates, they understand how to work together and maintain their sustainable pace. Such teams maintain focus and code quality. They have the flexibility to refactor the code and tests as they proceed, to create the best product possible. These teams are not under stress to do "more" when that "more" is an unreasonable request.

If anyone on the team wants to try more points per iteration, help that person see his or her data now. Consider asking how this person will create an experiment. See what happens. Maybe this team member can do more if the stories are smaller.

On the other hand, if someone outside the team wants the team to do more, explain that velocity is not acceleration. If this person wants the team to do more, the only way is to reduce the story size (not create tasks, but reduce the story size) so the team increases its throughput.

Trap: We Need Detailed Estimates for "All" of It

Sometimes the product owner thinks the team *must* estimate the entire feature set even though the feature set is large and the team will deliver the features incrementally. (This is related to, but is the estimation side of, *Trap: We Can't Release Anything Until It's "All" Done*, on page 171.)

The larger the feature set, the more difficult it is to estimate all of it. Combine that with the ideas that the stories might change, and your team has a recipe for potential estimation disaster.

Consider these options:

- As a leader, have a conversation with the product owner and ask that person what she or he needs. Is the product owner under pressure to provide a detailed or specific delivery date for that entire feature set? If so, ask if the team can work on only that feature set until it's complete. Consider asking the team to swarm or mob on the first several features in the feature set so the team can learn as it proceeds.

- Measure the cycle time for each feature as the team proceeds. It's possible the later stories will take less time, but I have not always seen that.

- Remind the people pressuring the team for the large estimate that the larger the thing the team estimates and the farther out that work is, the less accurate the estimate will be. Ask what these people want. They might want delivery as fast as possible. In that case, work with the product owner to make the stories as small as possible, and ask the product owner to rank all the stories in this feature set higher than any other story.

- Create smaller deliverables, and demo them to the people who want the estimate for "all" of it. This shows the team and the person who wants the estimate how the team is proceeding.

Consider using the graph Expected Value Over Time, on page 108, to help the product owner (or the people pressuring the product owner) to assess value over the entire feature set. It's possible the customers want the first few features *now* but could wait longer for other features.

Now Try This

1. If you need to estimate, decide who will receive the estimate. Is the estimate for management or the team?

2. Ask the team to discuss how it will estimate: story points, cycle time, or a combination. Consider estimating a small amount of work, doing the work, and reviewing the estimate to see how close the team was.

3. Consider making your stories small and asking the team to work together so you don't need to estimate.

Now that you know about estimation, let's discuss how the team gets to "done" on everything.

CHAPTER 11

Know What "Done" Means

What does "done" mean to your project? Here are some possibilities:

- The project met its date or scope commitments (or, if you're lucky, both), and there aren't too many problems, so the organization ships the product. The project is done.

- The project met its release criteria. The project is done and the organization ships the product.

- The project team is done. Someone else or another team packages the product in some way and releases the product later.

You might be accustomed to some rituals many nonagile projects use, such as "defect triage," to decide on showstoppers. Or product managers or some other managers took a day and played the rapid-descoping-of-"mandatory"-requirements game because of the time. Or, one of my favorites, someone played the defect-promotion/demotion game at the end of the project. All of these games helped us feel better about the work, even if we didn't make the work perfect.

With nonagile approaches, sometimes either a product manager or a senior manager will see a demo only the week before the project is supposed to end. That person may not like the way a feature works or looks. Or the team has so many defects, the managers say they can't release. The project goes on and on and on....

Agile approaches provide us much more flexibility with seeing value and releasing over the course of the project. I already talked about release criteria as being the definition of "done" for the project. (See *Develop the Release Criteria*, on page 76.) But how does a team know the features are done? How does a team know that the interim value is ready for the customers to see and use?

Teams need to know what "done" means at the release level, for a feature set, and for a given story. That way, the team can always work toward being done at every level.

In this chapter, I'll talk about the different levels of what done might mean for your team. I'll also discuss the problems when your team is not the final stop before the customer can see the finished work.

See the Different Levels of Done

You may have heard about "done," "done-done," and "done-done-done." Let's unpack those phrases.

People talk about "done" for a story being done. They use "done-done" for an iteration. They use "done-done-done" for a release. I don't find that differentiation helpful. I want the product to be *releasable* at any time. I want no friction for releasing.

But what about when the product owner accepts the story? Is that some other form of done? It depends on your board. If your board ends before the product owner accepts the story, you might call stories that the team thinks are done "done." Once the product owner accepts the story, you might call those stories "done-done." And if a story is accepted for a release, you might call that "done-done-done."

I think all these "done"s are a bit overdone. One way to manage the done problem is to define the Done column of your board as follows:

- The story meets the story-acceptance criteria. Consider adding acceptance criteria that discuss the larger environment for the story.

- The story meets the team's agreements for technical excellence.

- The product owner has accepted the story.

If the story meets all these criteria, the story is really done.

Define Acceptance Criteria for Each Story

Let's start at the micro level: how do you know when a team finishes a story? I want to know that the team met the acceptance criteria on the story *and* that the team met the working agreement on how it completes work.

For acceptance criteria, I like the Given-When-Then approach from behavior-driven development:

(Given) some context

(When) some action is carried out

(Then) you should see some set of observable consequences

This approach creates scenarios for a story. You might even use the number of scenarios as a guideline for how large the story is. For me, a guideline is four scenarios. Once I see more than four scenarios, I worry that the story isn't small enough. (You might prefer a different number than my four.)

Define What "Done" Means as a Working Agreement

I have found it useful to address what "done" means for a story as a working agreement. Here are some possibilities your team might consider:

- All the code is checked in.
- There are automated unit tests.
- There are automated system tests at the API level.
- All the automated tests are checked in.
- All the tests pass.
- The documentation for the feature is complete.
- There has been some sort of pairing or other eyes on the code and automated tests to prevent shortcuts.

Your team doesn't have to like these. It may want something different.

I find it helpful to specify what "done" means as a working agreement so no one takes shortcuts. If people think they need to take a shortcut, they can discuss the problem that requires them to take a shortcut.

 Joe asks:
Do I Need to Define "Done" for an Iteration?

If you use iterations, you might need to define what "done" means for an iteration, especially if you don't or can't release the stories as you complete them. That's because you're letting the stories become some form of WIP.

Instead of thinking about "iteration-done," consider creating a board that has an Accepted column as well as a Released column. The team demonstrates the story to the product owner and then can move the story into Accepted. Once the team is able to release the story, the story goes into the Released column.

Decide what might work for your team in your organization.

Consider When You Can Release to Customers

Sometimes new-to-agile product owners wonder about releasing something that's minimum. My opinion: when in doubt, release. Don't release nonsense. Make sure the story is an entire story, an MVP or an MVE, but release as early as possible. You will see several benefits:

- The more often you release, the more the team practices releasing safely. The team will build tests so it doesn't break anything.

- The earlier the team releases, the faster it's likely to receive feedback.

- The team has less WIP in the form of partially complete feature sets.

Back in the Potential for Release Frequency graphic on page 78, I suggested you locate your product on a continuum ranging from a totally digital product where the cost to release is quite low to a product with hardware where the cost to release is quite high. As a leader, can you move your product down toward the lower-cost-to-release part of the continuum? What would you have to do to the product to make that happen?

Understand When Customers Can Take Your Releases

As teams become more accustomed to agile approaches and they increase their throughput, some of their customers say, "We don't want new software every day or week. We want new releases only once every six months."

Customers might feel this way for any number of reasons:

- They want to "certify" or run the new product through some quality checks before they roll it out to their customers or organization.

- They have local changes that they have to integrate into your changes.

- They want to reduce any potential disruption from any changes you made.

They might have more reasons. Regardless of what you think, they prefer to manage their integration of your product.

Consider thinking about releasing in several ways:

- Internal releases, which we use internally to understand the product direction and for demonstrations.

- Incrementally grown releases, which we use when we bring new customers onboard.

- "Real" releases, which all customers take.

\//
:" Joe asks:
How Do I Release Partially Complete Feature Sets?

Let's assume the team has a feature set of 16 stories. Even if each of those stories only took one day to complete, you might want to release the completed stories into the code base. But the feature set isn't complete. Is it safe to release?

Here's the value in keeping the main code line current with all the features that are done. You don't have to manage branches in the code base or have to worry about regressions. On the other hand, what if the customers can't use the feature yet? Or what if these stories break some other part of the code because the whole thing isn't complete?

Many organizations use some sort of flag that prevents the customers from using only partially completed feature sets. If your organization does that, watch out for an increase in this potential waste: the number of items waiting to be unflagged and exposed to the customers. You'll see the cycle time for that feature set increase.

Consider flags for enabling features. Consider the ability to roll back any changes, including database changes. Do release as early as possible for feedback.

I like internal releases as often as we can make them reliable. I like to aim for at least one a day. That might not be possible for your team to do yet, so ask them what they want to aim for.

You might have an incremental release once a month and a "real" release once a quarter or every six months, depending on when your customers will actually install it.

We Differentiate Our Releases
by: Andrea, Customer Release Coordinator

We had a difficult time with demonstrating new features and fixes and releasing those features and fixes. Some customers wanted everything. Some customers we had to push and prod into taking new functionality every six months. But we want to onboard new customers more often than every six months. And we don't want to have to fix problems in older code bases, either.

We came up with a scheme to manage our releasing. We demonstrate new features to whomever wants to see those features. We release every month and roll over existing customers every April and October. We coordinate with our customers to make sure they are ready for the rollovers. We maintain a list of fixes and incremental value in the "current" release so customers can see if it's time for them to take it.

Oh, we didn't get here all at once. We had to learn how to release often and how not to make mistakes. I coordinate the releases to our different customers and I am starting to help some of them update once a quarter. We had to work to become as close to mistake-free as possible. And our customers now see our quality is far superior to what it was.

Building a Product Toward "Real" Doneness

One of the problems of "done" is ensuring the product acts in a way that satisfies the customer. These are often called "nonfunctional" requirements. The product needs usability, some form of reliability, and possibly some forms of security and performance before the product is really done.

How do you move from acceptance criteria in the small (for a story or feature) and move toward the release? Here are several ways to do so:

- Build automated tests for the scenario-based release criteria outlined in Table 4, *Possible Scenarios for Release Criteria*, on page 76. Any error from the test will trigger the team to determine what occurred.

- If the team thinks the release criteria are at risk, maybe it can do some architectural exploration with automated tests to verify the performance.

- Build the performance criteria as the product owner scales the story. If a story only has to work for 10 users, maybe the story doesn't need performance criteria. Once the product owner scales the story to 100 or 1000 users, it's time to add performance-acceptance criteria to that story.

Your team might have other ideas.

One team realized it needed to improve its search algorithm speed. The product owner and the team defined six common search scenarios. The testers created several automated tests for each scenario. The developers generated and coded several algorithms. They ran the tests against the algorithms on various data sets. It took the team a week to gain enough information to know which algorithm to select and what the team might have to do to the database schema. The team experimented longer and finally improved the algorithm by 50%. It codified those tests into automated tests to run against each build. The team now knows if a build degrades its product.

Build those nonfunctional requirements into acceptance criteria for every story and into release criteria.

Recognize "Done" Traps

Teams might not realize they encounter "done" traps. Here are three I've seen too often in teams:

- The team has no "done" criteria.
- It "all" has to be done before any of it can be released.
- The team requires "hardening" iterations or effort.

I've seen teams where these "done" traps prevent the team from releasing anything. Consider enlisting your leadership and your allies to help the team see what "done" means and how to release intermittent value.

Trap: The Team Has No Criteria for "Done"

In my experience, teams want to deliver value. Also in my experience, teams need to know what "done" means at various levels: for the story, for the iteration if the team works in iterations, for releasing, and for the project. If the team does not have working agreements or criteria for what "done" means, it will done-done-done everyone to death. "Oh, you meant done-done?"

Help the team create working agreements for what "done" means. Let's abolish this notion of done-done-done once and for all.

Trap: We Can't Release Anything Until It's "All" Done

I've seen product owners and teams create double-binds for themselves: they can't get feedback until they release something. And they can't release anything until it's "all" done. Their agile project has very few deliverables. The deliverables they have are quite large.

And the larger the deliverable, the more likely the team is to make mistakes or not quite deliver what the product owner or customer wants. The team becomes frustrated because it worked for a long time on this product. The customer or product owner is frustrated because that person isn't getting any value until too late. It's a mess.

As a leader, you can help the product owner create small stories. See *Write Small Stories*, on page 95, for more details. Encourage the team to build a culture of experimentation so the team can try an MVE or an MVP to gain feedback as early as possible.

Trap: We Need to "Harden" the Product

Sometimes teams don't realize that they have insufficient story-acceptance criteria. Or the team realizes at the end of an iteration or after some number of stories in flow that it didn't really finish its work.

Teams that are new to agile approaches might not realize this not-doneness for a while. Some teams use the idea of a "hardening iteration" (this seems to occur more often in iterations than it does in flow) to finish the work they didn't complete before.

Encourage the team to fix problems as soon as someone discovers them, especially if the work is not yet done. I don't recommend a regular practice of hardening iterations.

If your team realizes it didn't quite finish work it had previously marked as done, consider these options:

- Conduct a retrospective to understand what happened. Make sure not to blame anyone. Do unearth the data that led to people making what they thought was the best possible decision at the time.

- Watch any estimation efforts. Do people think they should forego or reduce testing to make a particular date or squeeze "more" into an iteration? This is another instance of "how much" thinking, which causes the team problems later. See if you can help everyone move to "how little" thinking instead.

- Revisit the idea of what "done" means for working agreements, for stories, for releases. Does the team need to refine any criteria to achieve technical excellence in its work?

If a team has trouble achieving its done criteria, reduce the work: the size of the stories and the work in progress. If the team encounters the need to "harden" its work infrequently, maybe you can ignore it. But I see teams that use hardening iterations or hardening activities every few weeks. That defeats the idea of finishing work so you never have to touch it again. Be wary of any "finish later" activities.

Now Try This

1. Does your team need to discuss working agreements for what "done" means for a story or an interim release?

2. Consider how often you can release and have your customers update their product.

3. Check with your team and see if it has considered technical excellence for its story-done criteria. Sometimes just asking that question helps the team think more about technical excellence.

Now your team knows what "done" means. It's time to discuss the measurements the team can use for itself and for status reporting.

CHAPTER 12

Agile Team Measurements

For years, project teams and project managers have tried to predict where the project was headed. Unfortunately, when teams don't release value on a frequent basis, it's quite difficult to tell where in the project the team is.

Agile approaches provide a team the chance to measure what it has finished and what's in progress, not what it anticipates doing. That means teams can directly measure their work and use that empirical data to predict a little farther ahead. If teams don't like what the data says, they can change something and see if that works better.

Consider two different approaches to agile team measurements: team-based measurements and project-based measurements. Teams can measure their work and work in progress to learn about their approach to the product and their process. In addition, there are project-based reporting measurements. See Chapter 14, *Report Your Project State*, on page 215, for reporting measures.

This chapter is about team-based project measures. These measures help a team see progress with respect to its planned and actual work, its WIP, and the effect defects have on the team's progress.

Teams Learn from Their Measurements

Team members learn from measuring their completed work and seeing their work in progress. Some of those measurements can predict—just a little—what a team can do in the near future.

Consider the following charts to understand what the team completed and how much more remains:

- Feature or story burnups to see feature progress.
- Feature charts to show what's done, what's added, and remaining features.
- Iteration contents to see what the team did, not just planned.

- Cumulative flow to see the WIP.
- Cycle time to see how long things take for this team.
- Defect escapes and bounce-back to understand how defects might affect the team in the future.

Consider which of these charts will be most applicable to your team and help the team learn from seeing the work on its board or in its retrospectives.

Measure and Create Charts as the Team Proceeds

 I used electronic tools for many of these charts for book-production purposes. You can use hand-drawn charts just as well as—maybe even better than—a tool. Measure as the team proceeds and don't worry about how beautiful the chart looks. The team needs data, not beauty.

Let's start with burndown, burnup, and velocity charts because many teams use some form of these.

Understand Burndowns and Burnups

Many teams that use iteration-based agile approaches use burndown charts, with which they measure progress against time, as shown in the following figure.

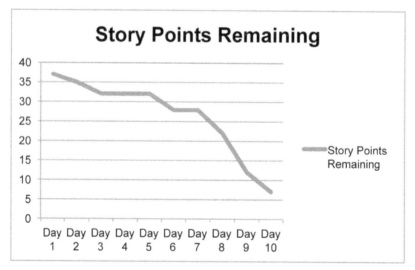

Many teams add an Ideal line to their burndown, as shown in the figure on page 175. The Ideal line is supposed to be a reality check—it allows the team to measure against time and what it thought it might do. The idea is that the team should make steady progress, completing work throughout the iteration.

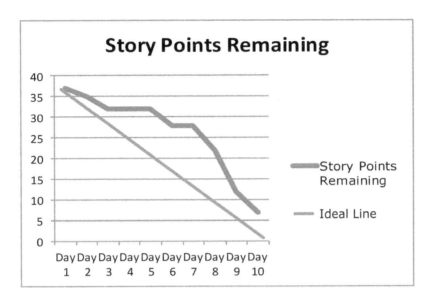

In either of these charts, you can see there are times when not much is done. Then, near the end of the iteration, the team finishes more. However, the team members don't finish "everything" before they run out of time.

An iteration is a timebox, by definition. Regardless of your "done" state on the stories, when the timebox is over, the team ceases its work and demonstrates and retrospects. Regardless of what the team has or has not completed, the demo and retrospective help the team understand what it did and did not do, and why.

These burndowns are from a specific team. When this team saw its original burndown, two interesting things happened. The team members beat themselves up for not finishing. And when they didn't finish everything, they didn't always do a retrospective. In addition, the product owner often took the unfinished work and added it to the next iteration's work. Yes, added—not replaced. That meant they never caught up.

When they tried to follow the burndown chart with the Ideal line, they realized they were "late" and off the Ideal line from Day 2. They felt worse about themselves. They stopped doing retrospectives, which meant they had no idea why they were "late."

I am emphasizing the word "late" here, because a team might not be late. It may have misestimated, or maybe someone was out sick for a couple of days, or someone got pulled into another project and is not working on the team's work. All of these problems are causes of "lateness." The burndown increases the idea of lateness.

A burndown shows what you have completed against time. A burndown with the Ideal line emphasizes what the team did and what the team *should* be doing.

A burndown is interesting, but not actionable. Think about what happens when you take a trip. You plug your destination into your favorite GPS (or app), and it calculates how long it will take to get to your destination. You know you have driven some number of miles, but to be honest, that's done. You can't change what's done—and you don't want to. What's interesting to you is what you have remaining. That's what a burnup chart helps you see.

A burnup is a way to see what we have accomplished and what's remaining. I can learn more from a burnup than I can from a burndown. The following figure illustrates a burnup of the same data.

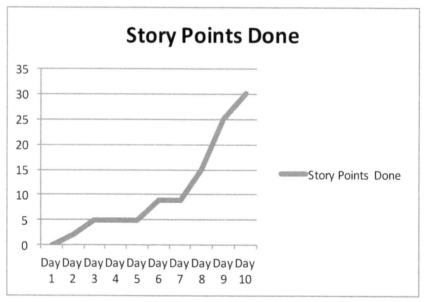

When I see the Story Points Done burnup chart without the Ideal line, I see a hockey stick. When I see a burnup with the Ideal line added, shown in the figure on page 177, I can tell by Day 3 that we are "behind" where we want to be. By Day 5, I know we cannot make up the time. As any team member, I can raise this as an impediment in the daily standup. If I am a leader of any sort, I will put this on my list to discuss in the retrospective, if not problem-solve beforehand.

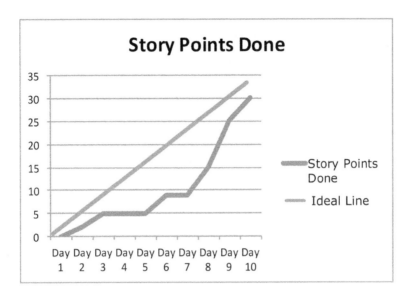

Maybe that's just the way my mind works. I like seeing where we are headed and what it will take to get there. I'm interested in what we've done, but that's in the past. I can't address the past except to retrospect. I can address the future and say, "Is there something we can do now to help us accomplish what we thought we could in this timebox?"

This team finally realized—when it changed to burnup charts—that it was trying to cram too much into an iteration. The team made its stories smaller. That put more pressure on the product owner, but then the team realized lack of product owner time was an impediment. The team had thought it was to blame with a burndown. It saw its data more easily with a burnup. Maybe we all had a mind-meld going on.

It doesn't matter which chart you generate. It matters how the chart makes you feel: what action will you take from your chart? If it's not prompting you to act early, maybe you need a different chart. One project truism is: You cannot "make up" time. You can choose actions based on what your data tells you.

Your team owns its data. Visualize it in a way that works for the team. I recommend you use a burnup, but that might not fit for the team. If you prefer to use burndowns, check out George Dinwiddie's great article on burndown charts.[1]

If the team works in an iteration-based agile approach, consider iteration burnups to help the team see its velocity and its rate of finishing.

---

1.   http://idiacomputing.com/pub/BetterSoftware-BurnCharts.pdf

Burnups Show You the Rate of Finishing

I don't use Ideal lines for my burnups. I tend to measure features completed as the iteration proceeds. Sometimes teams like to measure story points instead. One team had trouble finishing its work *during* the iteration. As shown in the following figure, that team had a hockey-stick look for its burnup.

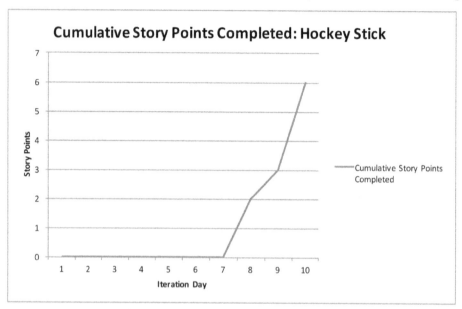

This next figure shows a team making steady progress toward finishing.

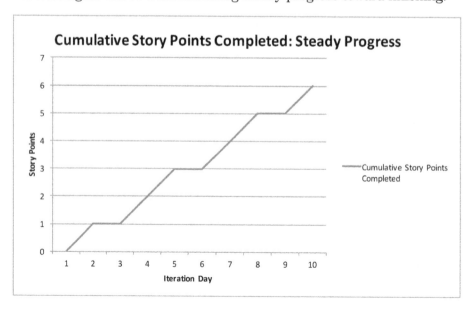

However, measuring points is not necessarily measuring progress. Points are activity. Stories are progress. To see progress, measure finished stories. You might want to see how many points you complete also, to see what you finish. This first graph is still a hockey stick.

Activity Is Not Progress

All the burnups and burndowns we've seen so far measure activity. They don't measure progress. That's because they measure points, not stories.

Completed points are activity. Completed stories are progress. That's why it's worth your time to *Count Stories Instead of Points*, on page 153.

If you use iterations and your stories are larger than one day long, you might need to measure your capacity, the number of points you normally complete in an iteration. Or you might measure your cycle time to see what an average story takes.

Don't confuse activity with progress. Until you start to measure stories completed, you don't know how much progress you make.

When you see hockey-stick completion in an iteration, address that in the retrospective. Does something prevent people from completing stories on a regular basis? You might see these causes:

- Everyone takes his or her own story at the start of the iteration.

- People get interrupted by other work that the team didn't know about when it started.

- The story was much more difficult than the team anticipated.

- The team members perform asynchronous code reviews. That means people don't want to interrupt their own work to review someone else's work.

You might have other problems. Seeing hockey-stick completion helps the team realize something is not quite right. Once it knows that, it can retrospect and decide what to do.

As shown in the figure on page 180, the first team has the same number of points as before. This graph shows when the team completes stories.

The next graph on page 180 shows the same steady-progress data for the second team, and we can see when the stories complete, not just the points.

Burnups or burndowns with story points only help teams learn how they work now, and how they might work a little while into the future. Teams need to measure more than story points. When they measure feature progress, they are able to report progress to other people who want to know where they are.

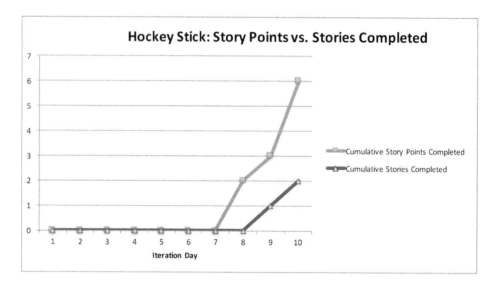

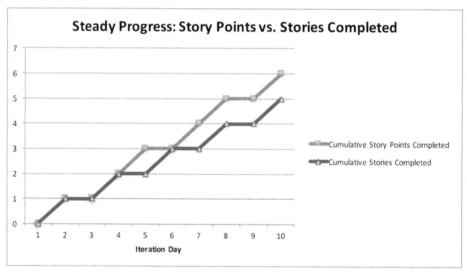

Points Are a Capacity Measure

In the same way as velocity is a capacity measure, measuring points is about the team's ability to measure its capacity and then fulfill what it thought it could deliver. (See *Velocity Is a Capacity Measurement*, on page 188.)

All the way through this book, I've suggested the team create and refine stories so that each story is a team-day or less. If you choose not to do that, and your stories are larger than a 1 (a team-day), you might need to use velocity. I would make my stories smaller, but that's me.

Iteration Contents Show What the Team Completed

The iteration contents chart that follows shows you what you have completed in a given iteration. Part of a team's capacity is the features it can complete, and any defects the team fixes, or changes the team takes. That's what the iteration contents chart can show you.

The following figure illustrates a team that can deliver nine features plus or minus a couple of defects. In addition, the team takes changes in the form of urgent work from a support queue.

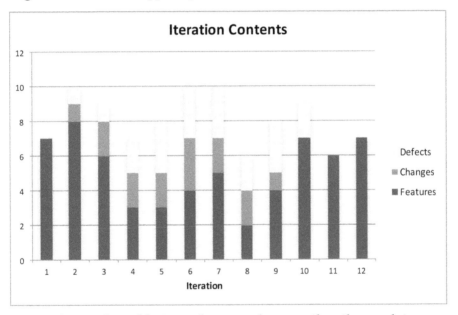

Notice as the number of features decreases because the other work increases, the defects rise. This team decided to pay attention to maintaining its technical excellence, so it stopped discovering defects after the end of the iteration.

Teams working in iterations often ask this question: "How much can we commit to for this iteration?" That leads to these potential problems:

- The team estimates that it can do more work than it really can, so team members "push" to complete work.

- The product owner (or the team) substitutes one story of the "same" size for another story after the iteration starts.

- The team doesn't find defects as soon as the team creates the defect, because in the rush to "finish" work, the developers move to another story while the testers attempt to catch up.

- The team doesn't fix the defects as soon as it discovers them. The team puts the problem in the backlog for another iteration.

The "how much" question nudges teams into shoving more potential work into an iteration. That creates multiple problems, such as shortcuts or technical-debt creation, the inability to refine a backlog in an hour or so, and stories or feature sets that are too large. See *Trap: We Need Detailed Estimates for "All" of It*, on page 162.

The iteration contents chart might help your team see if it has these problems.

Your team might find the following hand-drawn chart even easier to create to express what the team did this week. This chart shows that the team had steady progress, finishing at least one story per day. The team also fixed two defects during the week. This chart is fodder for the iteration contents chart.

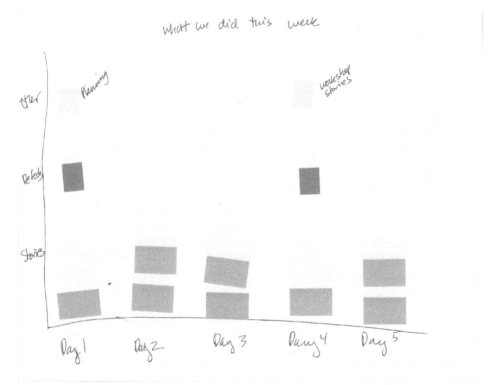

If the team adds start times and stop times to cards as the cards travel across the board, the team can calculate cycle time and lead time for each card.

Keep these charts next to your team's paper board, as discussed in *Start with a Paper Board*, on page 113. The team can see everything on one wall for easy viewing. I encourage you to draw your charts as you proceed and to use paper.

Cumulative Flow Shows Where the Work Is

If you've only used Gantt charts or a Scrum board, you may never have seen where the work in a project is. A cumulative flow chart shows how much work is in which state. The following is a cumulative flow chart from a real team after three iterations. The team made slow progress. This chart explains why.

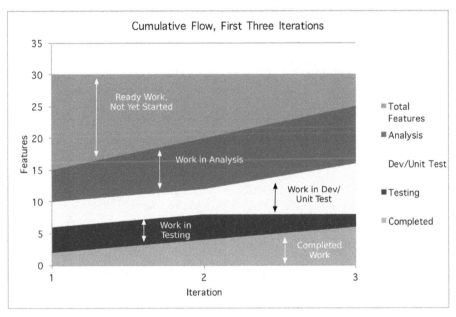

The product owner was working as an individual, churning out stories. He anticipated the team would need 30 stories to finish this short project. The team was confused about the work, so it had a number of stories in what it called Analysis.

During this review, the team met often with the product owner, as often as three hourly meetings each week. The more the team asked questions, the more it needed to bring in stories it would have to address later. That's why the total number of features in Analysis rose during the three iterations.

The team tried to finish work. The developers fell into the trap described in *Trap: Everyone Takes His or Her Own Story*, on page 123. The testers had questions for the developers or the product owner; everyone was busy. That team saw its cumulative flow and decided it would attack that problem in its retrospective.

The next chart on page 184 shows what happened after Iteration 3. The product owner learned that he had been creating feature sets instead of stories. That was okay, except the team couldn't complete the entire feature set in an iteration —nor did he want it to. He continued to create his roadmap, finally finishing

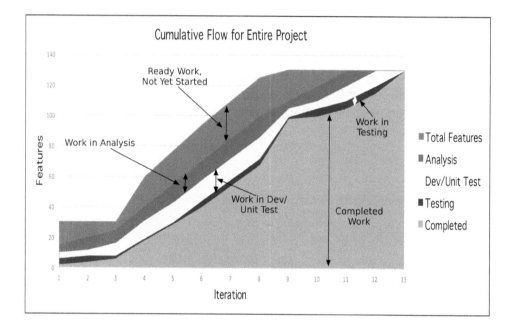

at 130 features. He still was ahead of the team, which is why that top stack of features is larger than what the team completed in any one iteration.

The team still worked a few iterations ahead with him on the features. It took the team a while to understand what a one-day story was for them. By about Iteration 7, they had a pretty good idea.

The team was still ambitious as to what the developers *and* the testers could complete in an iteration. It wasn't until about Iteration 10 that the team started to pull work across the board instead of push it.

The testers remained "behind" the entire project. In the last three iterations, when the developers finished writing code, they helped the testers with test automation. That test automation uncovered defects, so the developers alternated between fixing and test-automation help.

At the final project retrospective, the team decided it would always use cumulative flow to track where the work was. It also decided to try WIP limits and see what happened if the team limited its WIP and watched its cumulative flow. One of the team members said, "Cumulative flow actually helped us work as a team. We could see who had which work—not a person, but which parts of the team."

Note that in iteration-based agile approaches, I expect to see the cumulative flow—at least in Development and Testing—move to zero for each iteration. Sometimes the product owner works in advance, and that provides a look ahead for the team. But the team's accumulated work goes to zero at the end of the iteration, because the team completes what it committed to.

Flow-based teams might always have a constant number of stories in the Ready column. That constant number will look like WIP. In addition, because the flow-based teams might not care about seeing the WIP decrease to zero for an iteration, those teams might have some small WIP (whatever their WIP limits are for their columns) for their cumulative flow chart. I advise teams to keep the WIP in development and testing close to zero so the teams finish more work than they start.

Cycle Time Shows How Long Work Takes

You might wonder if your estimates are correct. Or you might wonder why some story is taking forever to finish. In that case, measure cycle time. In software, we have at least two ways to measure the time something takes: cycle time and lead time.

Cycle time
> The duration of time from when you put a card in the first in-progress column until when you mark the card as "done." Cycle time measures the time the team works on the story.

Lead time
> The duration of time from when a card goes onto the backlog until you release the feature to the customer. Lead time is the entire time from backlog to customer use. If you have a staging area before you can move your product to production, your lead time is at least the team time plus that time.

The top figure on page 186 illustrates the difference between cycle time and lead time. Here's what happened when one team measured its cycle time as feedback for its estimates. The team added one piece of data: the day and time the card moved from one column to the next as it progressed through the flow.

The team then added the times T0, T1, T2, and T3 together to see the entire cycle time, as shown in the bottom figure on page 186.

Possible Kanban Board

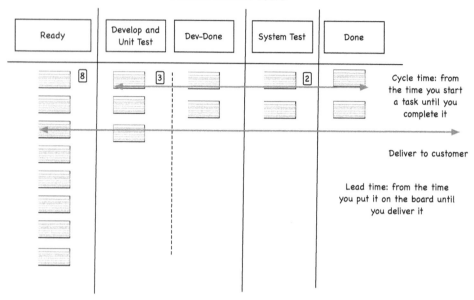

Team 1 Kanban Board

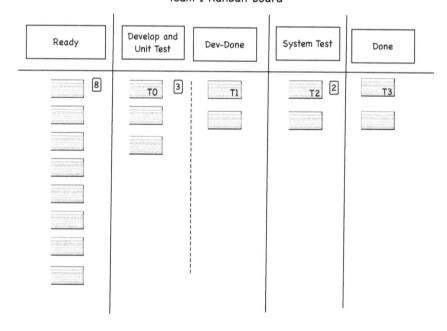

The team collected data for one iteration and discovered this:

Story	Duration
Story 1	1 day
Story 2	2 days
Story 3	3 days
Story 4	3 days
Story 5	Started, not done
Story 6	Started, not done
Story 7	Not started, not done
Story 8	Not started, not done

Table 10—One Team's Cycle Time

The team had estimated and thought it could finish all these stories in the iteration. The team thought that each story would take one day. It discovered that stories 2, 3, and 4 took much longer than expected. Why were these stories taking more than one day and why had the team started stories 5 and 6 and not finished them?

The team realized its board didn't describe the team's flow. The team learned what its flow was: it hadn't put WIP limits on the stories waiting for Check with UX or Integrate UX Fixes. (See the figure on page 188.) Until the team measured its cycle time, it had no idea that it had the wait state of Check with UX or the rework in Integrate UX Fixes.

The team's estimates were correct—the work inside the team was one day or less. However, it depended on other people and information in the organization to complete its work. Once the team realized that, it could decide what to do.

Cycle time helps the team see its flow and if it has bottlenecks. Cycle time might also be feedback for the product owner, to see that the stories are too large.

You can read average cycle time off a cumulative flow diagram. I don't recommend that, though, because I often want to see the variance. Teams have to measure their cycle time to see the variance, which is why I recommend measuring, not reading off a cumulative flow diagram.

Team 1 Kanban Board

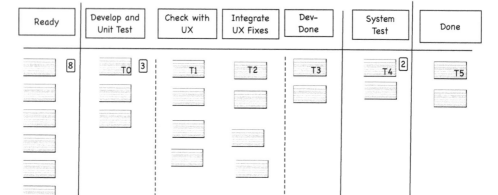

Use Cycle Time to Estimate Capacity

Many people think they need velocity to measure capacity. You can also measure a team's capacity with cycle time.

If you keep track of the average cycle time, you will learn how large the stories tend to be. If your team has stories that average two days each, then the team has a capacity of 2.5 stories per week.

A team's capacity will change if people are on vacation or sick. However, if the team tracks its cycle time, the capacity measurement might be more accurate than if a team uses velocity.

Velocity Is a Capacity Measurement

I already said velocity is not acceleration back in *Understand Velocity*, on page 148. Velocity can be a measure of capacity once the team is stable and understands how to work together.

A team's velocity (regardless of whether it uses points or story counts) will vary while it learns how to work together. (Many people think it takes somewhere between six and nine iterations for a team to learn how to work together.) A team's velocity might vary under other circumstances, as well:

- The team is learning a new domain.
- The stories vary in size and may be quite large.
- The team changed the iteration duration.

There are two potential drawbacks to measuring velocity. I said that velocity is the rate of change. That's what you deliver (features or story points) over time. If you change your iteration duration, you change the time, one of the inputs to the rate of change. If you use story points and you decrease or increase the size of the stories, you change one of the inputs to the rate of change. If you maintain the same iteration duration and use features instead of points, your velocity measurements will be more accurate.

Measure Cycle Time to Understand Capacity

 Many teams, especially those working in iterations, measure their velocity in story points to understand their capacity. Instead of points, consider measuring cycle time. When the team measures its cycle time—possibly different times for stories, fixes, and interruptions—the team has a better idea about its capacity. For me, points are too variable, especially in a team new to agile approaches.

Agile Approaches Change the Meaning of Defect Measurements

Assuming the team meets the acceptance criteria on a story, the team won't have defects during the iteration or while it works on the story. Any defects the team finds before it decides the story is done is work in progress. It's not until the team says the story is done that we need to count defects.

This means the defect counts should be much lower than on a more traditional project. However, the product owner and the team might not understand how the user will use the story. It's possible that in the entire product context, the team made a mistake and created a defect. One mistake I've seen is the product environment: the team assumed one environment and the customer uses the product in a different environment. That's a design defect.

You might find several defect measurements helpful: defect escape rates, the cost to fix a defect, the defect cumulative flow, and the fault feedback ratio.

Measure Defect Escapes

Sometimes the team doesn't fully understand some aspect of a story. Or maybe the product owner didn't fully explain the acceptance criteria. Or maybe the product owner or the team made a mistake writing the story and the acceptance criteria. Any number of things might occur and a defect escapes the team, even though the story met the acceptance criteria and the product owner accepted it.

Measuring the team's defect escapes can help the team see what's going on.

I would hope that the number of escaping defects is zero. However, if you are starting your agile journey, you might encounter several traps that prevent you from keeping your defect levels to zero or close:

- *Trap: Developers and Testers Work in Successive or Staggered Iterations*, on page 35

- *Trap: Your Team Has No Product Owner*, on page 67

- *Trap: You Have Iterations of Waterfalls*, on page 125

When you measure the number of defects that escape over time, you can then perform a retrospective to see what you might do.

In an agile approach, escaped defects are not the norm. If you see defects escape, address that as an impediment to fix.

Measure Your Cost to Fix a Defect

The software-engineering literature has references to exponential costs through the life cycle for how much it costs to fix a defect: If you have a cost of 1 in requirements, it's now 10x in analysis, 100x in coding, 1,000x in testing, and a whopping 10,000x post-release. Those costs have been debunked by *The Leprechauns of Software Engineering [Bos14]*.

My experience is that it does cost more, but not nearly that much. Even in one of my projects that did very little review or testing, the actual cost post-release was 16x. The problem was that there were so many defects that the overall cost to fix a defect was quite high. And given the number of defects, it was quite difficult to release and make progress on the *next* project. (See *Manage It! [Rot07]* for more details.)

The more the team works in a way to promote technical excellence, the fewer defects the team will see. That will make the number of escaped defects low. It should keep the cost to fix a defect low. If your team has trouble with escaped defects, start to measure the cycle time of defect-fixing. Once the team has the data, ask what actions the team might consider in a retrospective.

Measure the Defect Cumulative Flow

Especially if you have a legacy product where defect discovery overwhelmed the team, you might need to measure defect cumulative flow. The following chart illustrates the defects found, closed, and remaining as a line chart.

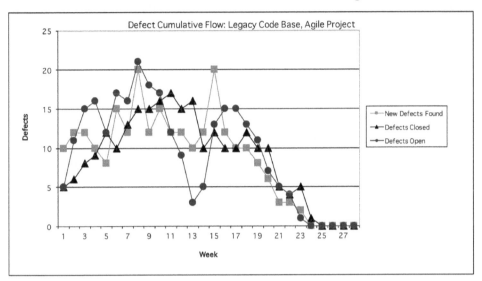

Your team might prefer a stacked chart, such as the one shown in the following figure, so that it can see the contribution from each part of the cumulative flow.

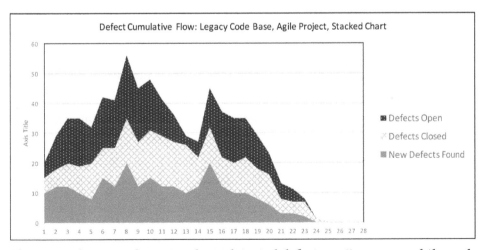

This team discovered previously undetected defects as it progressed through the project. That's because the team increased its test automation and refactored the code base as it worked on one small feature at a time.

Some weeks the team discovered 15 to 20 defects. The team learned, as it added those defects to the backlog, that it had cascading defects. It discovered and fixed one defect. Then it discovered that defect masked several more underlying defects.

As the team progressed through the project, it realized that it was able to stabilize the code base. As the number of discovered defects went to zero, the team's capacity for more features increased.

The team used this chart to help its management see that the team had unfinished work. It had debt from previous projects that it paid off in this project.

Measure the Fault Feedback Ratio

I bet you've seen problems that the team swore it fixed—and the problem returned. The team fixed it in one place and it popped back up in another place. What the team thought fixed the problem didn't. The team (and possibly the PO) rejects that fix.

We can measure the ratio of rejected fixes to total fixes. This is the fault feedback ratio (FFR).

The FFR is the ratio of the number of rejected fixes (fixes that don't actually fix the problem) to the total number of fixes. My experience is that an FFR of more than 10% says the developers don't make enough progress on finding and fixing the problems. They spend their time trying to discover the cause(s) of the problems and creating even more tests. I've also seen this occur when fixing one problem uncovered more problems.

If the team discovers defects as a matter of course, here are some possible actions to offer the team:

- Discuss the defects and their causes at a retrospective. What creates the defects?

- Is the team's definition of "done" sufficient for these kinds of problems? (See Chapter 11, *Know What "Done" Means*, on page 165, for more details.)

- Can the team pair or mob on the defects to discover the root cause and fix it?

The team may have other ideas once it realizes it has a problem that doesn't want to stay fixed.

If the team accomplishes the acceptance criteria (what "done" means for a story) and meets the "done" criteria for an iteration, the team tends not to have many defects. That means the escaped defects should be quite low.

Recognize Team-Measurement Traps

Measuring team-level work can lead to gaming the measurements, unless the team is able to also produce project-based measurements. Here are two traps I've seen in teams:

- The team measures points instead of features.
- The team doesn't measure as it proceeds.

You have options for managing these traps.

Trap: People Want to Measure Points Instead of Features

You've tried suggesting the team measure features completed, and someone still wants to use points. Here are some ideas for you to consider:

- Suggest that you or the team measure features and stories on the same graph so people can realize that one point is not a story.

- Ask the team to work with the product owner to make sure all the stories are one-day stories (or smaller).

- Move to flow and use cycle time and cumulative flow to estimate how long work will take and how much work is in progress.

I have had good results reminding my colleagues that customers buy features, not points. And, if you realize you can't win this argument, stop. The more you can help the team become a cohesive team, the more they will want to see the stories move across the board.

Trap: The Team Waits to Measure

One team had to use a prescribed board in a specific tool. Not everyone had a license to use the tool. As a result, the team didn't update its board on a regular basis. Nor did the team update its measurements. Instead, the person the team called the "Scrum master" asked everyone what they had done during the entire iteration and then he updated the measurements. The team received no interim value for its measurements.

Measuring every day provides the team feedback about its work and its process every day. Teams can see if they have steady progress or hockey-stick progress.

Teams can see their WIP when they create and use their own boards. And teams can see if they are making terrific progress.

The more often teams measure their progress, the more likely they are to create small stories so they can see their progress.

Now Try This

1. Measure the minimum cycle time or velocity for features.

2. If your team has WIP, measure cumulative flow so everyone can see where the WIP is.

3. Decide what status reporting you need to do and what to report.

Now that you know about measurements, it's time to think about the meetings your team needs to keep itself going.

CHAPTER 13

Help Your Meetings Provide Value

Do you wish you could abolish all project meetings? Too many meetings seem to be serial status meetings, or have no decisions, or have no action items. You could pull your hair out.

Here's a way to think about meetings: How can the team work together to accomplish its work?

Agile teams have these kinds of meetings:

- Meetings about the work and the work process: retrospectives, review of work in progress, demonstrations, and work-planning meetings

- Problem-solving meetings to address problems and risks teams discover that they want to manage as they review the work in progress

- Learning meetings so the team members can learn together and with other colleagues around the organization

Back in *Charter Your Project*, on page 74, I said I like to apply "how little" thinking to all parts of the project. That includes meetings, too. In this chapter, I'll explain how to make the most of your meetings and how to keep them short, with just the right number of people.

Let's start with the most important meeting a team can have: the retrospective.

Retrospectives Provide Valuable Data

When any team works for any period of time—even as short as a day—the team can examine its results (the work product) and its process (how the team worked). That's the idea behind the agile retrospective. A retrospective is a look back at the team's actions and output so the team can learn what to do next.

Too many agile teams shortchange their retrospectives. They stop doing them, the retrospectives become formulaic, or the team doesn't change what it does.

How often should your team reflect? Here are some possibilities:

- Reflect at a one- or two-week cadence, regardless of whether the team uses iterations.

- Reflect every time the team releases to the customer. (If your team uses continuous delivery, that might be too often.)

- Reflect at the start of the project to ask, "What do we want to keep, add, remove, or change from previous work we've done?"

- Reflect at the end of the project.

Don't wait until the end of the project to hold a retrospective. In the "general agile picture" on page 5, you saw the team demonstrate and reflect on a regular basis. The team has an opportunity to learn from its work together about the product and its process.

You may have heard the old project-management adage: "Plan the work and work the plan." That is an example of single-loop learning as illustrated in the following figure.

Single-Loop Learning

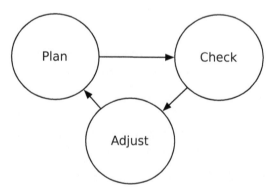

Single-loop learning is good. It helps a team deliver small value fast. Single-loop learning helps the team adjust the remaining features in the feature set as it proceeds.

Single-loop learning is insufficient to deliver on the promise of agile approaches, however. When the team and the product owner check their assumptions, not just the feature, they are able to replan, together and separately. The product owner can check her or his assumptions about the necessary minimum or even the overall content of the feature set. The team can check its assumptions about how it works, not just what it delivers.

Retrospectives encourage double-loop learning, as illustrated in the next figure. We can challenge and understand the assumptions we made in order to decide what to do and how to do it next. The more often the team creates opportunities to learn, the more often it can experiment. In *Learn Early Instead of Failing Fast*, on page 52, I suggested teams create small, safe-to-fail experiments. The more often the team reflects and creates experiments, the faster it will learn.

Double-Loop Learning

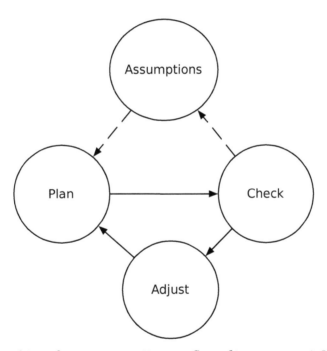

Your team might prefer a more continuous flow of improvement. In that case, the lean idea of *kaizen*, a change for the better, might be useful. The Lean Enterprise Institute presents the ideas of flow kaizen and process kaizen.[1] Flow kaizen looks at the value stream to see where the value is in all the activities. Process kaizen focuses on individual processes.

Instead of separating the two types of improvement, consider taking a holistic approach. Where is the value stream for this team? Are people working in a way that promotes the value of the product under development? Where are opportunities to improve and change? Two terrific books on organizing

---

1.   https://www.lean.org/lexicon/kaizen

retrospectives and kaizen activities are *Agile Retrospectives [DS06]* and *Getting Value out of Agile Retrospectives [GL15]*.

Make sure your team has an action-item list as it works through its retrospective. The team might discover numerous things it wants to improve. Consider helping the team decide on no more than three items to work on until the next retrospective. Some teams want to fix the accumulated years' worth of problems in two weeks. That's not possible.

Instead, help the team take an agile approach to improvement. The team might want a ranked backlog of improvements. It can select some small number of improvements so the improvement WIP remains small, too. The team is more likely to see progress that way.

Use a Parking Lot for the Improvement List

Teams new to agile approaches may have a long list of possible improvements. Instead of trying to work on all of those improvements at once, consider a visible parking-lot board, like the one shown in the following table.

Idea	Date Added	Value to Us	Notes	Progress
Figure out how to build learning into our normal week.	Feb. 10	We would have time to learn.	We are so full of WIP and new work we don't seem to have time to do this. If not started by Aug. 10 (six months) do something different.	Goal: Some kind of learning every week
Smoke test automation from API.	May 2	We would know about the builds.	Full API smoke tests take a few weeks. Chip away?	Goal: For all new features, another 10% every two weeks
Full system test automation from API.	May 2	We would have support for frequent changes.	Start with engine, add email, admin ASAP.	Goal: For all new features, another 10% every two weeks
Mob.	June 15	Improve throughput?	Mary to learn and explain.	None yet
Track cycle time as well as velocity.	May 15	Story size.	Just talking about it made some progress.	Need to change board. Tool doesn't allow us to do both.

Table 11—Possible Improvement Parking Lot

Although I've created this board in the text, some of the best parking lots are corkboards with index cards. You might not need the Progress column. As long as the team can track what it added and have a way of working through the parking lot, the team will continue to progress through its improvements.

When the team next plans its work, it can decide how many items to take off the parking lot, turn into stories, and work on. The nice thing about turning improvement into stories is that stories require acceptance criteria. The team might decide to *Learn from an MVP or an MVE*, on page 109, before it decides on this specific action. The team might discover an unexpected root cause.

If the team discovers a cluster of defects, or a similar problem occurring over time, consider asking the team to do a root-cause analysis so it can decide on corrective action.

Walk the Board

Teams retrospect often, but not every day. On the other hand, team members do need to connect with each other and see their work on a frequent, if not a daily, basis. And unless everyone mobs on all the work, the team needs to understand what everyone is doing, and especially if any work is stuck.

In the past, the team may have met once a week (or more often) to have a serial status meeting. Agile approaches save us from serial status meetings, which waste everyone's time. Instead, the team can walk the board—the board your team created back in *Make Your Own Board*, on page 120. That's how the team learns what everyone is doing and if any work is stuck.

Note the project manager or the Scrum master or whomever is a nominal lead does not necessarily lead the board-walking. Walking the board is a team responsibility. It's not the responsibility of any specific leader, although it might be convenient for someone to lead the board-walking activity. Consider asking a different person every day to lead the activity of walking the board. Or establish in the team's working agreements how the team will walk the board.

When the team walks the board, it doesn't have a serial status meeting. If team members start to blame another person for the state of something on the board, any team member can object to that blame.

We Walk the Board as a Team
by: Javier, Tester

When we first started our version of agile, we had a dev board and a testing board. You can imagine how well that worked. After our first retrospective, we decided to merge our boards. We decided to visualize our flow with a kanban board.

> We learn a ton about our WIP when we walk the board as a team. The first iteration of our joint board, we realized we needed buffer columns. The developers were too "fast" for the testers. We also realized we needed a UI column because we don't have a UI person on our team. We decided to calculate our delay so we now have a req for a UI person on our team.
>
> We update our board. We don't have serial status meetings. No one blames anyone for doing or not doing work. Our board makes our work transparent, whether we like it or not.

The board is for the team. The board represents the state of the team. If the team doesn't like what the board looks like, it can change the board by changing the team's process. When someone in a leadership position or a title-based authority position decides on a board for a team, the team might abdicate its responsibility for changing its process.

Regardless of your approach (iteration or flow) consider asking the team to start in the column just before the Done column and ask this question: "What do we need to move this to Done?" The reason you start at the column closest to the Done column is that the team creates its flow, a pull-based approach to work. You can't pull from the Ready column until you finish work in the right-most column and work left, to the front of the board. When you use WIP limits for a kanban board, you encourage the team to collaborate.

Even if your team uses iterations, consider asking, "What do we need to move this to Done?" Too many iteration-based teams fall into the *Trap: Everyone Takes His or Her Own Story*, on page 123, or *Trap: Experts Take Their Own Stories*, on page 160. The question changes the conversation from "how much work can we start" to "how much work can we finish."

Once you have a board, the team uses it by managing work in progress and finishing work. Many teams use standups to understand what's on the board. Boards help everyone see if a team is falling into any traps of not finishing work or having too much work in progress.

Standups Create Recommitment and Collaboration

If you are using some form of an iteration-based agile approach, where the team does not swarm or mob, you may find a standup useful. The purpose of a standup is to reveal the status of the team's work—the work on the board. The standup does not solve problems—the standup surfaces problems. The standup helps the team members recommit to each other and realize the impediments they face.

If you want your standups to work, consider when you will conduct them and how to make them work for your team.

Remember that standups are for the team. Standups help the team learn what it has completed since the last standup, the status of the work in progress, and if anyone has discovered impediments that will prevent the team from completing its work.

Your team might not need standups. If your team swarms or mobs on every story, the team doesn't need a standup.

We Never Use Standups

by: Jane, Product Owner

We started using iterations. But we had too many interruptions to predict anything. We transitioned to timeboxing spikes and experiments, limiting our WIP and pairing, swarming, and mobbing to finish larger stories faster.

We're not perfect. Sometimes Danny, our tester, feels pressure because he can see the incoming work. That's when we either stop taking in new stories or help Danny finish the testing.

We also walk the board when I'm worried about the cycle time and how long it's taking the entire team to complete a story, especially if it's on the urgent queue.

When we mob or swarm, we don't need to walk the board. We all know what we're doing. It makes our agile approach a lot easier.

Schedule Standups at a Consistent Time Every Day

Decide on the standup time. Make it the same time every day. I recommend a time just before lunch. That way, everyone on the team is at work. In addition, they are ready for a lunch break. They will respect the standup timebox of not more than 15 minutes.

I do not recommend first-thing-in-the-morning standups. It's too easy for weather or home responsibilities to prevent someone from participating. I also don't recommend post-lunch standups. It's too easy to get into problem-solving mode instead of problem-identification mode.

Standups at the end of the day can also be problematic because people have different schedules, and the person who needs to pick up his children at day care might not be able to devote as much attention as a person who does not have to pick up children.

Make sure everyone on the team, including the product owner, is present for the standup.

How to Conduct a Standup

The team gathers around its board. (See *Make Your Own Board*, on page 120.) Each team member answers these questions inside a 15-minute timebox:

- What have I/we completed since the last standup? (If people work together, they might answer what "we" completed.)

- What am/are I/we working on now?

- What are my/our impediments?

- How can I/we help move the work to Done?

The team facilitates itself. It might be a good idea for people to trade off who facilitates the standup. Remember, the standup is not a serial status meeting for the Scrum master or the agile project manager; the standup is for the team.

 Joe asks:
Do I Need to Stand Up at the Standup?

When I teach or facilitate standups, there is often someone who asks, "Must I stand up at the standup?" If you have a physical condition that prevents you from standing up, then no, don't stand up.

Here's why many teams have found standing improves their standups. When people stand, they tend to discuss just these questions. No more. Many teams discover that when they sit down, their standups go on and on and on, and don't get to the point.

Decide what fits for you and your team. If you must sit down, consider a 15-minute timer and then stop the meeting when the timer goes off. The first time someone hogs all the time, the team will provide feedback to that person. That's a part of the team learning how to work together.

I recommend the team decide how to collect its data and build its velocity chart as it proceeds throughout an iteration. If your team collaborates on the work by pairing or swarming in some way, the standup will focus on the work. However, too often teams focus on the person, not the flow of work.

Too many team members ask—or worse, the Scrum master or the product owner asks—"Why haven't *you* finished your work?" First, let's assume that people have a positive intent when they ask this question. They want to know the state of the work; they're worried about the team's ability to deliver; they have dependencies on your work.

Unfortunately, there are plenty of good reasons for someone to not have finished work: the work is more complex than anyone thought, the work is larger, the person answered questions for other people, and more.

Assume that people want to do the best job they can and that someone asks the question out of a desire to support others. On the other hand, if your team is blaming people for not finishing work, see the *Trap: Everyone Takes His or Her Own Story*, on page 123, and *Trap: Experts Take Their Own Stories*, on page 160, to see if the tips there will work for you.

Watch for Standup Antipatterns

While standups can be terrific ways for the team to recommit to its work and expose problems the team needs to solve, not all standups are sunshine and unicorns. Watch for antipatterns such as these in your team's standups:

- Blaming certain people for not finishing "their" work
- Allowing people to take other people's work while it was in progress
- The standup taking longer than 15 minutes
- The standup becoming a serial status meeting

Jason Yip's excellent article "It's Not Just Standing Up: Patterns for Daily Standup Meetings" discusses many ways teams fail with standups.[2]

 Joe asks:
Does the Team Need a Team Room?

If I were empress of the universe, every agile team would have a team room with plenty of wall space for the backlog, for cards being workshopped, and for the data the team needs. This room would have space for the entire team to mob, if it likes. The room would also lend itself to pairing or swarming, depending on the team. In addition, each person on the team would have a private office with a door, so team members could think alone or pair with another person when the need arises.

I'm not the empress of the universe.

At a minimum, the team needs enough wall area to be able to walk the board together. That means the board has to fit on a wall somewhere, along with all the necessary measurements. If the team is geographically distributed, the team needs a camera pointing at the wall all day and some capability for the team members to move items on behalf of other people.

I prefer my "empress of the universe" vision. However, I am a realist. Make sure your team has the room it needs to finish its work. If the team doesn't have the room it needs, that's an impediment that you, as a leader, can address.

Solve Problems Outside of Standups

Teams need a way to solve problems and manage risks. Don't use standups for that.

---

2. https://www.martinfowler.com/articles/itsNotJustStandingUp.html

Standups expose problems. Your team might surface an impediment to a specific feature. Maybe the people working on that feature need to discuss possible experiments or other designs for 15 to 30 minutes to solve the problem. That might be just enough to provide ideas for spikes, or multiple ideas that the team members can discuss with the product owner to see what they should try first.

Your team might recognize it has too much WIP. Someone might say, "I'm stuck on this because I'm waiting for a person on that other team" or "I don't know what to do." Your team members might surface other problems, too.

Your team needs to solve problems. That requires a meeting that's not a standup meeting. Not everyone needs to be at all problem-solving meetings. For example, if the problem is that your tester—your one and only tester—has a manager who asks him to multitask, the team doesn't need to be at that problem-solving meeting. You, as a leader, might gather some data with the tester first and then have a problem-solving meeting with the manager in question.

Maybe the team needs to discuss potential architectures or design patterns. Some teams take on the problem of smaller stories. Some teams want to solve problems of too much WIP in a meeting. Consider lean coffee (discussed next) and problem-solving meetings for managing risks and problems the team can address.

Lean Coffee Can Help Frame Problem Discussions

When you use lean coffee,[3] everyone brainstorms the list of issues on stickies. The team dot-votes on the stickies to rank all the stickies in order of importance.

The team takes the highest-ranking sticky and discusses that for a short timebox. Consider selecting a timebox of eight minutes and seeing if that works for you. You can always decrease the timebox duration to five minutes if you like. Do not start with a timebox longer than eight minutes. The idea behind lean coffee is that you discuss something as long as people have energy around it. Longer than eight minutes, and the discussion will sag.

At the end of the timebox, you thumb-vote to "continue" (thumbs-up), "don't care" (thumbs-sideways), or "change the topic" (thumbs-down). Your team might decide to continue with a shorter timebox (four minutes, maybe, if the original timebox was eight minutes). If you timebox your problem-solving meetings to one hour, you may be surprised by how many issues you can cover.

---

3. http://leancoffee.org

You might decide to summarize the list of action items or prepare a kanban board of the actions at the end of the meeting. If so, either add another five-to-ten-minute timebox to prepare the board, or include it in the meeting.

Especially if your team is new to lean coffee, consider a facilitator/timekeeper to manage the brainstorming and the timekeeping.

Problem-Solving Meetings Focus People on the Problem

Your team might prefer a more traditional problem-solving meeting. I have evolved this particular problem-solving agenda over time. You might find it useful.

Agenda for a problem-solving meeting:

1. Specify the location and participants. Send this out in advance so people have time to think.

2. Check in with everyone.

3. List the problem(s) of the week. You might find that people respond to "obstacle removal" or "impediment removal." Use terms that fit for your organization.

   - Discuss each problem. Consider whether you need to timebox the discussion. If your team can't resolve the problem, ask if you need to escalate the problem, and to whom.

   - If the team can't resolve this problem, put the problem on your kanban board or action-item list, with a time to resolve it. Don't let this work hide. It's WIP.

4. Review any outstanding action items or kanban items you have not resolved.

5. Adjourn the meeting.

If you don't like these options, select some other approach for solving problems. When teams solve their own problems, they are more likely to create solutions that work for them. And as a side benefit, the more teams can focus on the work (delivering value and solving problems to help them deliver value), the more they will coalesce around the work.

Consider Other Problem-Solving Approaches

If you are working on a problem that challenges the team's agility, consider other problem-solving approaches. One book that you might find helpful is

The Facilitator's Guide to Participatory Decision-Making [KLTF96]. You might consider using approaches from retrospectives, also.

Demonstrations Show Progress and Value

The smaller the story, the more the team can demonstrate value. Sometimes the team demonstrates for the product owner. The product owner can then accept, reject, or realize some other future story needs to change. If the team has small-enough stories, the team might demonstrate several times a day.

In addition, the team might demonstrate to other teams, a senior manager, or a customer. In that case help the people demonstrating show the people watching the demo how the product works—a holistic perspective. While a product owner might be fine seeing independent stories, customers or senior managers are much more likely to want to see how the product works.

Make sure your team knows who the demonstration is for, so the team is ready for it. For example, if the team demos to a customer once a month, it might be worth the team's time to decide who will run the demo. The team might want to (loosely) script the demo to show the customer what's working now.

Sometimes the product owner drives the demo. Sometimes team members do. Sometimes, depending on the data the team wants, the customer might drive the demo. These are all decisions the team and the product owner can make together.

 Joe asks:
What's the Difference Between Demonstrable and Releasable?

Demonstrable means the team can show its work to whomever is interested. Releasable means the team could release, at minimum, internally.

If your product has hardware, maybe you demonstrate the progress and you don't release it. If your team is concerned about releasing a feature before the entire feature set is done, the team might demonstrate it and not release it.

Creating demonstrable but not releasable digital products is a form of WIP. Watch for it and decide what to do about it.

If you have a product with hardware, you might only be able to demonstrate until you have working hardware. The team still has WIP because it can't check that the product works until the team can marry the software and the hardware. Recognize that the work is not actually done.

Plan the Backlog

The team needs a ranked backlog so it knows what to do for some time period. The ranked backlog is what's in the Ready columns on the team's board. In an iteration-based agile approach, that time period is the iteration duration the team selected. In a flow-based agile approach, the team only needs as much on the board as its WIP limit. The ranked backlog is what the team looks at *now*. The roadmap provides the longer perspective for the team.

Sometimes your product owner thinks he or she is fully capable of planning the backlog independently, without any input from the team. It's possible the product owner can do that. It's more likely, though, that the product owner would benefit from discussing the next set of work with the team.

Here's a possible structure for the backlog planning meeting:

1. Prepare stories: The product owner prepares stories, preferably on cards that the team can see and handle.

2. Ask for new information: Ask the team about new ideas and issues that arose during the most recent time the team worked. This might be a good time to look at Table 11, *Possible Improvement Parking Lot*, on page 198, to see what to address in this backlog. Prepare cards for discussion.

3. Explain each story: The product owner picks up a card and explains it. Ask if anyone has questions about that card. It's possible that the team wants to discuss acceptance criteria or other stories the team thinks depend on that card.

4. Estimate the work: Once the team understands all the cards, estimate the work if the team uses iterations.

5. Rank the work: The product owner ranks the cards. (See Chapter 7, *Rank the Work*, on page 105, for ranking possibilities.)

6. Create the backlog: Add the ranked cards to the Ready column.

There is give and take in this meeting, such as when the team estimates the work. If the team uses *How Do I Use Planning Poker?*, on page 152, it might realize this story is actually a feature set. The team might decide to spike the story, to break the story apart into multiple stories, or to go with either the larger or the smaller estimate. The team decides what to do.

There might be give and take in the ranking, too. If the team realizes one story will ease the way for a different story, the team should tell the product owner. Sometimes that discussion prompts the product owner to rerank or even select different work. This is the team's chance to influence which work it does when. The product owner decides, but the team can influence.

Create or Refine the Stories as Preparation for Future Work

Many teams that use iteration-based approaches refine the stories in preparation for the next iteration. Sometimes the team realizes it needs to workshop stories at that meeting so it'll be ready for the next iteration.

Teams that use flow might refine stories just in time to work on them.

There are several issues with planning the next set of stories for the team: the team often discovers valuable learning with its current set of stories; the product owner might hear from the product manager or support or customers about the stories the team released earlier; and the product owner might want to take advantage of more market knowledge.

Because the team finishes stories on a regular basis, the product owner continually plans and refines stories for the team. Sometimes the product owner can refine the stories alone, and sometimes not.

One way to refine stories so the entire team understands them is to use the Three Amigos approach.[4] When teams use the Three Amigos, they split into triads of one developer, one tester, and one product owner or business analyst. The idea is that each person has a unique perspective on the possible story:

- The developer thinks about how to implement the story.
- The tester thinks about what can go wrong.
- The product owner or business analyst thinks about what the customer or business wants to accomplish with this story.

The nice thing about all of these perspectives is that the three people discuss the story in its entirety. The more they discuss the story, the more they can clarify it. If they add acceptance criteria, especially in the form of Given-When-Then, the team is much more likely to understand the story.

Organize the Team's Meetings

Sometimes people spend too much time in meetings. Remember that none of these meetings are serial status meetings, so each meeting should provide value to the product owner and the team.

---

4. https://www.agileconnection.com/article/three-amigos-strategy-developing-user-stories

Here is an approach to managing the time people spend in meetings:

- If the team uses iterations, consider a standup during the day. I like just before lunch. Other people select 9 or 9:30 a.m. Avoid first thing in the morning because people's commute time can vary every day. If the team swarms or mobs, the team might not need a standup.

- Consider timeboxing the backlog planning meeting to one hour for a two-week timebox. If the team can't get through everything in that meeting, consider retrospecting on what the product owner and the team bring to that meeting. It's possible the team needs to workshop the stories with the product owner and limit what the product owner brings to a planning meeting.

- Consider timeboxing any backlog-refinement work to one hour to prepare for the next set of backlog items.

Here's how I recommend a team manage an iteration-based agile approach and meetings:

1. Start the iteration on a Wednesday after lunch.

2. Conduct the one-hour timeboxed planning meeting right after lunch. Start the iteration.

3. Consider standups every day just before lunch.

4. On the middle Wednesday, conduct a one-hour timeboxed refinement meeting in the morning.

5. On the last morning of the iteration, that next Wednesday, start a demo at 9 a.m.

6. Conduct a two-hour retrospective from 10 a.m. to noon. Break for lunch.

7. Start the next iteration after lunch.

I prefer starting and ending iterations in the middle of the week. I prefer Wednesday. Tuesday or Thursday can also work. The reason I prefer the middle of the week is so that people don't work over the weekend to hurry up and finish their work for Monday. That prevents the team members from realizing what their real velocity or cycle time is.

A flow-based team might decide to

1. Walk the board as a team if the team doesn't mob or swarm every day just before lunch.

2. Create a cadence for its backlog-refinement activities.

3. Create a cadence for its retrospective activities.

4. Decide about demos as part of its working agreements. For example, the team might demo every story as it's completed. The team might demo the product to sponsors or customers on a cadence.

Consider timeboxing any planning or refinement meetings. If people don't know exactly how long something will take or what it involves, it's time for a spike. Learning can be just as valuable as delivering functionality, especially if you learn you don't need to do any more work in this area for a while.

In agile approaches, we tend to have more meetings, touch points, about the work. These meetings are not serial status meetings. They are not for one person's benefit—they are for the entire team. If your meetings become too long, timebox them and see what happens.

Measure the Value from Meetings

You, your team, and even your management might be worried about the number of meetings the team has. Part of the problem is that agile is a collaborative approach to product development. It's possible no one has seen this kind of collaboration before. However, it might be worth seeing how much value your team gets from its meetings. In that case, consider measuring the return on time invested (ROTI). (See *Behind Closed Doors [RD05]*.)

Using a five-point scale similar to one shown in the following figure, ask people to report how much value they received for the time they invested in the meeting.

ROTI Ratings

0: No benefit received for time invested.

1: A little better than 0. Some benefit, but not commensurate with time invested.

2: Value received equal to time invested.

3: A little better than even return.

4: High benefit. Value received greater than time invested.

Post the ratings on a flip chart, and poll the group. Create a histogram that shows the results, as in the next figure.

ROTI Histogram

```
4    | |

3    | |

2    |

1    |

0
```

Then ask for information about what made the meeting worthwhile or not worthwhile.

- Ask the people who rated the meeting 2 or above what specifically they received for investing their time in the meeting.

- Ask people who voted 1 or 0 what they wanted but didn't receive for their investment.

- Ask what to keep, drop, and add for the next similar meeting.

If a majority of the participants rate the meeting an even return for their time invested, a 2, the meeting is valuable.

If a majority of the participants rate the meeting below 2, ask more questions. Was there a match between the people and the purpose of the meeting? Was the meeting run well enough? Was there something else that prevented people from gaining enough value from the meeting?

Agile approaches do require more meetings than people might expect initially. Make those meetings valuable.

Create Learning Opportunities

So far, we've discussed work-based meetings and opportunities to learn about the work. But that's not enough for any team.

In addition to the work-based meetings, people need time to learn about the product domain, their craft, and how other people work across the organization. Here are some possibilities to create learning opportunities for the team.

Learn About the Organization and Customers

In my experience, it's easy to learn who does what and learn about the customers and their challenges in a smaller organization. As the organization grows, people tend not to know who is in Marketing or Support or Sales. Yet the people in those departments might have great insight on the problems the customers want solved. They often know how little the team must do to solve those problems.

I happen to like lunch-and-learns, which help people learn about what's happening in the rest of the organization and with the customers. I like a regular cadence of these meetings, where someone provides a brief informal talk and encourage questions and answers. Consider a cadence of once every two to four weeks for some informal learning.

Learn About Other Ways to Work

When I visit teams, I often discover they barely know the agile approach they've been trying to practice. Or that they never really learned it—they picked up terms from their friends and colleagues.

It's possible your team could learn by osmosis, but one of the cheapest and fastest ways to learn is from a book club. Ask the team what it wants to study—or offer suggestions—and create a ranked backlog of subjects. Then buy everyone on the team a copy of a book that you think is useful for the team to study. Consider a chapter a week as a regular cadence. Your team might get through three or four books a year together, at one chapter a week.

Consider asking the team how it wants to learn. Maybe it prefers podcasts or some other medium. Teams don't have to choose books.

Learn from Others Across the Organization in Communities of Practice

In one assessment, several technical people had the same concern: "Now that I work as a member of a cross-functional team, I don't learn what my other developer/tester/writer colleagues are doing and how they are solving problems."

Communities of practice help solve that problem. Architects, product owners, developers, testers, coaches—anyone involved in the cross-functional teams—need a community of practice to surface issues in teams and learn how others solved or approached those problems. Communities of practice also provide mentoring and coaching in a particular function and help people consider options for their work.

Recognize Meeting Traps

Meetings can fail in spectacular ways. However, in agile approaches I've most often seen these traps:

- The standup becomes a serial status meeting.
- The team meets instead of delivering finished work.
- Team members don't have enough time in retrospectives to identify possible solutions or experiments.

You have options for managing these traps.

Trap: Standups Become Serial Status Meetings

For years, project managers and other managers asked team members about their status on projects. However, agile approaches move from individual work to team-based work. That change can challenge everyone: team members, project managers, and other managers. In addition, if the team falls prey to *Trap: Everyone Takes His or Her Own Story*, on page 123, or *Trap: Experts Take Their Own Stories*, on page 160, or if the stories are too large, the standups will feel like serial status meetings.

If you ever hear (or if you're tempted to ask), "Where are *you* with this story?" you know that the story is too large and people are not collaborating as a team.

You might say, "I'm nervous about the state of this story" and then explain why you are nervous. You can ask people for ideas to help you manage your nervousness.

Don't ask people about their individual work. (See *Beware of Board Tyranny*, on page 122.) Your team might also create a working agreement about how long any one person can be stuck.

Trap: The Team Meets Rather than Delivers

Some agile teams have a difficult time delivering value. Their stories are too large. They have too much WIP. And they spend forever in meetings.

One way to manage those problems is to ask the product owner to create one story that the team will work on, all together. If the product owner can make that story small, that's great. Even if not, ask the product owner to make the story as small as possible.

Next, have the team use Three Amigos—even if they all do it in parallel—to understand the story. Then it's time to estimate. The team estimates the story, then swarms or mobs on the story until it's done and meets the acceptance criteria the team defined in the Three Amigos activity. (See *Create or Refine the Stories as Preparation for Future Work*, on page 208.)

Now the team has succeeded on one story. It might choose to retrospect on this work. Ask the team to do one more story in the same way: use Three Amigos, estimate, and deliver.

Once the team gets a few stories done (maybe just three), ask it to do a retrospective and see what was different about these stories.

Too many or too-long meetings are a sign that the team or the product owner is asking the team to take on too much ill-defined and too-large work. Once the team understands what is too large or insufficiently defined, it will be able to change what it does.

Trap: Insufficient Time in a Retrospective to Solve Problems

Retrospectives are terrific for identifying problems. Sometimes the team can solve the problems in a retrospective just by seeing the data. And sometimes the problem is buried deep in the team's assumptions or work process. The retrospective time was sufficient to identify the problem. The team needs more time to solve the problem.

If you see your team struggling to solve a problem, consider suggesting a problem-solving meeting outside of the retrospective. You, as a leader, might facilitate this meeting. Or you might help by suggesting data the team can gather. Or you might not have a specific role except to make sure the meeting occurs with all the right people.

Some problems challenge the organization's culture, some challenge the team's data gathering, some require more time for root-cause analysis. Help your team see the problem and then create time to solve it.

Now Try This

1. Create a cadence of retrospectives so the team can choose what to improve and do one small thing after each retrospective.

2. Ask the team to decide how to work with the product owner to plan the backlog and define and refine the next set of stories.

3. If you are worried about the time the team appears to spend in meetings, consider measuring the meeting time and the value for that time.

Now that the team knows how to start and keep going, it's time to think about how to report status to your managers, sponsors, or customers.

CHAPTER 14

Report Your Project State

For any project, people outside the project—often managers—want to know when we think it might be done. They might want to know how much it will cost so they can manage expenses. Sometimes managers want to know other things, such as several measures around the project pyramid, as illustrated earlier, on page 80.

In this chapter, we'll work up from the team measures in the previous chapter. I'll explain what you can and might show your managers as *project* status as opposed to team measurements.

Your team has many ways to show its progress. Here are some possibilities:

- Show working product.

- Provide feature charts to show what's done, what's added, and what remains.

- Show the number of requests the team has received (and maybe what they are) in addition to work on its board.

- Show what's working but not yet released to customers.

- Show different project measures that relate to the *project's* progress.

Let's start with showing working product.

Show Working Product

The best way to show progress is to see the working product. That's because your customers buy and use features. They don't buy architectural progress or UI progress or any other kind of progress. They buy features and feature sets. If the team shows them finished features, the team and the managers/sponsors/customers build trust with each other.

Back in *Create a Walking Skeleton*, on page 90, I suggested the product owner define and the team implement small vertical slices that help people see the minimum skeleton of the product. As the product owner decides what's most important in the remainder of that feature set, the team implements it.

That process—implement small vertical slices around the product so people can see the intent—helps the managers (or sponsors or customers) *see* the team's progress. The more these people can see progress, the easier it is for them to understand and trust that the project is progressing well.

You might want to use the ideas described in *Demonstrations Show Progress and Value*, on page 206, for management/sponsor/customer demonstrations. When demonstrating to people outside the team, consider showing a "day in the life" of a customer. Consider using the scenarios that you defined for different users back in *Write Small Stories*, on page 95. Use the ideas in impact mapping or user story mapping to help define those scenarios. Then, demo by scenario.

Show Feature Progress

In the spirit of "customers buy features," consider showing the team's progress against the planned and additional features, as in the product backlog burnup chart shown in the following figure.

Product Backlog Burnup Chart

This chart is from a real team. This team created a walking skeleton by working on three different feature sets. The team made progress against each feature set at its interim dates. While each feature set grew, Feature Set 3 grew more than the other two. That feature set grew faster than the team could make progress on it. Showing this chart helped the product owner discuss what should be in the roadmap for management.

In addition to the product backlog burnup, consider the Product Features chart, shown in the next figure.

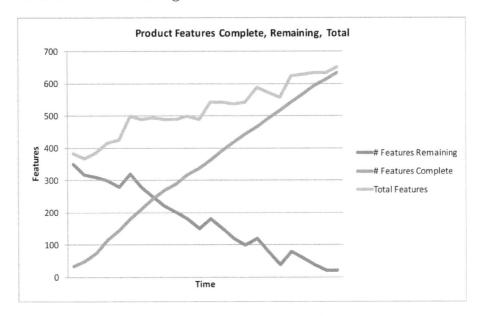

This graph helps people see that the number of features grows during the project (Total features, from our initial guess at the number of features to the upper right). The team makes steady progress, shown in the burnup of the Features Complete line, from bottom left to top right. And the Features Remaining burndown from the initial guess as to the number of features down to zero reflects what the team completes and the additional features.

You may have worked on projects in the past where your stakeholders (your managers, sponsors, and/or customers) wanted to know when the project would be done. And they added features. With the product features chart, all of these people can see approximately when the project will be done and the possible effect if they add more features—especially if they don't remove features.

Some people ask how to count the features in these two graphs. Count each feature in a feature set. If necessary, use the team's cycle time to measure an average cycle time for each feature. No, that does not account for the different complexities in each feature. If you think you have a complex feature set, break it into more features so the team can deliver smaller parts faster.

Show Other Requests in to the Team

Part of answering the "When will this project be done?" question is to assess other requests in to the team. I already said that multitasking makes estimation impossible and reduces throughput. Sometimes managers don't realize they are asking the team to multitask. Consider *showing* your managers how many multitasking requests the team receives, and the kinds of requests.

If your managers don't realize they are asking the team to multitask, consider creating a chart, such as the one outlined in the following table, that shows the day and the number of requests since the last time the managers saw the project state.

Day	Number of Requests	Individual or Team?	Notes
Day 1	2	Individual and team	Sandy for Project B and the team for support
Day 2	1	Individual	Sandy for Project B
Day 5	5	Individual	Each person for a different project
Day 6	2	Individual	Both: Sandy for Project B again
Day 8	1	Individual	Sandy for Project B again

Table 12—Number of Multitasking Requests for Individuals or the Team

The managers might explain, "Project B is more valuable to the organization than this project is." In that case, the team might ask why it is working on this project and not Project B.

There are several possibilities if Project B is more valuable:

- Neither the managers nor the team worry about the effect of multitasking on the team.

- The team might even lend Sandy to Project B for a while to help that team finish its work.

- The entire team might help Project B for a while so the more important project can finish first.

However, what I see more often is that Project B is not more valuable, and that managers don't realize the effect their multitasking requests have on the team. Here, Day 5 is particularly troublesome: each person on the team had requests from different projects.

If the team works on one-day or smaller stories, team members might be able to complete their work before servicing this interrupt. Or if this project is of lesser value than any of the other projects, team members might be fine with interruptions to their work.

More often, the managers are not assessing the project portfolio enough. (See how to do so in *Manage Your Project Portfolio [Rot16a].*) Or this team (or another) is not a cross-functional feature team. Or the managers don't realize multitasking causes delays in projects. Too often, managers don't realize team members create defects in one way or another when they attempt to multitask.

Multitasking requests are rarely something a team servant leader can resolve. More often, managers need to see the requests and decide what to do. Help your managers help you by showing them your data. You might add another column showing the effects of multitasking on the project, such as "Feature 1 is late now." Or you might show your cumulative flow graph, where your work is stuck in one column or several columns because the team cannot finish its work.

Show What's Done but Not Yet Released

Some teams have inventory (WIP): they have completed features hiding behind flags. (See *How Do I Release Partially Complete Feature Sets?*, on page 169.) One of the problems with that approach is that the team can create inventory of not-yet-released work.

Cards on the wall are an effective way to show what's done but not yet released. The sheer number of cards helps everyone—the team, the product owner, the sponsors/managers/customers—see what's going on. In the board shown in the figure on page 220, the columns Waiting for Release, Date Done, Why Not Released, and Anticipated Release answer the questions people might have about the WIP. The remaining column, Released Since Last Meeting, updates the status from the last time people looked at the team's output.

You might wonder why the Anticipated Release column does not have a full complement of cards. That's because this team doesn't know when it will have enough of the given feature sets done to know when it can release. The product owner has the team building walking skeletons in different areas of the product. The skeletons are enough to show people inside the organization, but the skeleton functionality is not enough for the customers to use.

The discussion about this WIP is much more important than the WIP itself. Sure, I would prefer if there were no WIP, if the team could release all the features whenever they were done. However, if the customers won't adopt the new functionality because it's not "enough," it's best to make that problem transparent.

Work That's Done and Not Yet Released

Waiting for Release	Date Done	Why Not Released	Anticipated Release	Released Since Last Meeting

Visualize Your Project's Delays

Maybe your team has all the people it needs. And your management makes decisions when they need to do so. And you have no delays in your releases—your team can release whatever it wants whenever it wants. You have no friction in your product development. If so, skip this section.

Many teams have some sort of delay in their projects. Sometimes management doesn't decide to start the project until the project is already late. Sometimes you have a geographically distributed team with built-in time-zone delays. Sometimes you need specialists from across the organization. And you might depend on other people to actually release the product to your customers.

You have delays in your project. Delays prevent teams from making progress. The diagram on page 221 illustrates how you can see your delays.

At time T0, management says, "Yes, let's do this." You might not see the item on your backlog until time T1. If your organization measures the difference between T1 and T0 in months, that's an enormous impediment. Make that impediment visible to everyone. You might need help to remove that problem. That delay from T0 to T1 is often a project portfolio problem. See *Manage Your Project Portfolio [Rot16a]* for ideas.

Organizational Lead and Cycle Time

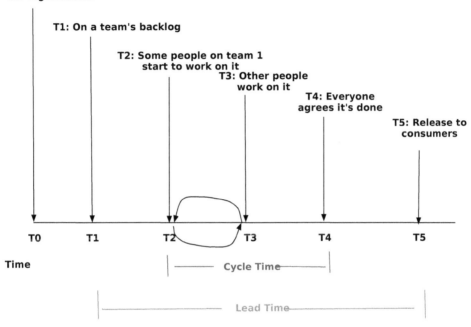

If your team has a large backlog, it might take weeks or months to *start* work on that item. That's what T2 means. Now, if you have a full cross-functional team that can deliver anything it needs, you won't have the extra time for the T3 and T4 cycles. However, if you have component teams or specialists, or shared-services "teams," your project will start work at T2, have the work cycle between the specialists and the team for T3, and not finish until T4.

If you have small stories in a complete cross-functional team, you might keep the difference between T4 and T2 to a day or so. However, once you need other teams to finish what one team starts, you have a cost of delay. (See *Diving for Hidden Treasures [RE16]* for more possible delays.) Once you see your delays, you can decide what to do. At the very least, raise the issue to your managers as an impediment.

The difference between T4 and T5 might be due to insufficient functionality for customers. Or it might be because you have a packaging process in your organization. For example, if you box your product in some way, you will see a delay between T4 and T5. If you have a different group that releases the product, possibly via a staging and production system, you will see a delay between T4 and T5.

Delays have implications on your ability to recognize revenue, acquire or retain customers, and better the customer's experience with your product. Delays—by themselves—are not the issue. The issue is what the delays cost the team and the organization. You can measure the effects of these delays once you see them.

Measure the Effects of Delays

Earlier in the book I suggested you consider *Use Cost of Delay to See Value*, on page 106, when ranking features. You can use a different measure to see the cost of delay when waiting for other people. That's a different measure: CD3, which means the cost of delay divided by duration. (See *The Principles of Product Development Flow: Second Generation Lean Product Development [Rei09]* and the explanation at "Cost of Delay Divided by Duration" for a fuller description.[1])

Imagine you have three features, each of which has a different duration and value to the organization, as outlined in the following table.

Feature	Estimated Duration	Estimated Value	CD3
Feature 1	2 weeks	$5,000	$5,000/2=$2,500/week
Feature 2	5 weeks	$10,000	$10,000/5=$2,000/week
Feature 3	8 weeks to an MVP	$100,000	$100,000/8=$12,500/week

Table 13—Calculating the Cost of Delay for Each of Three Features

Feature 1 is short—only two weeks of estimated duration. Because it's so much shorter than Feature 2, it is has a higher CD3. Feature 1 is more valuable, not because it's shorter, but because the value for the time is higher.

Now take a look at Feature 3. It's estimated to be much longer—eight weeks to an MVP. And the *value* of that MVP is significantly higher. The CD3 is five times more valuable than Feature 1. What prevents the team from starting and finishing Feature 3?

Here are circumstances under which I would create and show a table like this to the team and management:

- The team is multitasking. If the multitasking is self-induced, the team can discuss why it feels the need to multitask. More often, the managers ask the team to multitask. In that case, the managers can see the delay before they see the value.

---

1. http://blackswanfarming.com/cost-of-delay-divided-by-duration

- The team is waiting for other people during their work. Not only is the team's cycle time slower, but there is a real cost for having a team without all the skills and capabilities it needs.

- The team can't release completed work. The team might be able to finish all of its work, but it needs a deployment team or some other gatekeeper to release finished work. It's time for management to be aware of that impediment and decide whether to fix it.

CD3 is a helpful measure, often for management, to see the effects of their previous decisions and organization. They can choose a different path now. Now that you know about CD3, you might want to consider using it for ranking features. A caution: in my experience, the larger the item under discussion, the less we know about its real value and cost.

Recognize Project-Measurement Traps

Teams encounter several project-measurement traps, which you, as a leader, can help manage.

- Managers look at the team measures instead of project status measures.

- Managers try to compare teams using velocity or some other team-based measure.

- Too few people review the cost-of-delay measures, especially when the team has WIP.

Those traps—the gamification of team measures—can create risks for your project. Here's how to recognize and manage those traps.

Trap: Managers Review Team Measures Instead of Project Measures

Many teams use iterations and calculate their velocity as part of their measures. Velocity can help a team learn its capacity, as discussed in *Velocity Is a Capacity Measurement*, on page 188. However, just measuring velocity does not help anyone understand the team's progress. Teams make progress when they complete features, as discussed in *Show Feature Progress*, on page 216.

Here's the real problem: velocity is easy to measure. If teams have large features—really, feature sets—progress is much more difficult to see. However, managing velocity doesn't help anyone understand the team's progress.

If you can, avoid showing any manager a team's velocity. If you must, explain the team's capacity. Even better, ask the manager what information he or she wants. If the manager wants to know when to expect a particular feature, explain the roadmaps and the team's cycle time. You might say something like this: "That feature isn't on the roadmap for another three iterations. Once it gets closer, we can use cycle time—the average time it takes for us to release a feature—to tell you more about when in that iteration you might see it. And please check with the product owner to make sure the product owner knows how important this feature is for you."

If you can, show the manager what's working now, as the best measure of the team's progress.

Trap: Compare Teams' Velocity Instead of an Individual Team's Progress

Sometimes managers don't realize what velocity is. They only know it's some sort of team measure. They want to compare one team's velocity against another team's.

The problem is that teams work in different domains, in different code bases, and with a different number of people. Velocity is unique and personal to a team.

Consider asking the manager what he or she wants to know. Does the manager want to see the feature throughput? If so, consider using the product backlog burnup chart or the feature chart from *Show Feature Progress*, on page 216. If the manager wants to see delays, consider showing the cycle time chart from *Visualize Your Project's Delays*, on page 220. Maybe even measure the delays you see affecting the team.

Very few teams are comparable in an organization. Instead of comparison, ask the manager what she or he wants to know, and provide that.

Trap: WIP Is Everywhere

Teams have WIP for many reasons. One is when the team has partially completed feature sets, so those feature sets are not released. (See *Show What's Done but Not Yet Released*, on page 219.)

Sometimes it's reasonable for a team to produce a walking skeleton all over the product: a little in admin, a little in search, a little in billing. However, that approach has a cost in terms of WIP.

Sometimes the team has WIP in other ways. One team had a slow build system. Another team's product owner had feature-itis (see *Trap: The Product Owner Has Feature-itis*, on page 101), and kept asking the team to produce features. The team never finished a feature *set*, not by design. The team didn't finish a feature set because the managers and the product owner became impatient with the team's progress.

Some other teams have the *Trap: Experts Take Their Own Stories*, on page 160, or *Trap: Everyone Takes His or Her Own Story*, on page 123

Here are some possibilities for your team:

- Make the WIP visible. Consider a cumulative flow chart as discussed in *Cumulative Flow Shows Where the Work Is*, on page 183, and *Visualize Your Project's Delays*, on page 220.

- Measure the costs of those delays, possibly in the form of CD3. (See *Measure the Effects of Delays*, on page 222.)

- Create WIP Limits, even for work that's done and not yet released, as illustrated on page 220.

As a leader, your role is to help the rest of the organization see the costs of continuing to work the same way.

Now Try This

1. Demo vertical slices to managers/sponsors/customers as often as possible. If you have a product that is only demonstrable instead of releasable, demo vertical slices and help these people see where the product is headed.

2. Show feature-based completion in some way. Remember that customers buy features.

3. Show the effects of multitasking or other impediments for the team. Your team might not have multitasking problems. Show the team's specific problems with at least qualitative data. If that's not enough, show that the cycle time increases as a result of whatever problems your team has.

You understand how to design and manage an agile project for a cross-functional project team. If you have a group instead of a team, read the next chapter to see what's different.

Part III

Help Work Groups
and Managers Use Agile

CHAPTER 15

Create an Agile Work Group

You're part of a work group. You might be part of a customer-support team, a program team that works across the organization, or even a management team such as the project portfolio team.

You work mostly independently of a team. Even in your team, you don't tend to collaborate except during meetings. Can you still use an agile approach?

Of course. You rarely use iterations, although you might want a cadence for meetings and reporting. People and teams in your position often want to track cycle time and throughput. However, your meetings are likely different. Your metrics are different.

You can benefit from all the ideas in Chapter 3, *Build Teamwork with*, on page 41, because you will need to collaborate. However, you are not a cross-functional team in the same way as a product-delivery team is.

Let's see how an agile approach can work for you.

Work Groups Meet Differently than Teams

How does your group work? If you have interdependencies between people, you will need some form of checking on deliverables and recommitting to work. You might not need a daily standup. In fact, you might need a problem-solving meeting.

If you all work on similar kinds of work, as a customer-support group would, consider some form of retrospective to see how to improve your work.

You might need some form of planning if you make choices other than first-in/first-out work. For example, in more traditional customer-support organizations, managers might do the triage of tickets. In an agile customer-support group, the team might do the triage on some cadence—say, every morning.

There Is No One Right Agile Approach for a Work Group

Customer Support, Finance, Human Resources, and Sales can all benefit from using agile approaches. The difference is that you are part of a work group (where people work independently) rather than a team (where people are interdependent).

Suppose you work in Customer Support. You have a queue of work, which you might call "tickets." When you are done with one ticket, you take the next ticket that's at the top of the queue.

Every organization has a policy about what to do if you don't have sufficient knowledge to complete that ticket. There's no "agile" answer about what to do. However, I prefer to have people pair on work when at least one of them doesn't know enough to work on that ticket alone.

It's the same problem for other functional groups. Agile approaches—breaking work into small deliverables that have value, visualizing the work and the state of the work, and managing your work in progress—can benefit work groups. Consider what will work for your group.

The team would decide what to do when. You might need some planning approach that integrates team triage with management triage of tickets.

Consider which kind of meeting you need and how often. Especially, decide how often you would like to retrospect. Retrospectives provide valuable data for improvement. (See *Retrospectives Provide Valuable Data*, on page 195.)

How Will the Group Visualize Its Work and Data?

There is no "standard" kind of work group. That means there is no standard board. I have seen two major kinds of work groups: groups where people work on the same kind of work in the same kind of flow, such as Customer Support or Training; and groups where people work independently, such as HR or Marketing. They each have different kinds of work in different flows.

I'll talk about both kinds of work groups. If your work group is something different, consider the principles: visualizing all the work to do, tracking it, and noticing wait states.

Visualize Similar Kinds of Work in Similar Flows

In my experience, customer-support groups have a ton of interrupting work, so iterations are rarely helpful to organize their work. Instead, consider a flow-based agile approach with WIP limits.

Imagine your work group is able to maintain a steady pace with respect to tickets. As the tickets come in, someone places them in the Tickets queue, as shown in the following figure. The group takes some number of tickets—maybe what it thinks it can work on for a morning or an afternoon—and places them in the Ready for Ranking column. The group ranks some small number of tickets and ranks them in the Ready to Start column.

Tickets	Ready for Ranking	Ready to Start	In Progress	Escalate to R&D	Escalate to Product Mgmt	Test	Deploy	Done
			[3]	[3]	[1]	[2]	[2]	

Urgent Queue

This particular group has WIP limits on the next columns. In Progress means someone is (or several people are) working on the ticket. Sometimes the people working on the ticket have questions. That's what the Escalate to R&D and Escalate to Product Management columns are for. Once the people finish their work, they need to test it.

Different support groups manage testing differently. In this team's case, the testers are not the same people who created the solution. In your organization, maybe the work returns to a product-based team for testing.

Once the group completes the testing, it's ready for Deploy. Every organization has its own agreements on deployment or release. Once everything is done for that ticket, it goes into the Done column.

Many customer-support organizations have an electronic tool that manages the tickets and the flow. Consider if you need to add WIP limits to the flow, or if the work group can use a paper board once it's taken tickets into the group. It depends on the cycle time for the group.

Visualization for Independent Members in a Group

If you work in other groups, such as HR, Finance, or Sales, you might ask how you can use agile approaches, too. Again, look at your work to see how to create an information radiator.

I'll take HR as an example. HR has several *independent* work streams, such as recruiting, benefits, and performance administration. (Your HR department might have different streams from these.) Finance may have these streams: accounts payable, accounts receivable, purchasing, and taxes, depending on your organization. In Sales, the external salespeople grouped by region are often independent of each other, and interdependent with inside salespeople. Notice that the organization requires all of the people managing these work streams to finish their work. And the work streams themselves have different cadences, different workflows, and different measurements.

I recommend each part of an independent function have its own kanban board with its own WIP limits and cycle-time measurements. Then, once each part of the function visualizes and measures his or her own work, they can use the cross-organization approach for seeing all the work in the function as a whole. The following figure might help you think about how to visualize all the work for independent members of a work group.

Possible Kanban for a Functional Team, Such as HR

Ranked Backlog	In Progress		Risk Management or Mitigation	Decision Needed Post-Action	Waiting: Stuck Items	Done
	Action Item Analysis	Action Item Resolution				
[ ] [ ] [ ] [ ]	Item and date started. Who is working the item.					[ ] [ ] [ ]
Recruiting	[ ]					
Benefits				[ ]	[ ]	
Performance	[ ]					

The group has a Ranked Backlog on the left. In addition, each work stream has its own swim lane, so people can see at a glance where the work is. All work starts as In Progress in some way. This board has two pieces of In Progress: Action Item Analysis and Action Item Resolution. It's possible the members perform some sort of risk-management or risk-mitigation activities.

Sometimes the people need someone else across the organization for decisions—that's the Decision Needed Post-Action column. Always include a Waiting or Stuck column so everyone can see where the work is. And the Done column helps everyone see what's done.

Do think about what your work group's board should look like. What are common states? Where does this part of the group have wait states? Ask each part of the group to determine its own flow with its own wait states. Now, look at the different boards. See if the group can create one board to visualize all the work and wait states. The group might have to review each unique flow separately before it can create a board for the entire functional group.

Because every work group is unique, I can't provide the One Right Answer for your board. Consider starting in paper on the wall so you can track your work and see what value the board might bring.

 Joe asks:

When Does It Make Sense for Groups to Work Together?

If you read *Work as a Whole Team to Create the Product*, on page 131, you might wonder if pairing, swarming, or mobbing can help your work group increase its throughput. They might. It depends on how much solo expertise each person in your group has. The more each person has individual expertise, the more pairing or mobbing will help with the group's throughput. Pairing and mobbing help people learn together. Your group might have a challenging problem that requires several people's expertise. in that case, swarming or mobbing might help.

Consider all of these ideas: the expertise your group requires to complete this particular problem, the cross-training your group needs, and the urgency of solving this problem. There is no right answer. Check your context and see what might work for your group.

Visualize Work for a Management Team

For so long, we were taught that silos—development, testing, UX, whatever you had in your organization—were the Right Way to organize. While I lean much more toward a product organization, that might not be a reality for your organization now.

Functional managers collaborate to create the project portfolio. They might collaborate as part of a program or to remove impediments for cross-functional teams.

Managers have deliverables across the organization. Managers provide the leverage that the cross-functional teams or work groups require. When managers can see their work—and show their work to others—the entire organization can benefit from the transparency. The transparency might help several managers see how to collaborate, possibly as a cross-organization program team.

Programs are strategic collections of projects with one business objective. (See *Agile and Lean Program Management [Rot16]* for more information.) While your functional group (HR, Sales, Finance) might not deliver projects, the group does deliver value on a periodic basis.

One way you can see the overall function deliverables is to use a kanban board similar to the one shown here. You might not use WIP limits until you understand all the work your function is working on.

Ranked Backlog	In Progress		Risk Management or Mitigation	Decision Needed Post-Action	Waiting: Stuck Items	Done
	Action Item Analysis	Action Item Resolution				
☐ ☐ ☐ ☐	Item and date started. Who is working the item.					☐ ☐ ☐
Facilities Issues	☐				☐	
HR Issues			☐		☐	
Compensation Issues	☐			☐		
Internal Prod. Dev't Issues		☐				

This board has similar columns to the preceding one: Action Item Analysis and Resolution, Risk Management or Mitigation, Decision Needed, Waiting, and Done. However, look at the swim lanes below the big black line.

When managers explain they are working on facilities issues, such as team rooms or small private offices or the ability to collocate team members together, the teams can understand why it takes a while to resolve these issues. It's the same for HR issues: when and how does an organization move to team-based compensation for product-development teams and what does that mean for work groups?

As soon as agile approaches move past the team level, the managers have a difficult time understanding and working through the issues. When managers take the bold step of creating a board and showing the transparency as they deal with the issues, the people on the teams have more confidence in an agile transformation. Your management team(s) might need different boards. There is no One Right Board for management.

People need to see their work to see their throughput and cycle time. And the organization needs more information and data to understand the implications of those details.

Boards Don't Make You Agile

When you have people who can't collaborate on the work, such as recruiting and benefits administration, kanban boards for each function show you where the work is. Creating an overall kanban board to see what work is waiting where can help you explain the implication of the waiting work.

Having boards, using standups, measuring velocity—any kind of agile artifact—is not "being agile." Agile is the mindset of collaboration and frequent delivery. Refer back to *Create Your Agile Mindset*, on page 15, if you are confused.

Product Development Is Cross-Functional

Let me clarify: I recommend kanban boards for functions where people work independently. Product development, where a team or teams produce a working product that customers can consume, is *not* independent work.

Product development is *interdependent* work. Do not create a kanban board showing the developer work, another kanban with the testing work, another kanban with UX work, and so on and think you are agile. That's waterfall. That kind of a kanban board might help your team see its flow *before* you think about agile approaches that could work for you.

Every Group Decides How and When to Reflect

I recommend all work groups retrospect on a regular cadence. The retrospectives helps the people learn about their process, their throughput, and their assumptions. The more a work group reflects, the more everyone can collect and review data so they understand how the group works and what they might choose to address next.

Consider this data in preparation for your retrospectives:

- Cycle time for what you produce. For customer support, this means cycle time for tickets over a day, week, and month. If your cycle time increases, look for the root cause. Cycle time increases can be due to almost anything: the product developers let too many defects escape, some support people are on vacation, or each person in the group has specialized information and some people are overloaded.

- Cumulative flow for your work group. The charts in *Cumulative Flow Shows Where the Work Is*, on page 183, show the state of work on a team's board. When you have a board that reflects your work, you can see where the open work is.

- Incoming rate of work, closure rate of work, and remaining open work. For Customer Support, this data might refer to tickets. For HR, this data might be benefits investigation initiatives. Each group will measure different kinds of data. However, you can track what comes in, what you complete, and what remains open.

Use this data to decide what you might want to change.

Now Try This

1. Visualize your group's work with a kanban board to see the flow. Don't be afraid of adding wait or decision states if they exist.

2. Look at your board and ask the work group this question: "What data do we want to measure?" I recommend you measure cycle time for wait states as a minimum.

3. Ask how often your group needs to problem-solve as a group. Use that cadence to create group meetings where you can review the board and update the data. You might decide to retrospect at least that often or select another cadence for retrospectives.

Now let's see how managers can help an agile team or a work group.

CHAPTER 16

How Managers Help Agile Teams

Your organization might have technical leaders, managers, directors, vice presidents, and so on. All those people are organizational leaders. They have titles and some sort of organizational power. I'm going to call those people "managers" as shorthand.

Regardless of your team's project approach, you've seen managers who helped or hurt the team's momentum. And many people who try to use agile approaches say, "We don't need any managers in agile approaches." Those people are mistaken.

Managers hold the key to creating an agile culture. Managers remove impediments that teams can't remove. Managers make choices about removing or reinforcing these impediments all the time. Their choices create the culture for the organization. If you can help the managers see value in agile approaches, they'll work to create a more agile culture. If no one can help the managers see the value in agile approaches, the teams won't be able to sustain an agile culture.

Let's see some possibilities for managers to help your cross-functional team thrive in its chosen agile approach.

Here are primary areas in which managers can help the team become more effective with their agile approach:

- Removing impediments the team cannot remove on its own.

- Helping the team find or create its own workspace so the team can collaborate more easily.

- Managing the project portfolio with flow-efficiency thinking so people work on one project as part of one team.

- Helping HR understand how to transition to a team-based recognition and reward structure.

There are plenty of other actions managers might take to support agile approaches. For example, managers might help remove hierarchy by seeing if some people prefer to be technical leaders on teams instead of being managers removed from teams. Every organization I've consulted with has not enough product owners. Managers can offer people the role of product owner instead of project manager or manager. With the creation of communities of practice, people might be interested in technical work.

Let's start with looking at what managers might be able to do about four typical impediments:

- Resolve problems the team can't, especially systemic organizational problems.

- Create team workspaces.

- Manage the project portfolio.

- Start the transition to a team-based recognition and reward structure.

Managers Resolve Impediments the Team Escalates

In *Visualize Problems with a Board*, on page 121, there's a column on the board called Waiting for External Decision. The team escalates to the team's manager the problems it cannot resolve itself. (Yes, I am assuming every team has only one manager.)

Problems outside the team's control are often systemic problems. If your organization requires either change-control requests or a deployment team, the project team cannot release its product when it is done. Sometimes the annual budgeting process eliminates the possibility of making *product* advances in the marketplace because this project was not supposed to do that. Sometimes the team doesn't know enough about interpersonal skills or technical skills, so the manager can arrange for training.

Great managers start with this question: "What do I need to do to see a flow of value from this team?" If the manager optimizes for value flow, the manager will see what his or her role could be.

For more reading, see *Behind Closed Doors: Secrets of Great Management [RD05]* and "Agile Management: The Essence of Leadership."[1]

---

1.   https://www.jrothman.com/articles/2010/03/agile-managers-the-essence-of-leadership-2

Managers Help Create the Workspace Your Team Needs

I mentioned the idea of a team room in *Does the Team Need a Team Room?*, on page 203. Ideally, every collocated team would have a physical location where the team can work together. That work might be swarming, walking the board, and creating and updating the team's data.

When people work together, such as in pairs or mobs, they may find that being with other people all day exhausts them. Those people also need a private space where they can think quietly and recharge.

Managers have the title-based power in the organization to create the different spaces the team needs. Ask the team what kind of a space it would like to experiment with, and for how long it would like that space. Different teams need different kinds of spaces.

Seeing an Agile Team Work Convinced Me to Try Team Workspaces
by: Ben, CTO

My middle managers came to me with what I thought was a crazy request. They wanted the ability to collocate the team in one workspace. Oh, and yes, they wanted enough private spaces that people could go hide in a "cave"—that's what they called it—for a while.

I've spent my entire career doing and managing software. I'd never seen this team workspace nonsense before. One of the managers, Sarah, asked me to spend an hour walking around, seeing what the team did.

First, I saw a standup at a board. Okay, I have to admit I was impressed when people stepped up and said they could help each other finish work. But they're a team. What else would I expect?

Then I saw a pair—a developer/tester pair—working together to solve a problem. That was a bit of a surprise. What was even more surprising was the fact that they had to squish into his cube because she didn't have enough room. Sarah and I spoke with them and that's when the tester told me she liked to work from home because she had enough room there. I guess she told me.

I walked around and saw more people working in triads and even one quartet. I had been impressed with the team's throughput. When I realized I could run interference with Facilities, I was all in. Especially if they keep this throughput up.

Not all teams need a large physical room. For example, if your team is geographically distributed—not collocated—the team might only need a board with a camera pointed at it. Teams that are not collocated might need personal cameras so people can see each other to know who's interruptible. They might also need a variety of communication tools that help with immediate and not-immediate communication.

Managers Move from Resource-Efficiency to Flow-Efficiency Thinking

Too many managers were trained to think of "resources" as a term they can apply to people. They use terms such as "FTE," which is a full-time equivalent. They think of productivity, as if knowledge-work productivity can be measured with any kind of certainty. They think of percent utilization, which doesn't make sense for collaboration.

Great managers knew the words and measures were wrong. And they often saw no alternatives. Agile culture provides many alternatives.

When managers think of people as "resources," managers think they or the teams can split work to make people more efficient. We split this work by work type, creating experts. The name for this is "resource efficiency," as shown in the following figure.

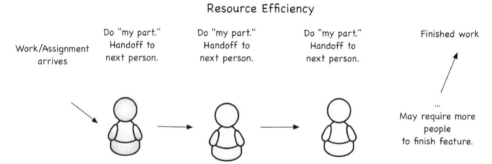

When managers think they can ask a team to work on several projects at once, or see 100% utilization, or reinforce narrow expertise, managers are victims of resource-efficiency thinking. High utilization makes no sense for knowledge work. People need time to think and to innovate. (See *This Is Lean: Resolving the Efficiency Paradox [MÅ13]* for a full discussion of resource efficiency versus flow efficiency.) One way to help people see the problems with resource efficiency is to *Visualize Your Project's Delays*, on page 220.

Instead of resource-efficiency thinking, explain to your management about flow efficiency, as illustrated in the figure on page 241. When we flow work through teams, we see the highest throughput. It doesn't matter if we talk about features or projects. Flow efficiency allows us to *finish* work faster.

This kind of thinking has several implications for managers:

- Managers need to manage the project portfolio to eliminate multitasking among projects.

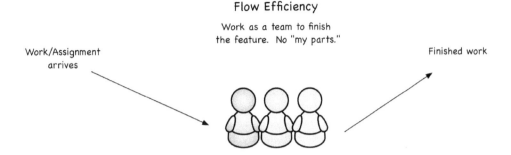

Flow Efficiency

Work as a team to finish
the feature. No "my parts."

Work/Assignment
arrives

Finished work

- Managers need to staff and retain stable cross-functional teams.

- Managers need to look for throughput measures instead of utilization measures.

When managers don't think about optimizing *up* for the team, the product, and the organization, they create management mayhem, as described in *Avoid Management Mayhem*, on page 243. In management's defense, too often the organization creates rewards that optimize for the individual, not the team, the product, or the organization.

One way to see if your organization is optimizing up is to see how many people try to control or direct the team's work. In agile approaches, the product owner is the single person who directs and controls *what* the team does. If managers try to control "their" developers, testers, writers, whatever, the team can't manage its work.

Those teams struggle to manage all their work because they are multitasking by person instead of working as a team. Teams can't depend on each other because managers move people around. Managers don't realize what they are or are not measuring because they don't understand agile measurement is different. Remember, *Work as a Whole Team to Create the Product*, on page 131.

Agile is a human-centered approach to work. Retraining your management will take time. Ask your managers to consider what they want: surrogate measures that create an individual approach to work, or measurements that encourage collaboration and delivery?

If you can help your managers change one idea about their thinking, ask them to consider flow efficiency instead of resource efficiency. Help your managers see the delays and the cost of those delays with *Visualize Your Project's Delays*, on page 220.

"Shared Services" Often Aren't

When the phrase "shared services" started, it often meant labs. Too often now, it means people.

Sometimes people think of product development as development plus "shared services." Those shared services were UX/UI, testing, and technical writers. Maybe your organization has other "services." People had the notion of shared services because in a serial-life-cycle environment, managers thought this approach sped the project completion. (I've never seen it work that way, but that was the idea.)

Agile approaches are about *product* development. There is no sharing of services. All these roles and capabilities need to be on each cross-functional agile team so the team can produce its features and release the product.

This requires a manager mindset change. Help your managers see the need for the abolishment of the idea of "shared services" and creation of cross-functional feature teams. Help them see delays in your team's multitasking and the cost of delay from this idea. Shared services are an artifact of resource-efficiency thinking instead of flow-efficiency thinking. When managers help teams move from component teams and other incomplete cross-functional teams, they increase flow and deliver value faster.

Managers Help with Team-Based Recognition

One byproduct of moving from resource-efficiency thinking to flow-efficiency thinking is realizing that managers can change how the organization recognizes and rewards people. Instead of recognizing and rewarding individual performance, an agile culture recognizes and rewards team performance.

That's a huge change.

Think about the agile team you are creating and working with. Can you tell the difference between people on the team? Is your team becoming a team of specializing generalists who help wherever the team needs them? If so, it's time to rethink the recognition and reward system.

Ranking for Compensation Doesn't Make Sense
by: Stacy, VP, Product Development

For years, I had a job that I hated. I was supposed to rank everyone in my organization. If I ranked everyone as a 5, HR would push back and tell me I couldn't possibly have that many stars. I did, but they didn't buy it. If I ranked everyone as a 3, I couldn't get the money I wanted for raises. I felt stuck between a rock and a hard place.

Then we moved to agile in the form of flow. I gotta say, I was blown away when every team's throughput increased because they now had WIP limits and they worked as teams. Blown away. What was I going to do about the compensation?

I brought HR around on what I called "a walking tour" so they could see how the teams worked. Sure, people were still developers and testers, but they gave each other feedback and coaching. They found and fixed problems before any of the managers could help.

And my managers? Wow, now they were coaching and giving feedback about the really difficult problems. We'd been doing flow for about 14 months, and everyone had stepped up their game. It was time to bring HR into the mix.

HR decided we could try giving teams a rank. I explained that ranking a team didn't make sense either. Each team worked on different work. We had to stop with ranking people against each other and talk with them about their careers and what they wanted to do. You should have heard the "Oooh." We're experimenting with results-based approaches. We're trying to create double-loop learning as an organization.

I wouldn't say we have rewards and compensation totally knocked. Each manager sits with a person to create that person's personal results in terms of her or his career. In addition, teams are responsible for results. We stopped ranking people last year, which makes everyone feel happy. We're on a path to reasonableness, which is what anyone, including me, wants.

Agile is a team-based approach to work. Consider a team-based approach to recognition and rewards.

Avoid Management Mayhem

Managers have power in the organization. That means that managers can create mayhem without even realizing it.

Here are some common management-created problems for agile teams:

- When managers yank people off or onto a team in the expectation that the team needs expertise

- When managers don't limit the work in progress for the organization by managing the project portfolio

- When managers don't realize that a team needs to be cross-functional, with all the capabilities and skills required to finish work

- When managers blame people for work—done or not done

When I Stopped Blaming, We Started to Use Agile Approaches
by: Cliff, VP, R&D

I had always worked in a culture of blame. I could swear all my managers came from the school of: "You do it, you own it. I don't like it? I blame you." I did the same thing with my managers and their teams.

I wanted to use agile approaches. I needed the features done and released. I kept managing the same way I had always managed.

One day, four of my managers asked for a meeting. They said they were all going to leave if I didn't change. What did I need to change? My blaming.

I talked to the first manager and she explained she was tired of working around me and trying to smooth things over when I had a screaming and blaming outburst in a meeting. She told me I never had "little" outbursts. She gave me feedback, as I now see.

The other managers gave me other examples. They were sick and tired of me. Me. Not the company. Me. My blaming had gotten out of hand and had changed my effectiveness as a manager.

I didn't think I could make things work without them. I told them that. They all smiled. That first manager told me she was happy I felt that way. They loved the product and their teams. I was the problem.

They taught me about feedback that day. I see now that they coached me. I am still a work in progress, but I'm working on my growth and agile mindsets.

They haven't quit and the teams started to really rock and roll after I started to learn how to manage. It's as if all they needed was a little reasonableness at the top.

This chapter is just the introduction to the idea of agile management. Even if your managers can do all of these things, that might not be enough to create and sustain your agile culture.

Recognize How Managers Can Help Agile Teams

In other chapters, I highlighted traps. I'm not highlighting traps here because it's difficult enough being a manager. Instead, I'm suggesting three things managers can do to help agile teams:

- Encourage collaborative work.
- Help the team consider "how little" instead of "how much."
- Optimize up wherever possible.

These kinds of ideas help a manager continue to create an agile environment. Unless the entire organization is already steeped in the agile mindset, managers have an ongoing responsibility to support teams in their agile approaches.

How Managers Can Encourage Collaborative Work

Agile is not just a project approach, but a cultural shift. One major shift is to teamwork from individual work. An agile culture creates the ability for the manager to flow work through the team. And the manager can provide team-based recognition and rewards.

Encourage your manager to manage the project portfolio, and flow just one project through a team. Encourage your manager to consider eliminating individual bonuses and work toward some form of team-based rewards.

How Managers Can Encourage "How Little" Thinking

In more traditional organizations, managers are accustomed to directing work. Sometimes they are accustomed to controlling what people do and how. Instead of saying, "Don't do that," consider asking the manager this question: "How little controlling or directing is it possible for you to do?"

Many managers are concerned with the effect of bad decisions and nonworking deliverables. You, as a servant leader, can help build trust first with your manager by helping the team deliver visible value, as often as possible. When managers see the team deliver value on a regular and sustained basis, they often start to think about other "how little" possibilities. Build trust with your manager by delivering value on a regular basis.

How Managers Can Help Optimize Up

Sometimes team members pull their hair out. They don't have the opportunity to solve problems where the problems are. Instead, the problem goes up the hierarchy, over to another function, and down where the people can solve the problem. Then the solution traverses the hierarchy again.

One way managers can help the team succeed is to help everyone think "up" a level. If you can help a manager think in a "lean" way, starting with *The Two Pillars of Lean*, on page 8, the manager will think about how to optimize the work for more value. Seeing the whole, eliminating waste, delivering as fast as possible—those ideas resonate with managers. You can help your manager see the whole by discussing how to optimize what the *team* delivers, not each individual person. Then, discuss what the department or product line delivers, not the teams.

Now Try This

1. Invite your manager to see the team at work. Help the manager see why a team workspace is useful and how the team might use it.

2. Help your manager see the value of collaborative cross-functional teams by using throughput or WIP or cost-of-delay calculations.

3. Start the discussion with your manager about what it would take or what it might look like to start to recognize and reward teams. This could be a discussion that evolves over many meetings, so start now.

Now that you've seen how you might use agile approaches at the team level, consider how you might start—especially if you're not so sure agile approaches are right for you.

CHAPTER 17

Start Somewhere

You might wonder if agile approaches have jumped the shark—whether agile is past its prime.[1]

Or maybe you or your managers thought agile approaches were merely a different project life cycle. Someone thought agile approaches were for teams only. No one thought the managers and the entire organization would need to change the culture. The transparency agile approaches bring is not what you had in mind.

You might have other concerns, such as no product owners for your teams. Or you might have too many managers who want to control what the teams do, threatening the teams' move toward self-management.

Use this chapter for ideas about what you can do. You might not be able to transform your team into an agile team, but here are two basic ideas that will help you deliver value faster: limiting work in progress and asking people to work as a cross-functional team.

Try these ideas only if the team wants to do so. Do not impose agile approaches on any team. If you aren't sure where to start, consider beginning with your work.

Limit the Work in Progress

One of the most powerful ideas in agile approaches is to limit what a team works on for now. Iteration-based agile approaches limit WIP by timeboxing the work. Flow-based agile approaches create explicit WIP limits.

---

1. https://en.wikipedia.org/wiki/Jumping_the_shark

When the team limits its work in some way, the team is more likely to finish the work it does. The team is more likely to use technical excellence as it completes work.

Consider creating a kanban board so the team can see its flow. On that board, create WIP limits. Make sure the WIP limits are no higher than the number of people on the team, divided by two. That will force people to collaborate on a limited amount of work.

Ask People to Work as a Cross-Functional Team

Agile approaches create change across the organization. One of the biggest changes is that of cross-functional teams who have allegiance to their team and their product, not their manager. That can be scary for the team members and for management.

Managers might fear their loss of organizational power when agile approaches change the reporting structure. Managers often "lose" people who formerly reported to them. Managers might fear being unable to pluck people from one project and push them onto another project to respond to an emergency.

Sometimes people don't want to leave their functional silos. The architects enjoy a certain status and they don't want to give it up. The developers or UX people or testers understand how to work now. How can they work as a cross-functional team?

My advice is to not reorganize first and change who people report to. Instead, leave the reporting structure alone and ask people to work as cross-functional teams. Help the team learn how to deliver value on a regular basis. The more the team can deliver value, the easier it will be for agile ideas to take hold.

Start with Yourself

Regardless of how your organization or team started with agile approaches, you can begin to create an agile culture by using the agile mindset yourself. Consider how you can use agile approaches in your work:

- How can you be transparent with your work? Consider a personal kanban board with WIP limits.

- How can you collaborate with the team and others? Consider when to bring other people into your work. Instead of writing a project charter alone, write it with the team, timeboxing the effort. Instead of having people ask you about the project's status, create a transparent way to report status on a daily basis. Instead of removing project impediments alone, consider enlisting other project leaders across the organization to see if you can all collaborate.

- How can you exhibit the growth mindset? Instead of being discouraged at setbacks, can you consider this an opportunity to learn early and create a better result?

People look up to their leadership. In your context, what can you do to use agile approaches as a person and as a team?

Last Thoughts

Remember, it's not about "being agile." The reason to use agile approaches is to deliver value faster, to work with the customer or with the business people, and to welcome change.

If you can do that, you're better off than where you were. And that's a form of success.

My best wishes for your successful agile approach.

Glossary

Agile approach Deliver small chunks of valuable finished work while collaborating with the customer (or customer surrogate). It's important that the people who want to use agile approaches use the mindset embodied in the Agile Manifesto and the 12 principles of agile software development.

Burndown chart A chart that measures progress against time.

Burnup chart A chart that tracks how much work the team has completed to date. Product backlog burnup charts look at the entire set of features, not just a small amount of work.

Cost of delay The effect of a delay on expected revenue. What it costs you in terms of revenue every week this project is delayed. Measure that cost from the maximum revenue, not the current revenue.

Cost of delay divided by duration (CD3) A way to compare different features with different value and duration to decide what to do first.

Cumulative flow A measure of the work in progress over time.

Generalizing specialist Someone who has one skill in depth, and is flexible enough to be able to work across the team to help move a feature to "done."

Hardening iteration If a team doesn't meet its "done" working agreements, or the acceptance criteria was insufficient, the team might realize it needs to do more work to finish the stories before it can release.

Iteration A specific timebox. For agile projects, that time is normally one to four weeks, with many teams preferring one or two weeks.

Kanban Literally the Japanese word for "signboard." A scheduling system for limiting the amount of work in progress at any one time.

Lean A pull approach to managing work that looks for waste in the system.

Mob When the team works as one to start and finish a feature. The WIP limit is 1 for the entire team. The team works off a single keyboard and monitor.

Pairing When two people work together on one piece of work.

Product owner The person who is responsible for creating and ranking the backlog for a team.

Program A collection of projects that, when released, together deliver significant business value.

Project A unique undertaking that involves risk and ends.

Roadmap A list, either by quarter or by month, of which features the organization desires in a product.

Spike If you cannot estimate a story, timebox some amount of work (preferably with the entire team) to learn about it. Then you will be able to know what to do after that short timebox.

Sprint An iteration in Scrum.

Swarming When the team collaborates to start and complete a feature. The team has a WIP limit of 1. People might work separately or together, but not all as one team, as in mobbing.

Timebox A specific amount of time in which a person will attempt to accomplish a specific task.

User story A requirement in the form of value to a specific user of the product.

Waste Work in progress, work that is started and not yet done.

WIP, work in progress Any work that is not complete. When you think in lean terms, it is waste in the system. Note that you do not get "credit" for partially completed work in agile.

Bibliography

[AE14]   Gojko Adzic and David Evans. *Fifty Quick Ideas to Improve Your User Stories*. Neuri Consulting LLP, London, UK, 2014.

[AK11]   Teresa Amabile and Steven Kramer. *The Progress Principle: Using Small Wins to Ignite Joy, Engagement, and Creativity at Work*. Harvard Business Review Press, Brighton, MA, 2011.

[Bec00]   Kent Beck. *Extreme Programming Explained: Embrace Change*. Addison-Wesley Longman, Boston, MA, 2000.

[Bec10]   Kent Beck. *Test Driven Development*. The Pragmatic Bookshelf, Raleigh, NC, 2010.

[Ber15]   David Scott Bernstein. *Beyond Legacy Code*. The Pragmatic Bookshelf, Raleigh, NC, 2015.

[Bos14]   Laurent Bossavit. *The Leprechauns of Software Engineering: How folklore turns into fact and what to do about it*. LeanPub, https://leanpub.com, 2014.

[Bro16]   Gil Broza . *The Agile Mind-Set*. 3P Vantage Media, Toronto, CA, 2016.

[CdL99]   Peter Coad, Jeff de Luca, and Eric Lefbvre. *Java Modeling In Color With UML: Enterprise Components and Process*. Prentice Hall, Englewood Cliffs, NJ, 1999.

[CG08]   Lisa Crispin and Janet Gregory. *Agile Testing: A Practical Guide for Testers and Agile Teams*. Addison-Wesley, Boston, MA, 2008.

[CG14]   Lisa Crispin and Janet Gregory. *More Agile Testing: Learning Journeys for the Whole Team*. Addison-Wesley, Boston, MA, 2014.

[CKM90]   Douglas P. Champion, David H. Kiel, and Jean A. McLendon. Choosing a
            Consulting Role: Principles and Dynamics of Matching Role to Situation.
            Training & Development Journal. 1990, February.

[Coh04]   Mike Cohn. *User Stories Applied: For Agile Software Development.* Addison-
            Wesley Professional, Boston, MA, 2004.

[Coh05]   Mike Cohn. *Agile Estimating and Planning.* Prentice Hall, Englewood Cliffs,
            NJ, 2005.

[DS06]   Esther Derby and Diana Larsen, Foreword by Ken Schwaber. *Agile Retro-
            spectives.* The Pragmatic Bookshelf, Raleigh, NC, 2006.

[Dwe07]   Carol Dweck . *Mindset: The New Psychology of Success.* Ballantine Books,
            New York, NY, 2007.

[Edm12]   Amy C. Edmondson . *Teaming: How Organizations Learn, Innovate, and
            Compete in the Knowledge Economy.* Jossey-Bass Publishers, San Francisco,
            CA, 2012.

[Fea04]   Michael Feathers. *Working Effectively with Legacy Code.* Prentice Hall,
            Englewood Cliffs, NJ, 2004.

[GL15]   Luis Gonçalves and Ben Linders. *Getting Value out of Agile Retrospectives:
            A Toolbox of Retrospective Exercises.* LeanPub, https://leanpub.com, 2015.

[Hac02]   J. Richard Hackman . *Leading Teams: Setting the Stage for Great Perfor-
            mance.* Harvard Business Review Press, Brighton, MA, 2002.

[HF10]   Jez Humble and David Farley. *Continuous Delivery: Reliable Software
            Releases Through Build, Test, and Deployment Automation.* Addison-Wesley,
            Boston, MA, 2010.

[HHM10]   Geert Hofstede, Gert Hofstede, and Michael Minkov. *Cultures and Organi-
            zations: Software of the Mind, Third Edition.* McGraw-Hill, Emeryville, CA,
            2010.

[Hig99]   James A. Highsmith III. *Adaptive Software Development: A Collaborative
            Approach to Managing Complex Systems.* Dorset House, New York, NY,
            1999.

[HT00]   Andrew Hunt and David Thomas. *The Pragmatic Programmer: From Jour-
            neyman to Master.* Addison-Wesley, Boston, MA, 2000.

[HT99]   Andrew Hunt and David Thomas. *The Pragmatic Programmer.* The Pragmatic
            Bookshelf, Raleigh, NC, 1999.

[Hun08]   Andy Hunt. *Pragmatic Thinking and Learning.* The Pragmatic Bookshelf,
            Raleigh, NC, 2008.

[Jef15]   Ron Jeffries. *The Nature of Software Development*. The Pragmatic Bookshelf, Raleigh, NC, 2015.

[Jon98]   Capers Jones. *Estimating Software Costs*. McGraw-Hill, Emeryville, CA, 1998.

[Kei08]   Kent M. Keith . *The Case for Servant Leadership*. The Greenleaf Center for Servant Leadership, Atlanta, GA, 2008.

[KLTF96]   Sam Kaner, Lenny Lind, Catherine Toldi, Sarah Fisk, and Duane Berger. *The Facilitator's Guide to Participatory Decision-Making*. New Society Publishers, Gabriola Island, BC, Canada, 1996.

[KS99]   Jon R. Katzenbach and Douglas K. Smith. *The Wisdom of Teams: Creating the High-Performance Organization*. HarperCollins Publishers, New York, NY, 1999.

[Kut13]   Joe Kutner. *Remote Pairing*. The Pragmatic Bookshelf, Raleigh, NC, 2013.

[Lik04]   Jeffrey Liker. *The Toyota Way*. McGraw-Hill, Emeryville, CA, 2004.

[LO11]   Jeff Langr and Tim Ottinger. *Agile in a Flash*. The Pragmatic Bookshelf, Raleigh, NC, 2011.

[Mar08]   Robert C. Martin. *Clean Code: A Handbook of Agile Software Craftsmanship*. Prentice Hall, Englewood Cliffs, NJ, 2008.

[McC96]   Steve McConnell. *Rapid Development: Taming Wild Software Schedules*. Microsoft Press, Redmond, WA, 1996.

[Mey93]   Christopher Meyer. *Fast Cycle Time: How to Align Purpose, Strategy, and Structure for Speed*. The Free Press, New York, NY, 1993.

[MM15]   Sandy Mamoli and David Mole. *Creating Great Teams*. The Pragmatic Bookshelf, Raleigh, NC, 2015.

[Moo91]   Geoffrey A. Moore. *Crossing the Chasm*. Harper Business, New York, NY, 1991.

[MÅ13]   Niklas Modig and Pär Åhlström. *This Is Lean: Resolving the Efficiency Paradox*. Rheologica Publishing, Sweden, 2013.

[Ohn88]   Taiichi Ohno. *Toyota Production System: Beyond Large Scale Production*. Productivity Press, New York, NY, First edition, 1988.

[Pat14]   Jeff Patton. *User Story Mapping: Discover the Whole Story, Build the Right Product*. O'Reilly & Associates, Inc., Sebastopol, CA, 2014.

[PP03]   Mary Poppendieck and Tom Poppendieck. *Lean Software Development: An Agile Toolkit for Software Development Managers.* Addison-Wesley, Boston, MA, 2003.

[RD05]   Johanna Rothman and Esther Derby. *Behind Closed Doors.* The Pragmatic Bookshelf, Raleigh, NC, 2005.

[RE16]   Johanna Rothman and Jutta Eckstein. *Diving for Hidden Treasures: Uncovering the Cost of Delay in Your Project Portfolio.* Practical Ink, Arlington, MA, 2016.

[Rei09]   Donald G. Reinertsen. *The Principles of Product Development Flow: Second Generation Lean Product Development.* Celeritas Publishing, Redondo Beach, CA, 2009.

[Rei97]   Donald G. Reinertsen. *Managing the Design Factory.* The Free Press, New York, NY, 1997.

[Rie11]   Eric Ries. *The Lean Startup: How Today's Entrepreneurs Use Continuous Innovation to Create Radically Successful Businesses.* Crown Business, New York, NY, 2011.

[Roc08]   David Rock. SCARF: a brain-based model for collaborating with and influencing others. *NeuroLeadership Journal.* 1-9, 2008, Issue 1.

[Rot02]   Johanna Rothman. Release Criteria: Is This Software Done?. *STQE.* 4[2]:30–35, 2002.

[Rot07]   Johanna Rothman. *Manage It!.* The Pragmatic Bookshelf, Raleigh, NC, 2007.

[Rot13]   Johanna Rothman. *Hiring Geeks That Fit.* The Pragmatic Bookshelf, Raleigh, NC, 2013.

[Rot15]   Johanna Rothman. *Predicting the Unpredictable.* The Pragmatic Bookshelf, Raleigh, NC, 2015.

[Rot16]   Johanna Rothman. *Agile and Lean Program Management.* The Pragmatic Bookshelf, Raleigh, NC, 2016.

[Rot16a]   Johanna Rothman. *Manage Your Project Portfolio, Second Edition.* The Pragmatic Bookshelf, Raleigh, NC, 2016.

[Rot99]   Johanna Rothman. How to Use Inch-Pebbles When You Think You Can't. *American Programmer.* 12[5]:24–29, 1999.

[Sch10]   Edgar H. Schein . *Organizational Culture and Leadership.* Jossey-Bass Publishers, San Francisco, CA, 2010.

[SF01]   Robert C. Solomon and Fernando Flores. *Building Trust in Business, Politics, Relationships, and Life.* Oxford University Press, New York, NY, 2001.

[SH06]   Venkat Subramaniam and Andy Hunt. *Practices of an Agile Developer.* The Pragmatic Bookshelf, Raleigh, NC, 2006.

[Sin14]   Andy Singleton. *Unblock! A Guide to the New Continuous Agile: Release software more frequently to fly past your competitors.* Assembla, Inc., Waltham, MA, 2014.

[SR98]   Preston G. Smith and Donald G. Reinertson. *Developing Products in Half the Time: New Rules, New Tools.* John Wiley & Sons, New York, NY, Second edition, 1998.

[Sut06]   Robert I. Sutton. *Weird Ideas That Work: How to Build a Creative Company.* The Free Press, New York, NY, 2006.

[TJ77]   Bruce W. Tuckman and Mary Ann C. Jensen. Stages of Small Group Development Revisited. *Group and Organizational Studies.* 2:419–427, 1977.

[TN86]   Hirotaka Takeuchi and Ikujiro Nonaka. The New New Product Development Game. *Harvard Business Review.* 1986, January.

[War07]   Allen C. Ward. *Lean Product and Process Development.* The Lean Enterprise Institute, Inc., Cambridge, MA, 2007.

[Wei15]   Gerald M. Weinberg. *What Did You Say? The Art of Giving and Receiving Feedback.* LeanPub, https://leanpub.com, 2015.

[Wei92]   Gerald M. Weinberg. *Quality Software Management: Volume 1, Systems Thinking.* Dorset House, New York, NY, 1992.

[WJ96]   James P. Womack and Daniel T. Jones. *Lean Thinking.* Simon and Schuster, New York, NY, 1996.

[WK02]   Laurie Williams and Robert Kessler. *Pair Programming Illuminated.* Addison-Wesley, Boston, MA, 2002.

Index

A

acceptance criteria, 166
acceptance test–driven development (ATDD), 137–138
Adzic, Gojko, *Fifty Quick Ideas to Improve Your User Stories*, 95
agile, *see also* collaboration, flow-based approach, getting started, iteration-based approach, servant leadership, teams, traps, visualizations
  approaches, 9–10, 12
  choosing an approach, 12–17
  coaches, 22
  culture of, 4–7
  customizing, xv, 247
  with lean, 11
  principles, 7–9
  roots of, 1–4
  value of management, 237–245
  work groups, 6, 229–236
Agile and Lean Program Management (Rothman), 26, 234
Agile Estimating and Planning (Cohn), 150
Agile in a Flash (Langr and Ottinger), 133
Agile Retrospectives (Derby and Larsen), 197

Agile Testing: A Practical Guide for Testers and Agile Teams (Crispin and Gregory), 142
Amabile, Teresa, *The Progress Principle: Using Small Wins to Ignite Joy, Engagement, and Creativity at Work*, 119
architecture, 81, 89
ATDD (acceptance test–driven development), 137–138
automation, 137

B

backlog, 207, 216
BDD (behavior-driven development), 137–138, 166
BDUF (Big Design Up Front), 81
Beck, Kent, *Test Driven Development*, 142
behavior-driven development (BDD), 137–138, 166
Behind Closed Doors: Secrets of Great Management (Rothman and Derby), 44, 47
Bernstein, David, *Beyond Legacy Code*, 133, 142
Beyond Legacy Code (Bernstein), 133, 142
Big Design Up Front (BDUF), 81
boards, *see also* charts, kanban boards
  advantages, 113
  choosing, 120

for groups, 230–235
iteration-based, 115
paper, 113, 122, 182
parking lots, 97–98, 198–199
Scrum, 183
traps, 123–126
visualizing problems, 121
walking, 199–200
work-focused, 122
bottlenecks, 117
budgets, 81
Build-Measure-Learn loop, 100
Building Trust in Business, Politics, Relationships, and Life (Solomon), 49
burndown charts, 174
burnup charts, 176–179, 216
Business Analyst as Product Owner trap, 64

C

cadences, 10–11, 14–15
Capability Maturity Model (CMM), 2
Capability Maturity Model Integration (CMMI), 2
capacity, 188–189
The Case for Servant Leadership (Keith), 60
Champion, Douglas, *Choosing a Consulting Role: Principles and Dynamics of Matching Role to Situation*, 47
change-focused feedback, *see* feedback

charters, 74–77

charts
backlog burnup, 216
burndown, 174
burnup, 176–179
creating, 174
cumulative flow, 183–185
cycle time, 185–188
hockey-stick completion, 176, 178–179
iteration contents, 181
paper, 182
product features, 217
types, 173

Choosing a Consulting Role: Principles and Dynamics of Matching Role to Situation (Champion, et al.), 47

Clean Code: A Handbook of Agile Software Craftsmanship (Martin), 141

CMM (Capability Maturity Model), 2

CMMI (Capability Maturity Model Integration), 2

coaching
external, 22, 47
internal, 46
of managers, 243
need for, 65
tracking collaboration, 48, 53
traps, 55

Coad, Peter, *Java Modeling in Color with UML: Enterprise Components and Process*, 85

Cohn, Mike
Agile Estimating and Planning, 150
User Stories Applied, 95

collaboration
communication, 24–25
facilitating, 244
in groups, 233
mobbing, 35, 132, 135
pairing, 35, 131–133
SCARF model, 53
standups, 200–204
swarming, 132, 134
tracking, 48
traps, 38, 123, 142, 160
workspaces, 239

communities of practice, 54

Compare Teams' Velocity Instead of an Individual Team's Progress trap, 224

Continuous Delivery (Humble and Farley), 130

costs
delays, 106–109, 222
fixing defects, 190
pairing, 132
releases, 79
technical debt, 138

craftsmanship, 127, 141

Creating Great Teams (Mamoli and Mole), 27

Crispin, Lisa
Agile Testing: A Practical Guide for Testers and Agile Teams, 142
More Agile Testing: Learning Journeys for the Whole Team, 22, 142

criteria
acceptance, 166
doneness, 171
release, 76–77

cross-functional teams
creating, 21–23
need for, 21
principles, 8
roles, 23
self-management, 27–28, 248
size, 24–27
stability, 24
workspaces, 239

Crossing the Chasm (Moore), 128

cruft, 138

culture, agile, 38

culture, organizational, 28–30, 38, 49–54, *see also* interpersonal skills

cumulative flow, 183–185, 191, 235

customers, *see also* feedback, releases
customer-support groups, 230
demonstrations, 206, 215
learning about, 212
product needs, 78, 129
releases, 79, 168–170

cycle times, 10, 154, 185–189, 235

D

defects, 94, 189–193

Defects Prevent the Team's Progress trap, 143

delays, 106–109, 220–223

delivery, continuous, 130

demonstrations, 206, 215

Derby, Esther
Agile Retrospectives, 197
Behind Closed Doors: Secrets of Great Management, 44, 47

Detailed Project Plans trap, 83

Detailed Schedule trap, 102

Developers and Testers Work in Successive or Staggered Iterations trap, 35

Dinwiddie, George, "Feel the Burn: Getting the Most out of Burn Charts", 177

Diving for Hidden Treasures (Rothman and Eckstein), 221

doneness
acceptance criteria, 166
definition, 165
for iterations, 167
levels, 166
measuring rate of finishing, 178
"real" requirements, 170
releases, 168–170
traps, 170–172
working agreements, 167, 171

Double Your Velocity trap, 161

double-loop learning, 197

Dweck, Carol, *Mindset: The New Psychology of Success*, 15

E

Eckstein, Jutta, *Diving for Hidden Treasures*, 221

Edmondson, Amy C., *Teaming: How Organizations, Learn, Innovate, and Compete in the Knowledge Economy*, 50

electronic tools, 113, 122

epics, 90

escapes, defects, 189

Estimating Software Costs (Jones), 138

estimation
  definition, 147
  feedback for, 185–188
  iteration-based approach, 152
  for management, 156–157
  purpose of, 155
  relative sizing, 149–151
  support work, 157
  task-based, 153
  team capacity, 188
  from team-based measurements, 173
  traps, 111, 159–163
  using cycle time, 154
  using previous data, 158
  using velocity, 148–149
  value of, 159
  Wideband Delphi, 150

Evans, David, *Fifty Quick Ideas to Improve Your User Stories*, 95

Everyone Takes Their Own Story trap, 123, 213

Experts Take Their Own Stories trap, 160, 213

F

The Facilitator's Guide to Participatory Decision-Making (Kaner, et al.), 205

"fail fast", 52

failure, mistake-proofing, 51

Farley, David, *Continuous Delivery*, 130

fault feedback ratio (FFR), 192

FDD (feature-driven development), *see* feature-driven development (FDD)

Feathers, Michael, *Working Effectively with Legacy Code*, 141

feature sets, 91

feature teams, 27–28

feature-driven development (FDD)
  advantages, 85
  architecture value, 89
  minimum viable products/experiments (MVPs/MVEs), 99–101
  parking lots, 97–98

  planning, 86
  releases, 88
  rolling-wave roadmaps, 96–98
  spiking, 94
  stories, 90–95
  traps, 101–103
  walking skeletons, 90, 106

Feature-itis trap, 101

features, ranking work, 105–112

feedback
  continuous delivery, 130
  continuous integration, 130
  demonstrations, 206
  for managers, 243
  measurements, 173
  meta, 46
  minimum viable products/experiments (MVPs/MVEs), 99–101
  not enough, 54
  pairing, 133
  peer-to-peer, 44–46
  ranking work with, 109–110
  release, 88
  sufficient, 46
  tracking collaboration, 48, 53
  traps, 46, 55–56
  user, 129
  using, 43
  value of, 7

Feedback Sandwich trap, 46, 56

"Feel the Burn: Getting the Most out of Burn Charts" (Dinwiddie), 177

FFR (fault feedback ratio), 192

Fibonacci sequence, 150

Fifty Quick Ideas to Improve Your User Stories (Adzic and Evans), 95

finishing, rate of, 178

firing, 31

flow efficiency, 35, 62, 132, 160, 240–241

flow-based approach
  cadences, 11, 14–15
  choosing, 13
  cumulative flow charts, 183–185

  for customer-support groups, 230
  cycle time charts, 185–188
  measuring defect cumulative flow, 191
  organizing meetings, 209
  overview, 10
  story refinement, 208

forming stage, group development, 32

functional groups, 231–235

G

Gantt charts, 102, 183

getting started
  architecture, 81
  budgets, 81
  customizing agile, xv, 247
  definitions, 73
  product types, 78
  project charters, 74–77
  risk assessments, 79
  traps, 82, 84

Getting Value out of Agile Retrospectives (Gonçalves and Linders), 197

Gonçalves, Luis, *Getting Value out of Agile Retrospectives*, 197

Gregory, Janet
  Agile Testing: A Practical Guide for Testers and Agile Teams, 142
  More Agile Testing: Learning Journeys for the Whole Team, 22, 142

group dynamics, 32–33, 38

groups
  advantages, 229
  choosing approach for, 230
  collaboration in, 233
  customer-support, 230
  functional, 231–235
  retrospectives, 235
  vs. teams, 6, 229
  types, 230

H

Hackman, J. Richard, *Leading Teams: Setting the Stage for Great Performances*, 30

hardening iterations, 171

hierarchies, 59

Highest Paid Person in the Office (HiPPO), 111

hiring, 31

Hiring Geeks That Fit (Rothman), 31, 52

hiring process, 52

Åhlström, Pär, *This Is Lean: Resolving the Efficiency Paradox*, 8, 240

hockey-stick completion, 176, 178–179

human resources (HR), 231

Humble, Jez, *Continuous Delivery*, 130

Hunt, Andrew, *The Pragmatic Programmer*, 141

Hunt, Andy
    Practices of an Agile Developer, 141
    Pragmatic Thinking and Learning, 47

I

Ideal lines, 174

incremental approach, non-agile, 6

individual work, 54

Inflicting Help trap, 47, 55

information radiators, 231

initiatives, 78

Insufficient Time in a Retrospective to Solve Problems trap, 214

integration, continuous, 130

interpersonal skills, *see also* coaching, collaboration, feedback
    importance, 41
    preferences, 42
    qualities, 42
    safety, 50–54
    traps, 54–56
    trust, 49

inventory, 219

iteration contents charts, 181

Iteration Zero, 77

Iteration Zero trap, 82

iteration-based approach
    boards, 115
    burndown charts, 174
    burnup charts, 176–179
    choosing, 13
    cumulative flow charts, 183–185

estimation, 152–153, 157

hardening, 171

iteration contents charts, 181

measuring velocity, 189

non-agile, 6

organizing meetings, 209

overview, 9

standups, 200–204

story refinement, 208

traps, 35, 125

iterations
    vs. cadences, 11
    counting days, 14
    doneness, 167
    length, 14–15

Iterations of Waterfalls trap, 14, 125

It's Not Done Until Everything Is Done trap, 102

"It's Not Just Standing Up: Patterns for Daily Standup Meetings" (Yip), 203

J

Java Modeling in Color with UML: Enterprise Components and Process (Coad, et al.), 85

Jones, Capers, *Estimating Software Costs*, 138

Jones, Daniel, *Lean Thinking*, 8

K

kaizen, 197

kanban boards
    customer-support groups, 230
    cycle time, 185, 187
    functional work groups, 231, 235
    management teams, 234
    reducing lag time, 36
    visualizing flow, 117–120
    waterfalls, 124

Kaner, Sam, *The Facilitator's Guide to Participatory Decision-Making*, 205

Keith, Kent, *The Case for Servant Leadership*, 60

Kessler, Robert, *Pair Programming Illuminated*, 133

Kiberle, Kathy, "Velocity—A Squishy Measure", 149

Kramer, Steven, *The Progress Principle: Using Small Wins to Ignite Joy, Engagement, and Creativity at Work*, 119

Kutner, Joe, *Remote Pairing*, 133

L

Langr, Jeff, *Agile in a Flash*, 133

Larsen, Diana, *Agile Retrospectives*, 197

lead time, 185

leadership, *see also* management
    creating workspaces, 239
    facilitation, 61–62, 149
    flow-efficiency mindset, 240–241
    management mayhem, 243–244
    management roles, 237, 244
    needs, 59
    overview, 60
    removing impediments, 238
    setting sustainable pace, 140
    team roles, 23
    traps, 66–70

Leading Teams: Setting the Stage for Great Performances (Hackman), 30

lean, 8, 11, 197

lean coffee, 204

Lean Enterprise Institute, 197

Lean Primer, 8

Lean Product and Process Development (Ward), 8

Lean Software Development: An Agile Toolkit for Software Development Managers (Poppendieck and Poppendieck), 8

Lean Thinking (Womack and Jones), 8

Liker, Jeffrey, *The Toyota Way*, 8

Linders, Ben, *Getting Value out of Agile Retrospectives*, 197

lunch-and-learns, 35

M

Mamoli, Sandy, *Creating Great Teams*, 27

Manage It! (Rothman), 38, 76, 150

Manage Your Project Portfolio (Rothman), 86, 101, 105, 220

management, *see also* leadership
  collaboration, 244
  creating workspaces, 239
  encouraging self-management, 245
  estimation, 156–157
  flow-efficiency mindset, 62, 132, 160, 240–241
  multitasking requests, 218–219
  optimizing up, 245
  recognizing teams, 242–243
  removing impediments for team, 238
  teams, 233–235
  traps, 37, 123
  value of, 237, 244

Management Mandates Your Boards trap, 123

management mayhem, 243–244

Managers Review Team Measures Instead of Project Measures trap, 223

manifesto, 4, 7

Martin, Robert, *Clean Code: A Handbook of Agile Software Craftsmanship*, 141

measurements, project-based
  advantages, 215
  delays, 220–223
  multitasking, 218–219
  not-yet-released work, 219
  product demonstrations, 215
  product features, 216
  traps, 223–225

measurements, team-based
  burndown charts, 174
  burnup charts, 176–179
  cumulative flow, 183–185
  cycle time, 185–188
  defects, 189–193
  feedback, 173
  iteration contents, 181
  rate of finishing, 178
  traps, 193, 223
  value of, 173
  velocity, 188

meetings
  backlog planning, 207
  demonstrations, 206
  lean coffee, 204
  for learning, 211–212
  organizing, 208–209
  problem-solving, 203, 205
  retrospectives, 195–199
  standups, 200–204
  story preparations, 208
  traps, 213–214
  types, 195
  value of, 210
  walking the board, 199–200

meta feedback, 46

mindset, 15–17

Mindset: The New Psychology of Success (Dweck), 15

minimum viable experiment (MVE), 100–101, 109

minimum viable product (MVP), 99, 109

mistake-proofing, 51

mobbing, 35, 132, 135

Modig, Niklas, *This Is Lean: Resolving the Efficiency Paradox*, 8, 240

Mole, David, *Creating Great Teams*, 27

Moore, Geoffrey, 128
  Crossing the Chasm, 128

More Agile Testing: Learning Journeys for the Whole Team (Crispin and Gregory), 22, 142

multitasking, 158, 218–219

MVE (minimum viable experiment, 100–101

MVE (minimum viable experiment), 109

MVP (minimum viable product), 99, 109

N

The Nature of Software Development, 22

No Product Owners trap, 67–69

#NoEstimates philosophy, 159

nonfunctional requirements, 170

nonsequential approach, 9

norming stage, group development, 32

Not Enough Feedback trap, 46, 54

O

Ohno Taiichi, *Toyota Production System: Beyond Large Scale Production*, 8

organizational culture, 28–30, 38, 49–54, *see also* interpersonal skills

Organizational Culture and Leadership (Schein), 28

Ottinger, Tim, *Agile in a Flash*, 133

P

pace, sustainable
  cumulative flow, 183–185
  setting, 14, 30, 140
  team capacity, 181
  traps, 37, 162

Pair Programming Illuminated (Williams and Kessler), 133

pair-wise communication, 25

pairing, 35, 131–133

paper, advantages of, 113, 122, 182

parking lots, 97–98, 198–199

Patton, Jeff, *User Story Mapping: Discover the Whole Story, Build the Right Product*, 95

People Want to Measure Points Instead of Features trap, 193

performing stage, group development, 32

planning, *see also* estimation
  approaches, 86
  creating stories, 92–95
  ranking work, 105–112
  releases, 88–89
  roadmaps, 86
  traps, 102
  value of stories, 90
  walking skeletons, 90, 106

planning meetings, iteration-based approach, 15

planning poker, 152, 207

points, 153, 176, 178, 180, 193

Poppendieck, Mary, *Lean Software Development: An Agile Toolkit for Software Development Managers*, 8

Poppendieck, Tom, *Lean Software Development: An Agile Toolkit for Software Development Managers*, 8

Practices of an Agile Developer (Subramaniam and Hunt), 141

The Pragmatic Programmer (Hunt and Thomas), 141

Pragmatic Thinking and Learning (Hunt), 47

Predicting the Unpredictable (Rothman), 151, 153, 156

The Principles of Product Development Flow: Second Generation Lean Product Development (Reinertsen), 106, 222

prioritizing, 105–112

problem-solving meetings, 205

product, cross-functionality of development, 235

product managers, planning, 86

Product Owner, Someone Else Pressures trap, 111

product owners
  external pressures, 111
  planning, 86
  responsibilities, 63–64
  role changes, 64
  traps, 66–70, 101, 162

products, *see also* projects
  architecture, 81
  definition, 73
  doneness, 165–172
  features progress measurements, 216
  identifying types, 78
  minimum quality, 128
  planning, 86
  release frequency, 78–79
  releases, 88, 129
  roadmaps, 86

programs, 233

The Progress Principle: Using Small Wins to Ignite Joy, Engagement, and Creativity at Work (Amabile and Kramer), 119

project boards, *see also* kanban boards
  advantages, 113
  choosing, 120
  for groups, 230–235
  iteration-based, 115
  paper, 113, 122, 182
  parking lots, 97–98, 198–199
  Scrum boards, 183
  traps, 123–126
  visualizing problems, 121
  walking, 199–200
  work-focused, 122

project managers, *see also* leadership, servant leadership
  command and control approach, 60
  defining release criteria for, 77
  responsibilities, 61–62
  role changes, 64
  roles, 23, 31, 52, 59
  traps, 37, 66–70

project portfolios, 86, 105

project-based measurements
  advantages, 215
  delays, 220–223
  multitasking, 218–219
  not-yet-released work, 219
  product demonstrations, 215
  product features, 216
  traps, 223–225

projects
  charters, 74–77
  definition, 73
  doneness, 165–172
  risks, 79
  traps, 83
  visions, 74

Q

quality
  continuous delivery, 130
  continuous integration, 130
  cruft, 139
  minimum, 128
  refactoring, 131
  sustainable pace, 140
  team collaboration, 131–136
  technical debt, 138
  technical excellence, 127, 141
  testing, 136–138
  traps, 142–143

Quality Software Management: Volume 1, Systems Thinking (Weinberg), 129

R

radar chart, 143

Rainsberger, Joe, 143

Rank Only by Estimation trap, 111

ranking work, 105–112

rate of finishing, 178

recognition, 242–243

refactoring, 131, 142

Reinertsen, Donald, *The Principles of Product Development Flow: Second Generation Lean Product Development*, 106, 222

reinforcing feedback, *see* feedback

releases
  continuous, 130
  criteria, 76–77
  definition, 73
  vs. demonstrations, 206
  differentiation, 168–169
  doneness, 168–170
  for feedback, 88
  frequency, 78–79, 129, 168
  nonfunctional requirements, 170
  "slice of cake", 89, 216
  traps, 171

Remote Pairing (Kutner), 133

resilience, 52

resource efficiency, 28, 35, 62, 132, 160, 240–241

resources, for this book
  agile manifesto, 4, 7
  charters, 76
  collaboration, 133
  efficiency, 240
  estimation, 149–151, 153, 156
  feature-driven development (FDD), 85
  interpersonal skills, 44, 47, 49–50, 52–53
  leadership, 60, 67
  lean, 8, 222, 245
  mindset, 15
  motivation, 119
  problem-solving, 205

product quality, 128
program management, 234
project management, 38, 86, 101, 105, 220–221
quality, 130
retrospectives, 197
scaling, xvi
standups, 203
stories, 95
team organization, 22, 26–28, 30–32
team-based measurements, 177
technical excellence, 141
testing, 138, 142
retrospectives
burndowns, 175
burnups, 179
double-loop learning, 197
frequency, 195
for groups, 235
iteration-based approach, 15
traps, 214
using parking lots, 198–199
rewards, 242–243
risks
assessments, 79, 110
budgets, 81
resilience approach, 52
traditional management, 51
visualizing with boards, 121
roadmaps, 86, 96–98
Rock, David, 53
rolling-wave roadmaps, 96–98
Rothman, Johanna
Agile and Lean Program Management, 26, 234
Behind Closed Doors: Secrets of Great Management, 44, 47
"Defining 'Scaling' Agile", xvi
Diving for Hidden Treasures, 221
Hiring Geeks That Fit, 31, 52
Manage It!, 38, 76, 150
Manage Your Project Portfolio, 86, 101, 105, 220
Predicting the Unpredictable, 151, 153, 156

S
safety, 50–54
scaling, xvi
SCARF (Status, Certainty, Autonomy, Relatedness, and Fairness) model, 53
SCARF: A Brain-Based Model for Collaborating with and Influencing Others (Rock), 53
Schein, Edgar, *Organizational Culture and Leadership*, 28
Scrum, 12–13, 62, 115, 183
servant leadership, *see also* management
creating workspaces, 239
expectations, 64
facilitation, 61–62, 149
flow-efficiency mindset, 240–241
management mayhem, 243–244
management roles, 237, 244
needs, 59
overview, 60
removing impediments, 238
setting sustainable pace, 140
team roles, 23
traps, 66–70
"7 minutes, 26 seconds, and the Fundamental Theorem of Agile Software Development" (Rainsberger), 143
"shared services", 242
shortcuts, 129, 141
shortest-work-first approach, 106
silos, 233
single-loop learning, 196
Singleton, Andy, *Unblock! A Guide to the New Continuous Agile*, 130
size, of teams, 24–27
"slice of cake" releases, 89, 216
"soft" skills, 42
Solomon, Robert C., *Building Trust in Business, Politics, Relationships, and Life*, 49
Someone Else Pressures the Product Owner trap, 111
spiking, 94, 110

stability, 36
Stages of Small-Group Development Revisited (Tuckman), 32
standups, 200–204, 213
Standups Become Serial Status Meetings trap, 213
Status, Certainty, Autonomy, Relatedness, and Fairness (SCARF) model, 53
stories
creating, 92–94
definition, 90
doneness, 166–168
estimating with, 149–151, 153
impact on velocity, 149
measuring with, 179
points, 176, 178, 180, 193
refinement, 208
rolling-wave roadmaps, 96–98
small, 95, 140, 151, 177
technical *vs.* user, 92
test-driven development, 138
traps, 123, 160, 213
types, 91
storming stage, group development, 32
Subramaniam, Venkat, *Practices of an Agile Developer*, 141
support work, 157
sustainable pace
cumulative flow, 183–185
setting, 14, 30, 140
team capacity, 181
traps, 37, 162
Sutton, Robert, *Weird Ideas That Work: How to Build a Creative Company*, 67
swarming, 132, 134

T
task-based estimation, 153
TDD (test-driven development), 137–138
Team Consists of Narrow Experts trap, 34
Team Has No Criteria for "Done" trap, 171
Team Meets Rather than Delivers trap, 213

Team Members Are Wary of Collaboration trap, 38

Team Membership Is Not Stable trap, 36

Team Pushes Its Pace trap, 37

Team Requires Permission from Distant Managers to Solve Problems trap, 37

Team Waits to Measure trap, 193

team-based measurements
  burndown charts, 174
  burnup charts, 176–179
  cumulative flow, 183–185
  cycle time, 185–188
  defects, 189–193
  feedback, 173
  iteration contents, 181
  rate of finishing, 178
  traps, 193
  value of, 173
  velocity, 188

Teaming: How Organizations, Learn, Innovate, and Compete in the Knowledge Economy (Edmondson), 50

teams, see also groups, interpersonal skills
  agile approaches, 5, 12–17
  architects, 81
  building trust, 49
  capabilities of members, 22
  capacity, 181, 188–189
  charter workshops, 77
  collaboration, 131–136
  common problems, 1
  cross-functionality, 8, 21–28, 248
  developing, 32–33
  distributed, 114, 122, 239
  hiring process, 52
  leadership needs, 59
  manager responsibilities, 61
  organizational culture, 28–30, 38
  product owners, 63–64
  recognition, 242–243
  roles, 23
  safety, 50–54
  self-management, 27–28, 30, 65, 120, 149, 245
  size, 24–27

stability, 24, 36
successful, 42
suggestions for, xv
tracking collaboration, 48, 53
traps, 27, 33–39, 123, 142, 160, 213, 223–224
value of management, 237–245
workspaces, 203, 239

technical debt, 138

technical excellence, 127, 141
  traps, 142–143

technical stories, see stories

Test Driven Development (Beck), 142

test-driven development (TDD), 137–138

testing, 136–139, 142

themes, definition, 90

This Is Lean: Resolving the Efficiency Paradox (Modig and Åhlström), 8, 240

Thomas, David, The Pragmatic Programmer, 141

Three Amigos, 208

timeboxing, 9, 105

Too Many Product Owners trap, 66

tools, charts, 174, see also charts, project boards

Toyota Production System, 8

Toyota Production System: Beyond Large Scale Production (Ohno), 8

The Toyota Way (Liker), 8

traps
  Business Analyst as Product Owner, 64
  Compare Teams' Velocity Instead of an Individual Team's Progress, 224
  Defects Prevent the Team's Progress, 143
  Detailed Project Plans, 83
  Detailed Schedule, 102
  Developers and Testers Work in Successive or Staggered Iterations, 35
  Double Your Velocity, 161
  Everyone Takes Their Own Story, 123, 213

Experts Take Their Own Stories, 160, 213
Feedback Sandwich, 46, 56
identifying, 6
Inflicting Help, 47, 55
Insufficient Time in a Retrospective to Solve Problems, 214
It's Not Done Until Everything Is Done, 102
Iteration Zero, 82
Iterations of Waterfalls, 14, 125
Management Mandates Your Boards, 123
Managers Review Team Measures Instead of Project Measures, 223
No Product Owners, 67–69
Not Enough Feedback, 46, 54
People Want to Measure Points Instead of Features, 193
Product Owner Featureitis, 101
Rank Only by Estimation, 111
Someone Else Pressures the Product Owner trap, 111
Standups Become Serial Status Meetings, 213
Team Consists of Narrow Experts, 34
Team Has No Criteria for "Done", 171
Team Meets Rather than Delivers, 213
Team Members Are Wary of Collaboration, 38
Team Membership Is Not Stable, 36
Team Pushes Its Pace, 37
Team Requires Permission from Distant Managers to Solve Problems, 37
Team Waits to Measure, 193
Too Many Product Owners, 66
Waiting for Other People or Teams to Test, 142
Waterfall Masquerades as Kanban, 124
We Can Do More, 162

We Can Go Faster Without Clean Code and Tests, 142
We Can't Release Anything Until It's "All" Done, 171
We Must Rank All of It, 111
We Need Detailed Estimates for "All" of It, 162
We Need to "Harden" the Product, 171
WIP Is Everywhere, 224
Your Team Consists of Experts, 27
Your Teams Are Component Teams, 33
trust, 49
Tuckman, Bruce, *Stages of Small-Group Development Revisited*, 32

U

Unblock! A Guide to the New Continuous Agile (Singleton), 130
user stories, *see* stories
User Stories Applied (Cohn), 95
User Story Mapping: Discover the Whole Story, Build the Right Product (Patton), 95

V

value over time graph, 107
velocity, 148–149, 158, 180
  comparisons, 224
  poor measure of progress, 223
  team capacity, 188
  traps, 161
"Velocity—A Squishy Measure" (Kiberle), 149
vision statements, 74
visualizations, *see also* kanban boards
  advantages, 113
  backlog, 216
  burndown charts, 174
  burnup charts, 176–179
  choosing, 120
  creating, 174

cumulative flow charts, 183–185
cycle time charts, 185–188
for groups, 230–235
hockey-stick completion, 176, 178–179
information radiators, 231
iteration contents charts, 181
iteration-based, 115
noting problems, 121
paper, 113, 122, 182
parking lots, 198–199
product features charts, 217
Scrum boards, 183
traps, 123–126
types, 173
walking the board, 199–200
work-focused, 122

W

Waiting for Other People or Teams to Test trap, 142
Wake, Bill, 89
walking skeletons, 90, 106
walking the board, 199–200
Ward, Allen, *Lean Product and Process Development*, 8
Waterfall Masquerades as Kanban trap, 124
waterfalls, 124–125
We Can Do More trap, 162
We Can Go Faster Without Clean Code and Tests trap, 142
We Can't Release Anything Until It's "All" Done trap, 171
We Must Rank All of It trap, 111
We Need Detailed Estimates for "All" of It trap, 162
We Need to "Harden" the Product trap, 171

Weinberg, Gerald
  Quality Software Management: Volume 1, Systems Thinking, 129
  What Did You Say? The Art of Giving and Receiving Feedback, 44
Weird Ideas That Work: How to Build a Creative Company (Sutton), 67
What Did You Say? The Art of Giving and Receiving Feedback (Weinberg), 44
Wideband Delphi estimation, 150
Williams, Laurie, *Pair Programming Illuminated*, 133
WIP (work in progress), *see* work in progress (WIP)
WIP Is Everywhere trap, 224
Womack, James, *Lean Thinking*, 8
work groups
  advantages, 229
  choosing approach for, 230
  collaboration in, 233
  customer-support, 230
  functional, 231–235
  retrospectives, 235
  vs. teams, 6, 229
  types, 230
work in progress (WIP)
  inventory, 219
  limiting, 5, 10, 35, 119, 184, 230, 247
  measuring, 36
working agreements, 29, 171
Working Effectively with Legacy Code (Feathers), 141
workspaces, 203, 239

Y

Yip, Jason, "It's Not Just Standing Up: Patterns for Daily Standup Meetings", 203
Your Team Consists of Experts trap, 27
Your Teams Are Component Teams trap, 33

Also by Johanna Rothman

More great titles from this popular author.

Manage It!

This book is a reality-based guide for modern projects. You'll learn how to recognize your project's potholes and ruts, and determine the best way to fix problems—without causing more problems.

Johanna Rothman
(360 pages) ISBN: 9780978739249. $29.95
https://pragprog.com/book/jrpm

Manage Your Project Portfolio, Second Edition

You have too many projects, and firefighting and multitasking are keeping you from finishing any of them. You need to manage your project portfolio. This fully updated and expanded bestseller arms you with agile and lean ways to collect all your work and decide which projects you should do first, second, and never. See how to tie your work to your organization's mission and show your managers, your board, and your staff what you can accomplish and when. Picture the work you have, and make those difficult decisions, ensuring that all your strength is focused where it needs to be.

This new edition features a free downloadable workbook that puts you on the fast track to creating your project portfolio. Pulling together key checklists, steps, and kanbans from the book, this workbook will help you get your ideas flowing and create something tangible. You'll find the workbook here.

Johanna Rothman
(240 pages) ISBN: 9781680501759. $36
https://pragprog.com/book/jrport2

Level Up

From data structures to architecture and design, we have what you need.

A Common-Sense Guide to Data Structures and Algorithms

If you last saw algorithms in a university course or at a job interview, you're missing out on what they can do for your code. Learn different sorting and searching techniques, and when to use each. Find out how to use recursion effectively. Discover structures for specialized applications, such as trees and graphs. Use Big O notation to decide which algorithms are best for your production environment. Beginners will learn how to use these techniques from the start, and experienced developers will rediscover approaches they may have forgotten.

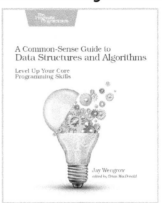

Jay Wengrow
(218 pages) ISBN: 9781680502442. $45.95
https://pragprog.com/book/jwdsal

Design It!

Don't engineer by coincidence—design it like you mean it! Grounded by fundamentals and filled with practical design methods, this is the perfect introduction to software architecture for programmers who are ready to grow their design skills. Ask the right stakeholders the right questions, explore design options, share your design decisions, and facilitate collaborative workshops that are fast, effective, and fun. Become a better programmer, leader, and designer. Use your new skills to lead your team in implementing software with the right capabilities—and develop awesome software!

Michael Keeling
(358 pages) ISBN: 9781680502091. $42.50
https://pragprog.com/book/mkdsa

Explore Testing and Cucumber

Explore the uncharted waters of exploratory testing and delve deeper into Cucumber.

Explore It!

Uncover surprises, risks, and potentially serious bugs with exploratory testing. Rather than designing all tests in advance, explorers design and execute small, rapid experiments, using what they learned from the last little experiment to inform the next. Learn essential skills of a master explorer, including how to analyze software to discover key points of vulnerability, how to design experiments on the fly, how to hone your observation skills, and how to focus your efforts.

Elisabeth Hendrickson
(186 pages) ISBN: 9781937785024. $29
https://pragprog.com/book/ehxta

The Cucumber Book, Second Edition

Your customers want rock-solid, bug-free software that does exactly what they expect it to do. Yet they can't always articulate their ideas clearly enough for you to turn them into code. You need Cucumber: a testing, communication, and requirements tool—all rolled into one. All the code in this book is updated for Cucumber 2.4, Rails 5, and RSpec 3.5.

Matt Wynne and Aslak Hellesøy, with Steve Tooke
(334 pages) ISBN: 9781680502381. $39.95
https://pragprog.com/book/hwcuc2

Start Great Teams, Keep Teams Great

See how to get great teams started, and keep them great by doing retrospectives the right way.

Liftoff, Second Edition

Ready, set, liftoff! Align your team to one purpose: successful delivery. Learn new insights and techniques for starting projects and teams the right way, with expanded concepts for planning, organizing, and conducting liftoff meetings. Real-life stories illustrate how others have effectively started (or restarted) their teams and projects. Master coaches Diana Larsen and Ainsley Nies have successfully "lifted off" numerous agile projects worldwide. Are you ready for success?

Diana Larsen and Ainsley Nies
(170 pages) ISBN: 9781680501636. $24
https://pragprog.com/book/liftoff

Agile Retrospectives

See how to mine the experience of your software development team continually throughout the life of the project. The tools and recipes in this book will help you uncover and solve hidden (and not-so-hidden) problems with your technology, your methodology, and those difficult "people issues" on your team.

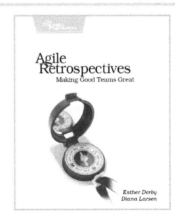

Esther Derby and Diana Larsen, Foreword by Ken Schwaber
(176 pages) ISBN: 9780977616640. $29.95
https://pragprog.com/book/dlret

Secure JavaScript and Web Testing

Secure your Node applications and see how to really test on the web.

Secure Your Node.js Web Application

Cyber-criminals have your web applications in their crosshairs. They search for and exploit common security mistakes in your web application to steal user data. Learn how you can secure your Node.js applications, database and web server to avoid these security holes. Discover the primary attack vectors against web applications, and implement security best practices and effective countermeasures. Coding securely will make you a stronger web developer and analyst, and you'll protect your users.

Karl Düüna
(230 pages) ISBN: 9781680500851. $36
https://pragprog.com/book/kdnodesec

The Way of the Web Tester

This book is for everyone who needs to test the web. As a tester, you'll automate your tests. As a developer, you'll build more robust solutions. And as a team, you'll gain a vocabulary and a means to coordinate how to write and organize automated tests for the web. Follow the testing pyramid and level up your skills in user interface testing, integration testing, and unit testing. Your new skills will free you up to do other, more important things while letting the computer do the one thing it's really good at: quickly running thousands of repetitive tasks.

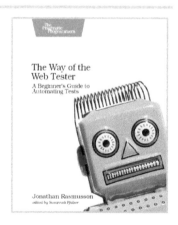

Jonathan Rasmusson
(256 pages) ISBN: 9781680501834. $29
https://pragprog.com/book/jrtest

Pragmatic Programming

We'll show you how to be more pragmatic and effective, for new code and old.

Your Code as a Crime Scene

Jack the Ripper and legacy codebases have more in common than you'd think. Inspired by forensic psychology methods, this book teaches you strategies to predict the future of your codebase, assess refactoring direction, and understand how your team influences the design. With its unique blend of forensic psychology and code analysis, this book arms you with the strategies you need, no matter what programming language you use.

Adam Tornhill
(218 pages) ISBN: 9781680500387. $36
https://pragprog.com/book/atcrime

The Nature of Software Development

You need to get value from your software project. You need it "free, now, and perfect." We can't get you there, but we can help you get to "cheaper, sooner, and better." This book leads you from the desire for value down to the specific activities that help good Agile projects deliver better software sooner, and at a lower cost. Using simple sketches and a few words, the author invites you to follow his path of learning and understanding from a half century of software development and from his engagement with Agile methods from their very beginning.

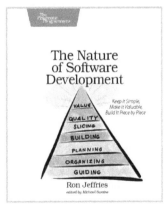

Ron Jeffries
(176 pages) ISBN: 9781941222379. $24
https://pragprog.com/book/rjnsd

The Pragmatic Bookshelf

The Pragmatic Bookshelf features books written by developers for developers. The titles continue the well-known Pragmatic Programmer style and continue to garner awards and rave reviews. As development gets more and more difficult, the Pragmatic Programmers will be there with more titles and products to help you stay on top of your game.

Visit Us Online

This Book's Home Page
https://pragprog.com/book/jragm
Source code from this book, errata, and other resources. Come give us feedback, too!

Register for Updates
https://pragprog.com/updates
Be notified when updates and new books become available.

Join the Community
https://pragprog.com/community
Read our weblogs, join our online discussions, participate in our mailing list, interact with our wiki, and benefit from the experience of other Pragmatic Programmers.

New and Noteworthy
https://pragprog.com/news
Check out the latest pragmatic developments, new titles and other offerings.

Save on the eBook

Save on the eBook versions of this title. Owning the paper version of this book entitles you to purchase the electronic versions at a terrific discount.

PDFs are great for carrying around on your laptop—they are hyperlinked, have color, and are fully searchable. Most titles are also available for the iPhone and iPod touch, Amazon Kindle, and other popular e-book readers.

Buy now at *https://pragprog.com/coupon*

Contact Us

Online Orders:	*https://pragprog.com/catalog*
Customer Service:	*support@pragprog.com*
International Rights:	*translations@pragprog.com*
Academic Use:	*academic@pragprog.com*
Write for Us:	*http://write-for-us.pragprog.com*
Or Call:	+1 800-699-7764

Milton Keynes UK
Ingram Content Group UK Ltd.
UKHW030148080224
437448UK00009BA/514